J. A. (James Aitken) Wylie

History of the Scottish Nation

J. A. (James Aitken) Wylie
History of the Scottish Nation
ISBN/EAN: 9783337008567

Printed in Europe, USA, Canada, Australia, Japan

Cover: Foto ©ninafisch / pixelio.de

More available books at **www.hansebooks.com**

HISTORY

OF THE

SCOTTISH NATION.

BY

REV. J. A. WYLIE, LL.D.,

AUTHOR OF "HISTORY OF PROTESTANTISM," ETC.

VOL. I.

PRE-HISTORIC, DRUIDIC, ROMAN, AND EARLY
CHRISTIAN SCOTLAND.

LONDON:
HAMILTON, ADAMS & CO.
ANDREW ELLIOT, EDINBURGH.
1886.

TO

THE PEOPLE OF SCOTLAND,

FROM WHOSE RANKS MAINLY HAVE SPRUNG

THE PHILOSOPHERS AND DIVINES,

THE POETS, WRITERS, AND MARTYRS,

WHO HAVE BEEN THE GLORY

OF THEIR COUNTRY.

CONTENTS.

CHAPTER I.
FIRST PEOPLING OF BRITAIN.

The Phœnicians the first Discoverers of Britain, 1—They trade with it in Tin, 2—Greatness of Sidon and Tyre partly owing to British Trade, 3—Triumphal Gates of Shalmanezer, 3—Tyrian Harbours, and probable size of Tyrian Ships, 4—When and whence came the first Inhabitants of Britain? 5—The resting-place of the Ark the starting-point of the enquiry, 5—Mount Ararat, 6—The Four great Rivers, 7—Their courses regulate the Emigration of the Human Family, 7—The Mountain-girdle of the Globe, 7—Divided by it into a Southern and Northern World, 8—For what purpose? 9—The Three Fountain-heads of the World's Population, 10—Ham peoples Egypt, 10—Shem,'Arabia and Persia, 11—Migration of Japhet's Descendants, 11—Two great Pathways, 11—The basin of the Mediterranean, 12—The slopes of the Caucasus running betwixt the Caspian and the Euxine, 12—The Sons of Japhet travel by both routes, 12—The one arrives in Britain through the Pillars of Hercules, 13—The other by the Baltic, 13—The Journey stamps its imprint on each, 14—Their foot-prints, 15—The Sons of Gomer, or Cymri, the first Inhabitants of Britain, 16.

CHAPTER II.
JOURNEY OF THE KYMRI TO BRITAIN.

Three guides to the Cradle of the Race, 17—Etymology, Mythology, Folk-lore, 18—All three conduct to Iran, 19—The Welsh Triads, 20—Division of the Earth among the Sons of Noah, 22—Nimrod's Tower, 23—An attempt to establish a Universal Monarchy, 24—Migration of the bands of Gomer, 25—Their journey to Britain, 25—Nomades, 26—The pasture-grounds of Europe the nursing-place of Warriors, 27—Character of the first Settlers, 29.

CHAPTER III.
HABITS, HABITATIONS, AND ARTS OF THE FIRST SETTLERS.

First Settlers bring the essentials of Revelation with them, 30—The first Ages the Purest, 31—Log huts of first Dwellers, 32—Aboriginal Dwellings on banks of Loch Etive, 32—Picture of the Inmates, 33—Food, Arts, Garments of the Aborigines, 34—Weems, description of, 36—Progress of the Arts, 37—Beauty of later Home Art, 38—Growth of Government and early Kings, 39.

CHAPTER IV.

THE STONE AGE.

The Stone Age coeval with Man, 40—The only record of the first Races, 40—The Cairn on the Moor, 41—The Sleeper within, 41—Glimpse into his Coffin, 41—Weapons interred with the Warrior, 42—Uses of the Stone Axe, 43—Flint Arrow-heads, 44—Battle in the Stone Age, 44—Mental horizon of the Men of the Stone Age, 46—The Landscape of the Stone Age, 46.

CHAPTER V.

THE BRONZE AGE.

The Celt brings Bronze with him into Britain, 47—Quickening in all the Arts, 47—First Irruption of the Celts into Europe, 47—Threaten Athens and Rome, 48—Europe known to Herodotus as the land of the Celts, 48—Nomades but fierce Warriors, 49—Their Tastes and Character, 49—Changes consequent on the introduction of Bronze, 50—In Ship building, 50—In House building, 51—In articles of Ornament, 51—In Domestic Utensils, 52—Cinery Vases, 54—Burning of the Dead, 55—Advance in Dress, 55—In Spinning and Weaving, 56—In Agriculture, 56—Invention of Bronze of unknown antiquity, 57.

CHAPTER VI.

THE IRON AGE.

Uses of Iron, 58—Power it confers on Man, 59—First historic traces of Iron in Asia, 59—Noric Swords, 60—Iron known to Caledonians in Cæsar's day, 60—Comes slowly into Use, 60—Revolutionises the Art of War, 61—Employed for Personal Adornment, 62—Iron Ring Money, 62—Interred with the Dead, 63—Changes with Iron, 64—Advance in Art, in War, in the Industries, 65—The Weaver and Potter, 66—Grain-stones, 67—Female Toilet, 67—Banquets and Cuisine of the Iron Age, 68—Brochs, 69—Their great number, 69—What knowledge of a Future State? 70—Divine Traditions transmitted from Noah, 70—No Idol or Graven Image dug up in Scottish soil, 71—Worship of Caledonians less gross than that of the Greeks and Romans, 72—Inference from mode of Burial, 72—Valhalla and its Delights, 73—Departed Heroes permitted to revisit their Barrow, 73—A Trysting place with earthly Friends, 74—Lesson of history, or Earth the picture of Heaven, 74.

CHAPTER VII.

THE DRUIDS—THE SUN-WORSHIP OF ASIA AND CALEDONIA.

Unwritten History or Testimony of the Barrows and Cairns, 75—Authenticity and Truth of these Records, 76—How did the Caledonian Worship? 77—Had he any Knowledge of a Supreme Being? 78—Testimony of the Stone Circles, 79—In what Age were they Erected? 79—Various Theories, 83—

These Theories considered, 81—Did the Vikings erect them? Are they Graveyards? 82—Monuments of Early Nations reared to their Gods, 83—Stone Pillars, 84—Biblical Examples, 84—The First Altars, 85—The Idols and Idol Groves of Early Canaan, 85—Rise and Progress of Stone and Sun Worship, 85—Travels westward and reaches Caledonia, 87—Stone Circles and Cromlechs of Ancient Moab, 88—Light thrown by them on the Early Caledonia, 89.

CHAPTER VIII.

DRUIDS, DEITIES, HIERARCHY, DOCTRINES.

Religion the most Potential of all Forces, 90—The Druidic Age as plainly written on the Face of Scotland as the Stone and Iron Ages, 91—Scottish Druidism imported from the East, 92—Its Comparative Purity in Early Times, 92—Testimonies of M. Reynaud, and others, 93—Druidism, a Branch of Sun Worship, 94—The Root Ideas of Revelation in all the Idolatries, 95—Explanation, 96—Identity of the Druidic and Greek Deities, 96—The Hierarchy of the Druids, 97—Their Studies in Science and Magic, 97—The Arch-Druid, 98—Their Political Power, 99—Their Annual Convention, 99—Their Emoluments and Privileges, 100—Their Doctrines, 101—Testimonies of Cæsar, Pliny, Tacitus, and Pomponius Mela, 102—A Supreme Being and a Life to come taught by them, 103—A Long Initiation demanded of their Disciples, 106—Their Tenets wrapt up in Mystery, 106.

CHAPTER IX.

THE DRUID'S EGG—THE MISTLETOE—THE DRUID'S SACRIFICE.

The Druid's Egg known to the Ancients, 108—Marvellous Process of Production, 109—Wonderful Virtues, 109—The Mistletoe, 109—Ceremony of gathering it, 110—Was it to Druid a Symbol of the Saviour? 110—No ground to think so, 111—Sacrifice of the Druid, 112—Was it Evangelical or Pagan? 112—Sacrificial Rites, 113—The High Priest, the Procession, the Victim, 113-The Three Acts and the Three Lessons in the Sacrifice of the Druid, 114—Universality of the Rite of Sacrifice, 115—Explanation, 115—Philosophy of Sacrifice as a Mode of Worship, 116.

CHAPTER X.

THE TEMPLES OR STONE CIRCLES OF THE DRUID.

The Stone Circle the earliest of Temples, 118—No Architectural Grace, 118 In Construction Simple, Rugged, Strong, 119—Stennes in Orkney, 120—A Temple to the Sun-God, 120—Its Antiquity, 120—Stonehenge, 120—Its Site and Size, 120—Supposed Description of Stonehenge by Hecatæus, B.C. 300, 121—Its Hippodrome, 121—Weird Appearance and Outline of its History, 122—Its Dimensions, 122—*Footnote*, Avebury, 123—Its Genera Arrangements, 123—Its Central Mount, 124—Its Grand Approaches, 124 Its surrounding Sepulchral Tumuli, 125—Beauty the Characteristic of the

Greek Temple; Strength and Size that of the Druid, 125—Mount Nebo a great Dolmen Centre, 126—Ruins of Dolmens and Stone Circles around Mount Nebo, 126—Universality of Stone Worship, 128—Human Victims offered by the Druid, 128—Human Sacrifice practised by Greeks and Romans, 129—"Stones of Remembrance," 130.

CHAPTER XI.

THE ALTEINS; OR, STONES OF FIRE— BELTANE; OR, MAY-DAY AND MIDSUMMER FESTIVALS.

Rise of Pagan Mythology, 131—*Footnote*, Indelibility of Aboriginal Names, 131—Key to Early History of Locality, 132—*Clachan*, 132—Its Meaning, 133—*Altein*, 133—Stone of Fire, 133—The Altein of Old Aberdeen, 134—Tragedies enacted at, 134—Stone of Liston, 135—Druidic Ceremonies of 30th October, 136—Extinction of Fire on Hearths, 136—Rekindled from "Stone of Fire-brands," 137—Link betwixt Phœnicia and Caledonia, 137—"Stones of Fire" of Tyre, 138—Beltane, or 1st May, 140—Beltane Rites at Crieff, 140—At Callander, 141—Midsummer Fires, 142—St John's Fires in Ireland, 143—In France, 144—Identity of these with the Fires of Moloch, 144—The Clocks of the Druid, 145.

CHAPTER XII.

VITRIFIED FORTS—ROCKING-STONES—DRUID'S CIRCLE—NO MAN'S LAND—DIVINATION—GALLOW HILLS—A YOKE BROKEN.

Vitrified Forts, 146—Probable Relics of Druidism, 147—Rocking-Stones, 147—Common to many Countries, 147—Known to the Egyptians, 148—Described by Pliny, &c., 148—Judgment Stones, 149—Stone at Boddam, 150—How Placed? 150—The Druid's Circle, 151—Its Virtue, 152—Surviving Druidic Usages, 152—The *teine eigin*, 153—Days on which the Plough was not to be Yoked, 153—Plots that must not be Cultivated, 153—Divination practised by the Druids, 154—Laws or "Gallow Hills," 155—Mounts of Divination, 155—Enslavement of the People by the Druid, 157—His Yoke broken, 158.

CHAPTER XIII.

SCOTLAND AS SEEN BY AGRICOLA AND DESCRIBED BY TACITUS AND HERODIAN.

History with her Torch, 159—Invasion of England by Cæsar, 159—Startling Reverse, 160—Agricola crosses the Tweed, 161—Penetrates to Firth of Forth, 162—Agricola probably accompanied by Tacitus, 162—The Time come for Scotland to be Born, 163—A Marvellous Transformation, 164—Picture of Scotland as seen by Tacitus, 165—Its Moors and Forests, 166—Its Rivers and Pathways, 166—Its Seas, 167.

CONTENTS.   xi

CHAPTER XIV.

THE CALEDONIAN AS PAINTED BY HERODIAN.

The Land and the Natives as Painted by Herodian, 170—Their Armour, 170—Their Bodies Painted or Tattooed, 171—Process of Tattooing, 172—Their Hair, 172—A Contrast, the Scotland of the First Century and the Scotland of the Nineteenth, 173.

CHAPTER XV.

CALEDONIAN HOUSES—LAKE DWELLINGS.

Picture of the Scotland of To-day, 174—The Architecture of Italy and the Architecture of Scotland in the First Century, 175—Not a Stone Edifice in Scotland in Agricola's Day, 176—First Dwellings in Caledonia an Underground Cave, 176—A Hut of Wattles, 177—Lacustrine or Lake Dwellings, 177—Method of Construction, 178—Utensils found in them, 178—Relics of their Feasts, 178—Second Class of Lake Dwellings, 179—Placed in the Lake, 179—Manner of Building, 180—Venice a Superb Specimen of a Lake Dwelling, 180—Crannog of Lochea, Tarbolton, Ayrshire, 181—Description, 181—Lochar Moss and its Buried Treasures, 182—The Site of Glasgow and its Embedded Canoes, 183—Changes in the Estuaries of the Forth and Tay, 183—The Modern Scotland bigger than the Ancient, 184.

CHAPTER XVI.

ROMAN PERIOD OF BRITAIN—ENGLAND INVADED BY CÆSAR, AND SCOTLAND BY AGRICOLA.

An Unpromising Land, 185—A yet more Unpromising People, 185—Roman Invasion, B.C. 55, 187—Fight off Deal, 188—Devastations of the Roman Sword in Britain, 189—Opinion of Tacitus, 189—Cæsar withdraws from Britain, 190—Aulus Plutius enters in A.D. 43, 189—The British Chief Caractacus before the Emperor Claudius, 190—Agricola arrives in A.D. 80, 191—Character of Agricola, 191—Crosses the Tweed and hews his way to the Forth, 193—The Caledonians and the Legions Face to Face, 194—Line of Forts and Skirmishes, 195—In Third Summer Agricola Traverses Fife to the Tay, 196—In the Fourth, constructs his Line of Forts, 196—In the Fifth, makes an Expedition to the West Coast, 196—Next turns towards the North, 197—His Fleet, 197—Tragic Fate of German Contingent, 198—Agricola's Hesitations, 198—Night Attack on the Roman Camp near Lochleven, 199—The Caledonian Tribes hold a Convention, 200—They Prepare for War, 200—Soldiers Enrolled and Weapons Forged, 201—If Agricola will not come to the Grampians, the Grampians will go to Agricola, 201.

CHAPTER XVII.

THE BATTLE OF MONS GRAMPIUS.

The Cloud on the North Hills, 202—March of the Roman Army Northward, 203—First Sight of the Tay, or *Ecce Tiberim*, 203—Strathmore or *Ecce Campaniam*, 203—Where was *Mons Grampius*? 204—At Ardoch? at Meigle? at Fettercairn? 204—The Fleet and Discovery of the Orkneys, 205—The

Romans approach the Grampians, 205—The Muster of the Caledonians, 206—Numbers of the Caledonians and of the Romans, 207—The War Chariots of the Caledonians, 208—Speech of Galgacus to his Soldiers, 209—Speech of Agricola to his Army, 210—Order of Battle, 210—Battle Joined, 211—Disadvantageous Armour of the Caledonians, 211—Fierceness and Carnage of the Fight, 212—Tacitus' Description of the Field, 213—The Caledonians Defeated, 213—Their Bravery, 214—Flight to their Mountains, 214—The Numbers of Fallen on both sides, 214—Night Rejoicings in the Roman Camp, 215—Sights which Morning Discloses, 215—The Wail among the Grampians, 216—The First of Scotland's Historic Battles, 216—Its Fruit, 217—It begins the long struggle for Scottish Independence, 218—Agricola retreats southwards, 219.

CHAPTER XVIII.

EXPEDITION OF SEVERUS AND WITHDRAWAL OF ROMANS FROM BRITAIN.

Northern Boundary of the Empire a moving line, 220—Antonine's Wall betwixt Forth and Clyde, 221—Hadrian's Wall betwixt Tyne and Solway, 222—Boundary again advanced to the Forth, 223—Pushed back to the Solway, 224—Severus' Expedition, A.D. 204-224—The Caledonians shun battle, 225—Traps set for the Legions, 225—Hardships of the March, 226—Severus reaches the Cromarty Firth, 226—Retreats and dies at York, 227—Rich and magnificent Realms subject to Rome, 227—Yet not content without the little Britain, 228—Changes effected by the Roman occupation, 229—Roads, 230—Husbandry, 231—Trade and Commerce, 231—Villas and Towns, 232—South England a favourite Residence of the Romans, 234—Law and Literature introduced, 235—Roman Civilisation swept away, 236.

CHAPTER XIX.

CHRISTIANITY ENTERS BRITAIN.

Entrance of two new Powers, 237—Why is the Scotland of to-day not a Land of Painted Men? 238—The Civilisation of Scotland other than that of the nations around it, 239—Its special Type or Characteristic, 239—A new Life descends on Scotland, 240—The two necessities, 240—Conscience or the Moral Sense the measure of a Nation's Liberty, 241—The Model of the Nations, 241—The second century and its facilities for the communcation of Thought, 242—Wide diffusion of Christianity by the end of second century, 242—Picture of the first British Convert to Christianity, 244—The Pudens and Claudia of Paul's Epistle, 245—The Pudens and Claudia of Martial's Epigram, 246—Chain of proof that they are the same couple, 246—Claudia most probably a British Lady, 247—Proof from Tacitus of the early entrance of Christianity into Britain, 247—Did Paul preach the Gospel in Britain, 248—Contention of Usher and Stillingfleet that he did, 248—Outline of their argument, 249—Rapidity of Christianity's spread in the first age, 251—Tertullian's Testimony, 251—Earliest Congregations in Britain, 252—Converts beyond the Roman Wall, 253—Prosperity of British Church after Dioclesian's Persecution, 255—British Pastors at Councils of Arles and Sardica, 255—Routes by which Christianity entered Britain, 257—Britain Christianised by Missionaries from the East, 258—Testimony of Neander, 259.

CHAPTER XX.
THE CRADLE OF THE SCOTS.

The Caledonian and Scot to form one Race, 262—The two branches of the Cymric Family, the Scythians and the Gauls, 264—The early Inhabitants of Britain Cymric, 265—Additional varieties, 265—Cæsar on the Britons of his day, 266—Scythia a fountain-head of Nations, 267—Picture of the Scythians, 267—Ancient testimonies to the Virtue and Valour of the Scythians, 268—They overthrow Rome, 269—Scythia the original cradle of the Scottish Race, 270—*Scythæ* and *Scoti*, two Names for one People, 270—Journey south over Germany and France, 271—They arrive in Spain, 272—Cross to Ireland, 273—Division of the Scythic Stream, 273—The Picts, 273—Their physical Prowess, 274—Their Mode of Fighting, 275—Burials, Dress, Food, Feasts, 275—Their War Songs and Music, 276—The one extant Pictish Word, 276.

CHAPTER XXI.
THE COMING OF THE SCOTS TO IRELAND.

The Scots first mentioned by Ammianus Marcellinus in end of Fourth Century, 279—Arrive in Ireland probably in the First Century, 279—The Scots formed the van in the descent of the Gothic Nations, 280—A marked Individuality, 281—The Inhabitants of Ireland in Patrick's time, 281—Scots give Kings to Ireland, 282—Their Fighting qualities, 283.

CHAPTER XXII.
THE PLANTING OF THE SCOTTISH NATION.

First Appearance of the Scots in Scotland, 284—Join the Picts in Ravaging the Territory betwixt the Two Walls, 285—Penetrate to the South of England, 286—Forced back by Theodosius, 287—A Second Irruption of Pict and Scot, 287—Again Repulsed, 288—A Third Raid, 288—A Third Repulse, 289—Fall of Rome, 289—Miseries of Britain on Departure of the Romans, 290—Groans of the Britons, 291—Four Nations in Britain, 292—The ANGLO-SAXONS, 293—Their Territory extends from Portsmouth to the Forth, 294—The BRITONS, 294—Their Kingdom Stretches from Cornwall to the Clyde, 294—The PICTS or CALEDONIANS, 295—Their Kingdom from the Forth to the Pentland Frith, 295—The SCOTS, 296—Boundaries of their Kingdom, 296—Identical nearly with Argyleshire, 297—The *Scotia* of the Early Centuries, 298—Fergus Mor leads the Scots from Antrim to Caledonia, 298—The Scottish Settlers Christian, 299—Angus and Loarne, 300—First Capital of Scots, 300—Early System of Government, 300—Peace between the Scots and Picts, 302.

CHAPTER XXIII.
KINDLING OF THE LAMP OF IONA.

A Coracle crosses the sea from Ireland, 303—Columba and his Twelve Companions, 303—They step ashore on Iona, 303—First Survey of the Island, 304—One of the Great Voyages of History, 305—Columba obtains a Grant of the Island, 306—Conversion of King Bruidi, 307—A Century's Peace in Caledonia, 308—Anglo-Saxon Conquest of England, 309—English Christianity swept away, 310—A Partition Wall of Heathenism betwixt Scottish and Latin Christianity, 311—Iona and Rome, or the Two Principles at the two opposite extremities of Europe, 312—Work of the Men of Iona, 313—Their Mission Field Christendom, 313—Brief Sketch of their Mission Tours, 314—Their Dress, Dangers, Bravery, 314.

CHAPTER XXIV.

BATTLES POLITICAL AND ECCLESIASTICAL.

Early Light Bearers, 316—Ninian and Kentigern, 316—Servanus, 317—Patrick, 317—Columban Institution, 318—Its Work, Training of Missionaries, and Evangelisation of Scotland, 319—The School and the Plough, 319—A Spirit of Peace Breathes over the Land, 320—King Aidan anointed by Columba, 321—Summary of his Reign, 321—Ethelfrith of Northumbria Slaughters the Monks of Bangor, 321—Arrival of Augustine and his Monks in England, 323 —What comes out of it, 324—Oswald of Northumbria finds asylum in Scotland, 325—Sits at the Feet of the Elders of Iona, 325—King Edwin Converted to the Roman Rite, 326—His Death in Battle, 326—Oswald Ascends the Throne of Northumbria, 326—Sends to Iona for Evangelists to Instruct his People, 327—Aidan sent, 327—Aidan and the King Evangelise together, 328—Oswald dies and Oswy ascends the Throne, 328—Perversion of King Oswy, 329—He drives the Columban Missionaries out of Northumbria, 329—War breaks out, 330—Bloody Battle at Nectan's Mere, 330—It saves Iona, 330—Lindisfarne, or "Holy Island," 331—Cuthbert of Melrose, 332—His beautiful Life, 332—Goes to Lindisfarne, 332—His touching Deathscene, 333

CHAPTER XXV.

IONA AND ROME, OR THE SECOND ROMAN INVASION.

Calm after Tempest, 334—Two Learned and Wise Princes, 334—Venerable Bede, 334—Outline of his Life and Labours, 334—What he Lacks, 335—Eugene VI. of Scotland, 337—His Learning, 337—The Eighth Century of Scotland Rises in Haze, 337—Romish Missionaries at the Court of Nectan, King of the Southern Picts, 340—Questions of Easter and the Tonsure, 341—Nectan Listens and Submits, 342—The Clergy who refuse to have their Heads Shorn are driven out, 342—They find Refuge among the Scots, 343— War follows, 343—Nectan Retires to a Monastery, 343—Confusions and Battles, 345.

CHAPTER XXVI.

UNION OF THE SCOTS AND PICTS—THE SCOTTISH NATION.

Invasion of the Vikings, 346—Form of their Ships, 346—Prodigies in the Sky, 346—Their Terrible Ravages as described by Simeon, 347—Lindisfarne

Destroyed, 347—Iona Ravaged, 347—Slaughterings in the Western Isles, 347—Iona Finally Destroyed, 348—Removed to Kells in Ireland, and Dunkeld in Scotland, 349—Changes, 349—Picture of Scotland at Opening of Eighth Century, 349—Pre-eminent among the European Countries, 349—War between the Northern and Southern Picts, 350—The Scots Join the Northern Picts, 350—These Wars Traced to the Romanizing Monks, 351—The Various Indications and Proofs of this, 352—Learned Scotsmen in France, 355—Gradual weakening of the Picts, 356—The Religious Divisions and Wars of the Picts pave the Way for the Ascendancy of the Scots, 356—Extinction of Royal Line of the Picts, 357—Throne Claimed by Alpin the Scot, 357—Death of Alpin on the Battle-field, 358—His Son Kenneth resumes the War, 359—Extraordinary Stratagem, 359—The Final Battle near Perth, 361—The Scots Victorious, 361—Kenneth MacAlpin Ascends the Throne, 362—The One Scottish Nation, 362.

HISTORY OF SCOTLAND.

CHAPTER I.

FIRST PEOPLING OF BRITAIN.

WHILE Alexander was overrunning the world by his arms, and Greece was enlightening it with her arts, Scotland lay hidden beneath the cloud of barbarism, and had neither name nor place among the nations of the earth.[1] Its isolation, however, was not complete and absolute. Centuries before the great Macedonian had commenced his victorious career, the adventurous navigators of the Phœnician seaboard had explored the darkness of the hyperborean ocean. The first to steer by the pole-star, they boldly adventured where less skilful mariners would have feared to penetrate. Within the hazy confine of the North Sea they descried an island, swathed in a mild if humid air, and disclosing to the eye, behind its frontier screen of chalk cliffs, the pleasing prospect of wooded hills, and far expanding meadows, roamed over by numerous herds, and dotted by the frequent wattle-built hamlets of its rude inhabitants. The Phœnicians oft revisited this remote, and to all but themselves unknown shore,[2] but the en-

[1] Dion Casius says, Book xxxix., that "Britain was unknown to the more ancient of the Greeks and Romans."
[2] Strabo, Lib. iii.

riching trade which they carried on with it they retained for centuries in their own hands. Their ships might be seen passing out at the "Pillars of Hercules" on voyages of unknown destination, and, after the lapse of months, they would return laden with the products of regions, which had found as yet no name on the chart of geographer.[1] But the source of this trade they kept a secret from the rest of the nations. By and by, however, it began to be rumoured that the fleets seen going and returning on these mysterious voyages traded with an island that lay far to the north, and which was rich in a metal so white and lustrous that it had begun to be used as a substitute for silver. In this capacity it was employed now to lend a meretricious glitter to the robe of the courtezan, and now to impart a more legitimate splendour to the mantle of the magistrate.

In process of time other sea-faring peoples, taught by the example of the Phœnicians to sail by the stars, and to brave the terrors of unknown seas in pursuit of wealth, followed in the track which these early merchants had been the first to open. The tin of Cornwall and of the Scilly Islands, the "Cassiterides"[2] of the ancients, began to circulate among the nations of Asia Minor, and was not unknown even to the tribes of the Arabian desert. It is interesting to think that Britain had already begun to benefit nations which knew not as yet to pronounce her name. But it was on the Syrian shore, and among the maritime tribes that nestled in the bays of Lebanon, that the main stream of this traffic

---

[1] The Phœnicians had sailed beyond the Straits of Gibraltar before Homer's time. Gades (Cadiz) in Spain was founded by them centuries before Carthage. See Huet, *Commerce des Anciens*.

[2] So called by Herodotus, Book iii. 115. It is generally supposed that he used the term vaguely to designate Britain and Ireland. Aristotle calls it *Celtic* tin, because the *Celts* were the first inhabitants of Europe. Diodorus Siculus informs us that it was the people of Cape Balerium (Cornwall) that digged the tin.

continued to diffuse its various riches. The wealth and power of the Phœnician state were largely owing to its trade with Britain. Its capital, Sidon, was nursed by the produce of our mines into early greatness. The site of Rome was still a morass; the cities of Greece were only mean hamlets: the palaces of Babylon were brick-built structures; and Jerusalem was but a hill fort; while Sidon had risen in a splendour and grown to a size that made men speak of her, even in the age of Joshua, as the "Great Sidon."

Nor was Sidon the only city on that shore that owed its greatness to the remote and barbarous Britain. Tyre,[1] the daughter of Sidon, feeding her power at the same distant springs, came ultimately to surpass in wealth, and eclipse in beauty, the mother city. No sublimer ode has come down to us than that which has as its burden the greatness and the fall of Tyre—the number of her ships, the multitude of her merchants, the splendour of her palaces, the exceeding loftiness of her pomp and pride, and the dark night in which her day of glory was to close.

The bronze gates set up by Shalmanezer to commemorate his triumphs, exhumed but the other day from the ruined mounds of Assyria, present to modern eyes a vivid picture of the greatness of the Phœnician cities. On these gates Tyre is seen seated on her island-rock, encompassed by strong walls, with serrated battlements and flanking towers. A broad avenue leads from her gates to the sea. Down this path is being borne her rich and various merchandise, which we see ferried across to the mainland. Ingots of gold and silver, rare woods, curious bowls, precious stones, spices, dyed cloths, embroidered garments, and similar products,

[1] The priests of the temple of Melcarth told Herodotus that Tyre was founded at a date that corresponds with B.C. 2750. Josephus is content with a less high antiquity for this famous seaport, and fixes its rise at B.C. 1250. He is probably nearer the true date.

brought from far off lands, form the tribute which we here see laid at the feet of the conqueror Shalmanezer. The monarch in his robes of state, a tiara on his head, stands a little in advance of a brilliant staff of officers and princes, while an attendant eunuch shades him with a richly embroidered umbrella from the hot Syrian sun, and a deputation of Tyrian merchants offer him the submission of the now tributary city. This was in the year B.C. 859.[1]

But though the doom foretold by the prophet has long since fallen upon this ancient mistress of the seas, her ruin is not so utter but that we may trace at this day the dimensions of those harbours from which the fleets engaged in the traffic with Britain set sail, and where, on their return, they discharged their rich cargoes. The harbours of Tyre, as their ruins, still visible below the waves, show, had an average area of twelve acres. The ports of Sidon were of a somewhat larger capacity. Their average area was twenty acres,—so do the scholars of the "Palestine Exploration" tell us. We who are familiar with the "Leviathans" that plow the deep in modern times, cannot but feel surprise at the diminutive size of the craft employed in the Tyrian traffic, as judged of by the limited capacity of the basins in which they unloaded their wares. A modern ironclad would hardly venture into a port of so diminutive a size. But if the ships of Tyre were of small tonnage, so much greater the evidence of the skill and courage of the crews that manned them, and the enterprise of the merchants that sent them forth on such distant voyages. And it is pleasant to reflect that even at that early age, the riches of our mines formed an important factor in the commercial activity, the artistic taste, and the varied grandeur,

---

[1] These gates were discovered by Mr Rassam in the mound of Bellowat in 1877. They are now in the British Museum.

of which the narrow strip of territory that stretches along on the eastern shore of the Mediterranean, beneath the cliffs of Lebanon, was then the seat.[1]

The palmiest era of the Phœnician commerce was from the twelfth to the sixth century before Christ. It follows, that Britain, with whom these early merchants traded, was then inhabited, and probably had been so for some considerable time previous. At what time did the first immigrants arrive on its shore, and from what quarter did they come? We cannot tell the year, nor even the century, when the first wanderer from across the sea sighted its cliffs, and moored his bark on its strand; nor can we solve the question touching the first peopling of our island, otherwise than by an approximating process. In a brief discussion of this point, we shall avail ourselves of the guidance furnished by great ethnological principles and facts, as well as of the help given us by historic statements.

The earliest and most authentic of all histories—for the monumental and historic evidence of the Bible does not lessen but grow with the current of the centuries—tells us that the Ark rested, after the flood, on one of the mountains of Ararat. Here, at the centre of the earth, is placed the second cradle of the human family, and to this point are we to trace up all the migrations of mankind. The Ark might have been set down by the retiring waters on the verge of Asia, or on the remotest boundary of America; or it might have been floated on currents, or driven by winds far into

[1] Numbers xxxi. 22, shows that *tin* was one of the metals in use among the Syrian nations when the tribes entered Canaan; and Ezekiel xxii. 18, 20, tells us that it was imported in the ships of Tyre. There were only two countries in those days where *tin* could have been obtained—Spain and England. In the Spanish mines the ore lay deep, and the yield was not over-abundant; the probability, therefore, is that the main supply of tin for the markets of Phœnicia and the East was brought from Cornwall and the Scilly Islands.

the polar regions. Escaping all these mischances, here, in the central regions of the world, and probably within sight of those plains with which Noah had been familiar before the flood overspread the earth, did the Ark deposit its burden. It was the first great providential act towards the human family in post-diluvian times.

Let us take our stand beside "the world's grey fathers," and survey with them, from the summits where the ark is seen to rest, the singular framework of rivers, mountains, and plains spread out around the spot. The various fortunes and destinies of their descendants lie written before the eyes of the first fathers of mankind on the face of the silent earth; for undoubted it is that in the geographical arrangements of the globe is so far laid the ground-work of the history, political and moral, of its nations. The physical conditions of a region assist insensibly but powerfully in shaping the mental and moral peculiarities of its inhabitants, and prognosticate dimly the events of which any particular region is to become the theatre. The mountain-chains that part kingdoms, the oceans that divide continents by diversifying the climatic influences of the globe, enrich that "one blood" of which all the nations of the earth partake, and by engendering a difference of temperament and aptitude, and stimulating to a variety of pursuit prepare more variously endowed instrumentalities for the world's work, and impart to history a breadth, a variety, and a grandeur which otherwise would have been lacking to it.

From this new starting point of the race great natural pathways are seen to stretch out in all directions. In the heart of the Armenian mountains, close to the resting place of the ark, four great rivers take their rise, and proceeding thence in divergent courses, flow towards the four quarters of the globe. A tribe or colony in quest of habitations naturally follows the course of some great stream, seeing the fertility which its waters create along its banks afford pasture for their flocks and food for themselves. Of the four great rivers which here have their birth, the Euphrates turned off to the west, and pointed the way to Palestine and Egypt and Greece. The second of these great streams, the Tigris, sending its floods to the south, and traversing with rapid flow the great plains which lie between the mountains of Armenia and the Persian gulf, would open the road to India and the countries of the East.

The Araxes and the Phasis, rising on the other side of the mountain-chain which here forms the water-shed between Asia and Europe, and flowing towards the north, would draw off, in that direction, no inconsiderable portion of the human tide that was now going forth from this central region to people the wilderness, into which, since the flood, the earth had again reverted. The settlers who proceeded along the banks of the Araxes, whose waters fall into the Caspian, would people the northern and north-eastern lands of Asia. Those who took the Phasis as the guide of their exploring footsteps, would arrive in due time in the west and north of Europe. By the several roads spread out around their starting-point, do these emigrants journey to those distant and unknown homes where their posterity in after ages are to found kingdoms, build cities, become great in arms, or seek renown in the nobler pursuits of peace.

But farther, this mountain-girdle, which is drawn round the middle of the globe, and which has two great rivers on either side of it flowing in opposite directions and in divergent channels, parts the earth into two grand divisions. It gives us a northern and a southern world. In this striking arrangement we see two stages prepared in anticipation of two great dramas, an earlier and a later, to be enacted in after time. The one was destined to introduce, and the other to conclude and crown the business of the world. Let us mark what a difference betwixt the natural endowments of the two zones, yet how perfect the adaptation of each to the races that were to occupy them, and the part these races were to play in the affairs of the world!

On the south of the great mountain-chain which bisected Asia and Europe was a world blessed with the happiest physical conditions. The skies were serene, the air was warm, and the soil was molient and fertile. How manifest is it that this favoured region had been prepared with a special view to its occupancy by the early races, whose knowledge of the arts did not enable them meanwhile to construct dwellings such as should suffice to protect them from the cold of a northern sky, and whose skill in husbandry was not enough, as yet, to draw from less fertile soils the necessaries of life in sufficient abundance. In this genial clime the inhabitants could dispense with houses of stone; a tent of hair-cloth would better meet their wants; and hardly was it necessary that their exuberant soil should be turned by the plow; without labour almost it would yield the food of man. Here then was meet dwelling-place for the infancy and youth of the human family; the brilliant light, the sparkling waters, the gorgeous tints of the sky, and the rich fruitage of field and tree, would combine to quicken the sensibilities and stimulate the imagination of man, and so fit him for those more elegant acquisitions and those lighter labours in which his youth was to be passed. Here the arts of music and painting grew up, and here, too, passion poured itself forth in poetry and song. In these voluptuous climes man perfected his conceptions as regards symmetry of form and melody of speech, and from these ages and lands have come to us the incomparable models of statuary, of architecture, and of eloquence.

"Graiis dedit ore rotundo
Musa loqui."

Nor, even yet, has the glow of morning altogether left the sky of the world. The pure and beautiful *ideals* which these young races succeeded in perfecting for us still continue to delight. They exert to this day a refining and elevating influence on the whole of life. Our graver thoughts and more matter-of-fact labours wear something of the golden lacquering of these early times.

On the north of the great mountain-wall which, as we have said, parts the world in two, the ground runs off in a mighty downward slope, diversified by forests and lakes, and furrowed by mountain-chains, and finally terminates in the steppes of Tartary and the frozen lands of Siberia. This vast descent would conduct man by slow journeys from the genial air and teeming luxuriance of his primeval dwelling to the stony soils, the stunted products, and the biting sky of a northern latitude. The boundless plains spread out on this mighty decline refuse their harvests save to the skill of the hand and the sweat of the brow. In vain the inhabitant holds out his cup to have it filled with the spontaneous bounty of the earth. But if nature has denied to these regions the feathery palm, the odorous gum, and the precious jewel, she has provided an ample compensation in having ordained that products of infinitely greater price should here be ripened. This zone was to be the training-ground of the hardier races. Here, in their contests with the ruggedness of nature, were they to acquire the virtues of courage, of perseverance, and of endurance, and by that discipline were they to be prepared to step upon the stage, and take up the weightier business of the world, when the earlier races had fulfilled their mission, and closed their brief but brilliant career. Here, in a word, on these stern soils, and under these tempestuous skies, was to be set that hardy stock on which the precious grafts of liberty and Christianity were to be implanted in days to come. With the advent of the northern races the real business of the world began.

When Noah comes forth from the Ark we see him accompanied by three sons—Shem, Ham, and Japhet. These are the three fountain-heads of the world's population. "These are the three sons of Noah, and of them was the whole earth overspread."[1] "Peleg," who lived in the fifth generation from Noah, is set up as a great finger-post at the parting of the ways, "for in his days was the earth divided."[2] And it is strikingly corroborative of the truth of this statement, that after four thousand years, during which climate, migration, and numerous other influences have been acting unceasingly on the species, all tending to deepen the peculiarities of race, and to widen the distinctions between nations, the population of the world at this day, by whatever test we try it, whether that of physical characteristic, or by the surer proof of language, is still resolvable into three grand groups, corresponding to the three patriarchs of the race, Shem, Ham, and Japhet.

The descendants of Ham, crossing the narrow bridge between Asia and Africa, the Isthmus of Suez to wit, planted themselves along the banks of the Nile, finding in that rich valley a second plain of Shinar, and in the great river that waters it another Euphrates. Egypt is known by its inhabitants as the land of Mizraim to this day. From the black loamy Delta, which reposes so securely betwixt the two great deserts of the world, and which the annual overflow of the

[1] Genesis ix. 19.   [2] According to Usher, B.C. 2247.

Nile clothes with an eternal luxuriance, Ham spread his swarthy swarms over the African continent. Shem turned his face towards Arabia and India, and his advancing bands, crossing the Indus and the Ganges, overflowed the vast and fertile plains which are bounded by the lofty Himalyas on the one side, and washed by the Indian Ocean on the other. An illustrious member of the Semitic family was recalled westward to occupy Palestine, where his posterity, as the divinely-appointed priesthood of the world, dwelt apart with a glory all their own. Japhet, crossing the mountainous wall which rose like a vast partition betwixt the north and the south, poured the tide of his numerous and hardy descendants down the vast slope of the northern hemisphere over Europe, and the trans-Caucasian regions of Asia, with, at times, a reflex wave that flowed back into the territories of Shem. Thus was the splendid inheritance of a world divided amongst the three sons of Noah.

Our main business is to track the migration of the sons of Japhet, and see by what route they travelled towards our island. From their starting point in the highlands of Armenia, or on the plain of the Euphrates, two great pathways offer themselves, by either of which, or by both, their migrating hordes might reach the shores of the distant Britain. There is the great hollow which Nature has scooped out between the giant Atlas and the mountains of the Alps, and which forms the basin of the Mediterranean Sea. Moving westward through this great natural cleft, and dropping colonies on the fair islands, and by the sheltered bays of its delicious shores, they would people in succession the soil of Greece and the countries of Italy and Spain. Pushed on from behind by their ever increasing numbers, or drawn by the powerful attraction of new habitations, they maintain their slow but inevitable advance across the rugged Pyrenees and the broad and fertile plains of France. The van of the advancing horde is now in sight of Albion. They can descry the gleam of its white cliffs across the narrow channel that separates it from the continent; and passing over, they find a land, which, though owned as yet by only the beast of prey, offers enough in the various produce of its soil and the hidden treasures of its rocks to reward them for the toil of their long journey and to induce them to make it the final goal of their wanderings.

By this route, we know, did the clans and tribes springing from Javan—the ION of the Greeks—travel to the west. We trace the footprints of his sons, Elishah, Tarshish, Kittim, and Dodanim all along the northern shore of the Mediterranean, from the Lebanon to the Pyrenees, notably in Greece and Italy, less palpably in Cyprus and Spain, attesting to this day the truth of the Bible's statement, that by them were the "isles of the Gentiles," that is, the western seaboard of Asia Minor and the northern coast of the Mediterranean, "peopled."

Meanwhile, another branch of the great Japhethian family is on its way by slow marches to the northern and western world by another route. This great emigrant host proceeds along the great pathways which have been so distinctly traced out by the hand of Nature on the surface of the globe. The Araxes and the Phasis are the guide of their steps. They descend the great slope of northern Asia, and winding round the shores of the Euxine, they thread their way through a boundless maze of river and morass, of meadow and forest, and mountain-chain, and stand at length on the shores of that ocean that washes the flats of Holland and the headlands of Norway: and thus of the human tide which we see advancing towards our island, which is still lying as the waters of the flood had left it, the one division, flowing along

through the basin of the Mediterranean, finds egress by the
Pillars of Hercules, and the other, rolling down the great
northern slope of the Caucasian chain, issues forth at the
frozen doors of the Baltic.

This parting of the emigrant host into two great bands,
and the sending of them round to their future home by two
different routes, had in it a great moral end. There are
worse schools for a nation destined for future service, than
a long and arduous journey on which they have to suffer
hunger and brave danger. The horde of slaves that left
Egypt of old, having finished their "forty years" in the
"great and terrible wilderness," emerged on Canaan a disciplined and courageous nation. The route by which these
two Japhethian bands journeyed to their final possessions,
left on each a marked and indelible stamp. The resemblance between the two at the beginning of their journey,
as regards the great features of the Japhethian image, which
was common to both, was, we can well imagine, much
altered and diversified by the time they had arrived at the
end of it, and our country, in consequence, came to be
stocked with a race more varied in faculty, richer in genius,
and sturdier in intellect than its occupants would probably
have been, but for the disciplinary influences to which they
were subjected while yet on the road to it. The aborigines
of Albion combined the strength of the north with the
passion of the south. Of the two great hosts that mingled
on its soil, the one, passing under the freezing sky of the
Sarmatian plains, and combatting with flood and storm on
their way, arrived in their new abode earnest, patient, and
courageous. The other, coming round by the bright and
genial shores of the Mediterranean, were lively and volatile,
and brimming with rich and lofty impulses. Though sprung
of the same stock, they came in this way to unite the

qualities of different races and climes—the gravity of the Occident with the warm and thrilling enthusiasm of the Orient.

The stream that descended the slopes of the Caucasus, passing betwixt the Caspian and the Euxine, would arrive on our eastern sea-board, and people that part of our island which fronts the German Ocean. The other current, which flowed along by the Mediterranean, and turned northward over France and Spain, would have its course directed towards our western coasts. In the different temperaments that mark the population of the two sides of our island, we trace the vestiges of this long and devious peregrination. The strong Teutonic fibre of our eastern sea-board, and the poetic fire that glows in the men of our western mountains, give evidence at this day of various original endowments in this one population. These mixed qualities are seen working together in the daily life of the people, which exhibits a sustained and fruitful industry, fed and quickened by a latent enthusiasm. The presence of the two qualities is traceable also in their higher and more artistic pursuits, as, for instance, in their literary productions, which, even when they kindle into the passionate glow of the East, are always seen to have as their substratum that cool and sober reason which is the characteristic of the West. Most of all is this fine union discernible, on those occasions when a great principle stirs the soul of the nation, and its feelings find vent in an overmastering and dazzling outburst of patriotism.

We do not know the number of links which connected the Patriarch of the Armenian mountains with that generation of his descendants, who were the first to set foot on the shores of Britain; but we seem warranted in concluding that Gomer and Ashkenaz were the two great fathers of the first British population. The nomadic hordes that we see descending the vast slope that leads down to the Scandinavian countries and the coast of the White Sea, are those of Gomer. This much do their footsteps, still traceable, attest. They gave their names to the lands over which their track lay, and these memorials, more durable than written record or even pillar of stone, remain to this day, the ineffaceable mementoes of that primeval immigration by which Europe was peopled. Here is Gomer-land (Germany) lying on their direct route: for this track was far too extensive and fertile not to commend itself to the permanent occupation of a people on the out-look for new habitations. "The Celts, from the Euxine to the Baltic," says Pinkerton, "were commonly called *Cimmerii*, a name noted in Grecian history and fable; and from their antiquity so obscure that a Cimmerian darkness dwells upon them. From the ancients we learn to a certainty, that they were the same people with the Cimbri, and that they extended from the Bosphorus Cimmerius on the Euxine, to the Cimbric Chersonese of Denmark, and to the Rhine."[1] The main body of these immigrants would squat down on the soil at each successive halt, and only the front rank would be pushed forward into the unpeopled wilderness. Their progress, often retarded by scarce penetrable forest and by swollen river, would be at length conclusively arrested on the shores of the North Sea; and yet not finally even there. Passing over in such craft as their skill enabled them to construct—a fleet of canoes, hollowed out of the trunks of oaks, felled in the German forests—they would take possession of Britain, and begin to people a land, till then a region of silence or solitude, untrodden by human foot since the period of the Flood, if not since the era of the creation.

The new-comers brought with them the tradition of their

[1] Pinkerton, vol. ii. pp. 48, 49.

descent. They called themselves Cymry or Kymbry. They are the Gimirrai of the Assyrian monuments. The Greeks, adopting their own designation, styled them *Kimmerioi*, and the Latins *Cimbri*. Cymry is the name by which the *aborigines* of Britain have uniformly distinguished themselves from the remotest antiquity up to the present hour; and their language, which they have retained through all revolutions, they have invariably called *Cymräeg*, which means the language of the aborigines, or "the language of the first race."[1] "It is reasonable to conclude," says Pinkerton in his learned "Enquiry into the History of Scotland," "that the north and east of Britain were peopled from Germany by the Cimbri of the opposite shores, who were the first inhabitants of Scotland, who can be traced, from leaving Cumraig names to rivers and mountains, even in the furthest Hebudes."[2]

[1] James's Patriarchal Religion of Britain, p. 13. London, 1836.
[2] Pinker. Enquiry, vol. ii. 52. Edin., 1814. Pinkerton appears to make the Cimri and the Celtæ one people. The two were kindred, sprung of the same stock, but the Celtæ were preceded by an earlier immigration into Europe (see chap. v., *seq.*). And these earlier immigrants, and first inhabitants of Britain, we can scarce doubt, were the people whom we trace up through the *Cimri* of the Latins, the *Kimmeriri* of the Greeks, and the *Gimirrai* of the Assyrian tablets to the *Gomer* of the Bible.

CHAPTER II.

JOURNEY OF THE KYMRI TO BRITAIN.

THERE are three guides which we can summon to our aid when we set out in quest of the cradle of the tribes, races, and nations that people the globe. The first is Philology, or language: the second is Mythology, or worship: and the third is Tradition, or folk-lore. These are three guides that will not lie, and that cannot mislead us.

As regards the first, no great power of reflection is needed to convince us that in the first age men conversed with one another in a common language; in other words, that man started with one speech. May not that one speech linger somewhere on the earth, slightly changed and modified, it may be, by time and other influences, but still containing the roots and elemental characteristics of those numerous tongues which are diffused over the earth, and of which it is the parent? This is not a supposition, but a fact. Philology holds in its hand the clue by which it can track all the tongues of the world through the perplexed labyrinth of diverse grammars, idioms, and dialects, to the one primeval tongue of the race. And when we permit philology to perform its office, it conducts us to the great central plain of Asia, called Iran. The researches of Max Müller, Sir William Jones, and others, appear to have established the fact, that we find the ancestor of all the numerous tongues of the nations, not in the classic languages of Greece and

Rome, nor in the more ancient Semitic, but in the speech of the Indo-European races, or Aryans. The Sanscrit possesses the root-affinities, and stands in a common relation to all the languages of the East on the one hand, and the West on the other. It presents its proud claim to be the parent of human tongues, and it identifies Iran as the spot whence the human family was spread abroad. "After thousands of years," says Mr Dasent, "the language and traditions of those who went East, and of those who went West, bear such an affinity to each other, as to have established, beyond discussion or dispute, the fact of their descent from a common stock."

Let us next attend to the evidence, on the point before us, of the second witness, Mythology, or worship. The first form of worship—keeping out of view the one divinely appointed form—was Nature worship. By nature worship we mean the adoration of the Deity through an earthly symbol. The first symbol of the Creator was the sun, and consequently the earliest form of nature worship was sun-worship. Where, and in what region of the earth was the first act of sun-worship performed? All are agreed that this form of worship took its rise in the same region to which philology has already conducted us and identified as the father-land of mankind. On the plains of Shinar rose the great tower or temple of Bel, or the Sun. There was the first outbreak of a worship which quickly spread over the earth, continually multiplying its rites, and varying its outward forms, becoming ever the more gorgeous but ever the more gross, but exhibiting in every land, and among all peoples, the same seminal characteristics and root-affinities which were embodied in the first act of sun-adoration on the Chaldean plain. Thus a second time we arrive on those great plains on which Ararat looks down.

There is a third witness, and the testimony of this witness is to the same effect with that of the former two. There exists a unique body of literature which is found floating in the languages of both the East and the West. It is mainly popular, consisting of traditions, fables, and tales, and is commonly styled *folk-lore*. These Tales bear the stamp of being the creation of a young race: they are bright with the colours of romance, and they embody, in the guise of allegory and fable, the maxims of an ancient wisdom. Whether it is the Celtic or the Teutonic, the classic or the vernacular tongue, in which we hear these tales rehearsed, they are found to be the same. They have the same groundwork or plot though diffused over the globe. This points to a common origin, and in tracing them up to that origin we pass the tongues of modern Europe, we pass the Latin and Greek tongues, we come to the language spoken by the Aryan races of Asia, and there we find the fountain-head of these unique and world-wide tales. This is another link between the East and the West, between the peoples that beheld the "grey dawn" and those on whom the world's "eve" is destined to descend. Such is the witness of these three—Philology, Religion, Tradition. They are the footprints which the human family have left on the road by which they have travelled; and following these traces we are led to Iran, where lived the men who were the first to "till and ear" the soil.

Thirty years ago it would have required some little courage to mention, unless to repudiate, the authority which we are about to cite. At that time it was fashionable to stand in doubt of the early traditions of all nations. The first chroniclers were believed to display a vein for legend rather than a genius for history. Lacking the critical acumen of the wise moderns, they were supposed to delight in garnishing their pages with prodigies and marvels, rather than storing them with ascertained facts. But this spirit of historic scepticism has since been markedly rebuked. The graven tablets dug up from the ruins of Nineveh, the treasures exhumed from the mounds of Babylon, and the secrets of a bygone time with which the explorations on the plain of Troy have made us acquainted, have signally attested the veracity of the early writers, and shown us, that instead of indulging a love of fable, they exercised a scrupulous regard to fact, and an abstention from poetic adornment for which the world, in these latter days, had not given them credit. The consequence is that the early historians now speak with a justly enhanced authority. This remark is specially true of the sacred writers, and also, to a large extent, of the secular historians.

We in Great Britain likewise possess the records of an ancient time. These writings have been preserved, not in the dust of the earth, like the written cylinders and graven slabs of the Tigris and the Euphrates valley, but in the sacred repositories of the aboriginal race whose origin they profess to record. We refer to the "Welsh Triads." These documents are the traditions received from the first settlers, handed down from father to son, and at last committed to writing by the Druids, the priests of the aborigines. They are arranged in groups, and each group consists of three analogous events; the design of this arrangement obviously being to simplify the narrative and aid the memory. We do not claim for them the authority of history; we use them solely as throwing a side light on the darkness of that remote age, and as confirmatory, or at least illustrative, as far as it is now possible to understand them, of the sketch we have ventured to trace of the peopling of Europe, and the first settling of Britain, from the etymological and historic proofs that remain to us.

The fourth Triad says: "There are three pillars of the nation of Britain. The first was Hu the Mighty, who brought the nation of the Kymry first to the isle of Britain; and they came from the summer country, which is called Defrobani (the shores of the Bosphorus), and they came over the Hazy Sea to the Isle of Britain, and to Armorica (Gaul) where they settled. The other two pillars of the nation of the Kymri were Prydain and Moelmud, who gave them laws, and established sovereignty among them."

The fifth Triad says: "There were three social tribes of the Isle of Britain. The first was the tribe of the Kymry who came to the Isle of Britain with Hu the Mighty, because he would not possess a country and land by fighting and pursuit, but by justice and tranquillity. The second was the tribe of Lloegrians (the Loire) who came from Gascony; and they were descended from the primitive tribe of the Kymry. The third were the Brython, who came from Armorica, and who were descended from the primitive tribe of the Kymry, and they had all three the same language and speech." This Triad offers a rough sketch of two migrations which are seen moving towards our island, each by a different route. The one comes over the Hazy Sea (most probably the German Ocean[1]), and the other from Gaul across the channel. But both are sprung of the same stock, the Kymri, the descendants of Gomer that first peopled Europe.

The Triads go on to speak of two subsequent arrivals of settlers by whom the first great immigration into Britain was followed and supplemented. The two later immigrations were doubtless passed on to the remoter, and perhaps as yet,

---

[1] Claudian calls the ocean opposite the Rhine the Cimbric.
[2] The Duan, says Pinkerton, puts the Cumri as first possessors of Albain, and then the Piks.—II. p. 234.

uninhabitated districts of our country. The first arrivals, it is natural to suppose, would plant themselves in the fertile and grassy plains of England, and would refuse, not without reason, to surrender to new-comers lands in which they had already established, by cultivation, the right of ownership. These last explorers would have to move onward and seek a settlement in the less hospitable and more mountainous regions of Scotland. Those whom we now see arriving in our island, and retiring to the straths and slopes of the Grampians, are probably the ancestors of the men who came afterwards to bear the name of Caledonians.

At what period the sons of Gomer—for their migration only does it concern us to trace—took their departure from their original seats in the East, no history informs us. It is natural to suppose that before his death Noah gave to his sons no uncertain intimation of how he meant the earth to be parted amongst them, and the quarter of the globe in which they were to seek their several dwellings. As the great Patriarch of mankind he possessed the princedom of the world. This vast sovereignty he could not transmit entire. Like some great monarchs who have lived since his day, he must needs distribute his power among his successors; and in this he acted, we cannot doubt, in conformity with the intimations which had been made to him of the will of a yet greater monarch than himself. For we are told that "the Most High divided to the nations their inheritance." But rivalships and conflicts would, not unlikely, spring up in connection with the distribution of so splendid a possession. Some might be unwilling to go forth into the unknown regions allotted to them, and instead of a long and doubtful journey, would prefer remaining near their original seat. The fruitful hills and well-watered vales of Armenia, and the broad plains of the Tigris and Euphrates, would not be easily forsaken for a climate less hospitable and an earth less bounteous. Noah would judge it expedient, doubtless, that while he was yet alive the three Septs into which his descendants were parted should begin their journey each in the direction of its allotted possession.

Ham must direct his steps toward his sandy continent on the West. Japhet must cross the mountains on the North, and seek a home for his posterity under skies less genial than those of Assyria. Shem must turn his face towards the burning plains of India. To leave their sheltered and now well-cultivated valley for unknown lands whose rugged soils they must begin by subduing, was a prospect far from inviting. The command to go forth seemed a hard one. They would lose the strength which union gives, and be scattered defenceless over the face of the earth. And if we read aright the brief record of Genesis, the mandate of Heaven, delivered to mankind through their common Father, that they should disperse and settle the world, met with an open and organised resistance. They broke out into revolt, and in token thereof built their tower on the plain of Shinar. There is one name that stands out, bold and distinct, in the darkness, that hides all his contemporaries; that even of the leader in this rebellion. Nimrod saw in this strong aversion of the human kind to break up into tribes and disperse abroad, a sentiment on which he might rest his project of a universal monarchy. His plan was to keep the human family in one place, and accordingly he encouraged the rearing of this enormous structure, and he consecrated it to the worship of the Sun, or Bel. This tower on the plain of Shinar was meant to be the great temple of the world, the shrine at which the unbroken family of man should meet and perform their worship, and so realise their unity. The tower was the symbol of a double tyranny, that of political despotism and that of religious superstition. The policy of Nimrod was the same with that of many an autocrat since, who has found priestcraft the best ally of ambition, and concluded that the surest way to keep a people under his own yoke was first to bend their necks to that of a false god. It was the policy adopted by Jeroboam in an age long posterior, when he set up his golden calves at Dan and Bethel, that the ten tribes might have no occasion to resort to Jerusalem to worship, and so be seduced back into their allegiance to the House of David.

This bold and impious attempt met with speedy and awful discomfiture. "The Lord came down," says the inspired historian, using a form of speech which is commonly employed to indicate, not indeed a bodily or personal appearance on the scene, but an occurrence so altogether out of the ordinary course; a catastrophe so unlooked for, and so tremendous, that it is felt to be the work of Deity. We can imagine the lightnings and mighty tempests which accompanied the overthrow of this earliest of idolatrous temples, and centre of what was meant to be a world-wide despotism. There was after this no need to repeat the patriarchal command to go forth. Pursued by strange terrors, men were in haste to flee from a region where the Almighty's authority had been signally defied, and was now as signally vindicated. If Noah outlived this catastrophe, as he had survived an earlier and more awful one, he now beheld the insurrection against his patriarchal government quelled, and his posterity forced to go forth in three great bodies or colonies to seek in the primeval forests and wildernesses of the world each its allotted home. We cannot be very wide of the mark if we fix the epoch of this great exodus at about the three hundredth year after the Flood.

The length of time occupied by the bands of Gomer in

their journey from their starting-point to the shores of
Britain would depend not so much on the space to be
traversed, as on the incidents which might arise to facilitate
or retard their journey. They had no pioneers to smooth
their way, and they could have no chart to guide them over
regions which they themselves were the first to explore.
The speed of the single traveller, and even the caravan, is
swift and uninterrupted: the movements of a million or two
of emigrants are unwieldy and laborious. Their flocks and
herds accompany them on their march. They had to cross
innumerable rivers, passable only by extemporised bridges,
or in canoes scooped hastily out of great oaks felled in the
neighbouring forest. They had to traverse swampy plains,
hew their way through tangled woods, and struggle through
narrow mountain defiles. A march of this sort must necessarily be slow. They made long halts, doubtless, in the
more fertile regions that lay on their route. In these spots
they would practise a little husbandry, and exchange their
nomadic habits for the pursuits of a more settled mode of
life; and only, when the place became too narrow for their
increasing numbers, would they send forth a new swarm to
spy out the wilderness beyond, and find new habitations
which would become in turn radiating points whence fresh
streams might go forth to people the plains and mountains lying around their track. Their progress would
exhibit the reverse picture of that presented by the army
whose terrible march an inspired writer has so graphically
described. The locust host of the prophet pursued its way,
an Eden before it, a wilderness behind it. It was otherwise
with the invading, but peaceful, millions, whose march we
are contemplating. Wherever their footsteps passed the
barren earth was turned into a garden. It was beauty, not
blackness and burning, which lay behind them. They

advanced to make war upon the desert only. The swampy pool and the black wood disappeared as they went on, and behind them on their track lay smiling fields and the habitations of men.

Forty years sufficed to carry the Goths from the banks of the Danube to the shores of the Atlantic. But their steps were quickened by their love of war and their thirst for plunder. No such incentives animated the emigrant horde whose march we are tracing, or urged on their advance. Their movement would bear not a little resemblance to what we see in America and Australia at this day, where there is a gradual but continuous outflow from the centres of population into the wilderness beyond, and the zone of desolation and silence is constantly receding before the face of man. Hundreds of years—we know not how many—would these early intruders into the silent wastes of the northern hemisphere occupy as they journeyed slowly onward and gave the first touch of cultivation to what is now, and has long been, the scene of fair kingdoms and flourishing cities.[1]

The men whom we now see stepping upon our shores are shepherds and hunters. They had learned something in their long journey, but they had forgotten more. That journey had not been conducive to their advance in knowledge, nor to their refinement in manners. The epithet "barbarian" was doubtless more applicable to them on their arrival at their new homes than when they took their departure from their original abodes. Whatever skill in husbandry and the arts they possessed in their native seats, would be diminished, if not well nigh lost in its transmission

---

[1] "No savages have yet been discovered," says Pinkerton (Vol. II. chap. 1), "over the whole globe, who had no navigation. From the North Pole to the South Pole, where there were men, there were canoes."

through successive generations in the course of their wandering and unsettled life. Their daily combats with the ruggedness of the earth, with the storms of the sky, or with the beast of prey, would brace their bodies and discipline their courage, but it would at the same time tend to roughen their manners, and impart a tinge of ferocity to their tempers and dispositions.

Counteractive influences, such as the modern emigrant from the old centres of civilization carries with him into the wilds of the southern or western world, they had none. We are accustomed to invest the shepherd's life with the hues of poetry, and we people Arcadia with the virtues of simplicity and innocence, but when from this imaginary world we turn to the contemplation of real life we are rudely awakened from our dream. We are shocked to find brutality and cruelty where we had pictured to ourselves gentleness and love. It is the pasture grounds of Europe that have sent forth its fiercest warriors. Its nomadic tribes have been its most ruthless desolators. In proof of our assertion we might appeal to the portrait which Herodotus draws of the Scythians of his day; or to the ravaging hordes which issued from the banks of the Borysthenes, or of the Volga; or to the sanguinary halberdiers which in later times so often descended from the mountains of the Swiss to spread battle and carnage over the Austrian and Italian plains. The influences which moulded these dwellers amid sheep-cots into warriors and plunderers would operate, though with greatly modified force, on the army of nomades which we see pursuing their way, century after century, down the great slope which conducts from the highlands of Armenia, and the ranges of the Caucasus, to the shores of the North Sea. They could hardly avoid catching the colour of the savage scenes amid which their track lay. There are souls to which the gloom of the far-extending forest, the grandeur of the soaring peak, and the darkness of the tempest impart a sentiment of elevation and refinement: but as regards the generality of mankind, they are but little moved by the grandest of nature's scenes, and are apt to become stern and hard as the rocks amid which they dwell.

The tendency of these injurious influences on the host whose movement we are tracing would be aggravated by other circumstances inseparable from their condition. They could carry with them no magazine of corn. Their daily food would be the flesh of their slaughtered herds, or of the animals caught in the chase. This is a species of diet, as physicians tell us, which is by no means fitted to cool the blood or allay the passions, but rather to inflame the irritability of both. Besides, this host was subjected to a natural process of weeding, in virtue of which only the hardiest and the most daring were sent onward. The less adventurous would remain behind at each halt to be transformed into tillers of the soil, or dressers of the vineyard, and this process of selection, repeated time after time, would result at last in the creation of a race singularly robust in body and equally indomitable in spirit. And such, doubtless, were the physical and mental characteristics of that band of immigrants that ultimately stepped upon our shore. They were not like the Scythians of Herodotus, or the Goths of the Roman invasion, or the treacherous and cruel Arab of our own day. They were men occupied in the first great humanizing mission of subduing and cultivating the earth. Battle they had not seen all the way, if we except the contests they had to wage with the forces of nature. Blood they had not shed, save that of bullock or of beast of prey. But if their long journey had schooled them in the peaceable virtues of patience and endurance, it had engendered not less a keen relish for their wild freedom, and stalwart in frame and strong of heart, they were able and ready to defend the independence which had been theirs ever since the day that they rallied beneath the standard of their great progenitor, and contemning the double yoke of despotism and sun-worship which Nimrod had attempted to impose upon them, turned their faces toward the free lands of the North.[1]

[1] "Originally," says Pinkerton, "the northern Celts or Cumri, were superior to the southern or Gael, in strength of mind and body, as the conquests of the former over the latter prove."—Vol. II. p. 49.

CHAPTER III.

HABITS, HABITATIONS, AND ARTS OF THE FIRST SETTLERS.

WE see these emigrants from the land of Armenia arriving on our shore, but the moment they pass within the confine of our island the curtain drops behind them, and for ages they are completely hidden from our view. What passed in our country during the centuries that elapsed between the period when it was taken possession of by the sons of Gomer and the advent of Cæsar with his fleet, we can only dubiously conjecture.

As regards one important particular, we have tolerable grounds, we apprehend, for the conclusion we are now to state. These emigrants brought with them the essentials of Divine revelation. When they left their original dwelling, the world's first Christianity, the Edenic to wit, had not been wholly obscured by the rising cloud of nature-worship. The first idolatrous temple had already been reared, and the earliest form of idolatrous worship, that of the sun and the heavenly bodies, had been instituted; but the dispersion which immediately followed had removed the Japhethian emigrants, whom we now see on their way to the far north, from contact with the rites of the rising idolatry, and from those corrupting and darkening influences which acted powerfully, doubtless, on those who remained nearer the seat of the Nimrod instituted worship. Besides, the heads of this emigration had conversed with the men who had been in the ark with Noah, and stood beside the altar whereon the Common Father offered his first sacrifice to Jehovah after the flood. It is not conceivable that Japhet had joined in the rebellion of Nimrod, or ever worshipped in the great temple on Shinar. From Japhet they had learned the knowledge of the one true God, and the promise of a Redeemer, who was to appear in after ages, and in some not yet clearly understood way, though dimly foreshadowed in the victim on the Patriarchal Altar, was to accomplish a great deliverance for the race. This great Tradition would journey with them, and some rays of the primeval day would shine on the remote shores of Britain. We have been taught to picture the earliest condition of our country as one of unbroken darkness. A calm consideration of the time and circumstances of its first peopling warrants a more cheerful view. Believing in a God, invisible and eternal, and knowing that He heareth those in every land who pray unto Him, who can tell how many "devout fearers" of His name there may have been among the first inhabitants of our country? How many lives may this knowledge have purified, and how many death-beds may it have brightened! The Patriarchs themselves had not much more than was possessed by those whom we behold setting out towards our distant shore.

Our idea that the earliest ages of all nations were the purest, and that as time passed on mankind receded ever the farther from the knowledge of the true God and sank ever the deeper into idolatry, is corroborated by the fact that the oldest known Egyptian manuscript, and of course the oldest known manuscript in the world, contains no traces of idolatry, and does not mention the name of one Egyptian god.[1]

[1] This is the manuscript known to Egyptologists as the Prisse Papyrus. It was found at Thebes, and is now in the library of Paris. Its author

These settlers found the climate of their new country more temperate—its summers less hot, and its winters less cold—than that of the continental lands over which they had passed on their way thither. Its plains wore a covering of luxuriant grass, and afforded ample pasturage for their flocks and herds. Forests covered the mountain sides, and in places not a few stretched down into the valleys and straths. These would furnish in abundance materials for the construction of dwellings, one of the first requisites of the emigrant. The new-comers go about this task in the following wise. They clear a space in the forest, or on the jungly plain, felling the trees with a stone hatchet. On the open area they plant stakes of timber, intertwine them with wattles, and roof them with straw. There rises a little cluster of huts. A wall of palisades is run around the hamlet to defend it from the beast of prey, for, as yet, human foe they have none to dread.

In at least one instance, if we mistake not, we come upon the traces of these aboriginal settlers, and the memorials, disclosed after so long an interval, touchingly attest the truth of the picture we have drawn. The relics in question occur as far north as Loch Etive, Argyleshire. Under a black peat moss, on the banks of the loch just named, are found, here and there, patches of stone pavement of an oval form. These pavements, on being dug down to, are found strewed over with wood-ashes, the remains of fires long since extinguished; and around them lie portions of decayed hazel stakes, the relics of the palisading that once formed the defences of the encampment. Here stood a cluster of log huts, and at a period so remote that the moss that now

was Ptah-hotep, son of King Tatkara Assa of the Vth dynasty, of Elephantine. It contains moral maxims and admonitions to the practice of virtue, and most remarkable of all, mentions not one Egyptian god.—Harkness, *Egyptian Life and History*, p. 18.

covers the site to a depth of eight feet has had time to grow above it.[1] It is touching to think that in these memorials we behold the oldest known "hearths" in Scotland. We picture to ourselves the forms that sat around their fires. They may not have been just the savages we are so apt to fancy them. They had their joys and their sorrows as we at this day have ours. The human heart is the same whether it beats under a garment of ox-hide or under a vesture of fine linen. It ever goes back into the past, or forward into the future, in quest of the elements of hope and happiness. These settlers cherished, doubtless, as their most precious treasure, the traditions which their fathers had brought with them from their far-off early home. They will not let them die even in this rude land. And when the winter draws on, and the storm lowers dark on the hill, and the winds roar in the fir wood, or lash into fury the waters of the lake, beside which they have raised their huts, the inmates gather in a circle round their blazing hearth, and the patriarch of the dwelling rehearses to ears attent the traditions of an early day and a distant land. Tales of the flood and of the ark, who knows, may here have had their eloquent reciters and their absorbed listeners. The "glorious hopes" carried to our island by the first pilgrim settlers would be clung to by their descendants. The knowledge of them alone kept their head above the darkness. To part with them was to obliterate by far the brightest traces by which to track their past. But gradually, veiled in legend, or disfigured and darkened by fable, these "hopes" died out, or, rather, were crystallized in the ritual of the Druid.

The sons of Gomer, who erected these frail structures on the shores of Loch Etive, were probably coeval with the sons of Ham, who were the first builders of the pyramids on

---

[1] Wilson, *Pre-historic Annals of Scotland*, p. 76, Edin. 1851.

the banks of the Nile. The monuments of the workers in granite, thanks to the durability of the material, still remain to us. The perishable edifices of the workers in wattle and sod have also been preserved by the kindly moss which, growing with the centuries, at last covered them up for the benefit of future ages. We can now compare them with the huts in which their brethren of the Gomer race, on the other side of the German Ocean, were found still living, in times not so very remote. Simple, indeed, in both style and material, was the architecture of these Cymric houses, whether on German plain or on Scottish moor. A circular row of wooden piles formed their wall. The roof was of straw; the fire was kindled on the stone floor, and the smoke made its escape by an opening left for that purpose in the centre of the roof.

The habits of the inmates were simple. They were compelled to accommodate their life to the conditions of the country in which they found themselves. A humid atmosphere, the necessary accompaniment of a swampy soil, would darken the sky with a frequent haze, and diminish the sun's power to ripen the grain. Corn they did not grow. Their long devotion to the shepherd's life had made them unfamiliar with the art of tillage. What of the husbandman's skill they had known and practised in their ancestral homes had been unlearned on their long journey. It hardly matters, for their wants are supplied by the milk of their flocks, by the game in which their forests abound, and the fish with which their rivers are stocked, which they spear with sharpened stakes. Their hardihood is maintained by the daily combats in which they are compelled to engage with the beast of prey. The weapons with which they do battle against these depredators of their herds, and, at times, assailants of their villages, are simple indeed. The club, the stone hatchet, the bow, the spear tipped with flint or bone, the snare, the sling, are the instruments they wield, being the only ones then known to them.

Invention sleeps when the wants of man are few. Necessity rouses the dormant faculties, and impels to the cultivation of the arts, slow and tardy at the best. It is easier transforming the shepherd into a warrior than training him into an artizan; the wild freedom of the hills is not easily cast off for the minute diligence and close application of the workshop. Yet were there handicrafts which these pilgrim-shepherds were compelled to learn. We find them expert at canoe-building. They had had frequent occasion to practise this art on their long journey, and the friths and lakes of their new home were too numerous to permit their skill in this important department to rust. New needs as they arise prompt to new devices. A tent may suffice as a dwelling on the plains of Asia, but not on the bleak Caledonian moor. The inhabitants of the latter must dig a chamber in the earth, or erect a hut above ground of dry sods, or of unhewn stones, would they protect themselves from the rains and frost. Garments of some sort they must needs have; for though some historians have pourtrayed the Caledonian as running *nude* on his mountains, or covering his person with paint instead of raiment, we submit that this was incompatible with existence amid the snow and ice of a Scottish winter. A succession of rigorous seasons, such as are incident to our high latitude, would have wound up the drama of the race before it had well begun, and instead of flourishing in stalwart vigour for centuries, the Caledonian would have perished from the land, and left it as desolate and silent as when he first set foot on it. It is the historian, we suspect, who has *painted*.

If the Caledonian dispensed with clothing, it was only at

times. He stript himself that he might give greater agility to his limbs when he chased the roe, or greater terror to his visage when he grappled with his enemy in battle; or he disencumbered himself to wade his marshes and swim his rivers. Raiment he not only needed, but raiment of a very substantial kind. The hoar frosts of Caledonia were so famous as to be heard of at Rome, and the light fabrics woven on the looms of later days would have afforded but small protection from the haars and icy blasts of the then Scotland.

The skin of sheep or the hide of ox formed a substantial and comfortable garment for the native. This was his winter covering. The stitching of it together taught him a little tailoring. He used a needle of bone with a sinew for a thread. His summer robe was lighter, and, moreover, admitted of a little gaiety in the way of colour, which would bring out in bright relief the figure of the wearer as he was seen moving athwart brown moor or blue hill. This was fabricated from the wool of his flock or the hair of his goats. The manufacture of these homely stuffs initiated the Caledonian into the useful arts of carding, spinning, and weaving.

The aboriginal dwellings merit a more particular description. They are commonly known by the name of *weems*. These weems have been discovered in groups in almost every county of Scotland, more particularly in Aberdeenshire, in Buchan, in Forfarshire, and even in the wildest districts of the Highlands. They are nearly as common as the sepulchral cairn. Generally the surface of the ground gives no clue to the existence of these underground dwellings. The moor or heath looks perfectly level and unbroken, and the traveller may pass and repass a hundred times without once suspecting that underneath his feet are houses that were constructed thousands of years ago, still containing the implements and utensils of the men who lived in them—the quernes in which they ground their corn, the bones and horns of the animals they hunted, the relics of their meal, and the ashes of the fire on which they cooked it.

These weems in their construction show both ingenuity and labour. Those found in Aberdeenshire are built of blocks of granite more than six feet long. They vary, of course, in their details, but the general style and structure are alike in all of them. Some of these subterranean abodes are upwards of thirty feet long, and from eight to nine feet wide. The walls converge as they rise, and the roof is formed in the same way as in the cyclopean edifices of early Greece and the colossal temples of Mexico and Yucatan, whose builders would appear to have been ignorant of the principle of the arch. The great slabs have been made to overlap each other; the intervening space is reduced at each successive row, and at last the opening a-top is so narrowed as to be covered in by a single block, and the vault completed. Not unfrequently small side chambers are attached to the main chamber. These are entered by passages not above three feet in height, and as a proof of the inefficiency of the tools with which these primitive builders worked, the stones in the wall forming the partition between the two chambers, though placed flush in the side which presents itself to the great chamber, project their narrow ends in the side turned to the small apartment. The workmen evidently lacked metal tools to dress and smooth the stones. If one may judge from the indications in the case of the best preserved of these weems, the doorway was formed of two upright slabs; the width between being sufficient for the occupant to glide in, and by a slanting passage find his way to the chamber below. It was in many cases the only opening, and served the purpose of door, window, and chimney all in one. In some instances, however, a small aperture is found at the farther end, which might give egress to the smoke, or permit the entrance of a little light.[1] On the approach of an enemy, the entire population of a district would make a rush to these narrow apertures, and vanish as quickly and noiselessly as if the earth had swallowed them up, or they had melted into thin air, leaving the intruder partly amazed and partly awed by their sudden and complete disappearance.

These underground massy halls were the winter abodes of their builders. Once safely below, a little fire to dispel the darkness, their larder replenished from the spoils of the chase or the produce of the flock, they would make a shift to get through the long months, and would not be greatly incommoded by the fiercest storms that raged above ground. But we can imagine how glad and joyous the occupants would be when the winter drew to a close, and spring filled the air with its sweetness, and the beauty of the first green was seen on strath and wood, and the early floweret looked forth, to exchange these dreary vaults in the earth for the huts above ground, built of turf and the branches of trees, in which they were wont to pass the warm days of their brief summer.

When at last, after centuries had passed by, the Phœnician navigator, penetrating the recesses of the North Sea, moored his bark beneath the white cliffs of Albion, or under the dark rocks of Caledonia, the ingenuity and resource of the natives were quickened afresh. The Invention of the Caledonian was set to work to create new forms of art which might tempt the distant trader to re-visit his barbarous shore. New artistic designs, some of them of rare ingenuity and

---

[1] Wilson, *Pre-historic Annals of Scotland*, pp. 78-84, Edin. 1851.

exquisite beauty, arose in an after-age on our soil, all of them native to the land. Shut in by their four seas, these early artists had no foreign models to copy from. Nevertheless, though they had studied in no school of design, and despite the farther disadvantage under which they laboured of being but ill-served by the tools with which they worked, the products of their home-born art surprise and delight us by their purity, their ingenuity, their elegance, and the finish of the workmanship. More graceful designs were not to have been seen in the famous studios of Phœnicia, or even in the more celebrated workshops of Greece.

As their numbers grew other necessities dawned upon them. The pilgrim-bond, so strong when they arrived in the country, now began to be relaxed and to lose its hold. They felt the need of laws and of a stronger authority than the Parental to govern them. First came the chief, whose rule extended over a tribe. When quarrels broke out between tribe and tribe, a higher authority still—a chief of chiefs—was felt to be needed for the government of the community, and the administration of the laws. Now came the king. This brings us to that long procession of august personages which Fordoun and Boethius make to defile past us, and which they dignify with the title of monarchs. These far-off and dimly-seen potentates may not be mere shadows after all; they may have had an actual existence, and exercised a rude sovereignty in those obscure times; but it does not concern us to establish their historic identity, and celebrate over again the glory of those valorous and worthy exploits which they have been made to perform on the battle-field, and which, doubtless, if ever they were achieved, received due laud from the age in which they were done.

CHAPTER IV.

THE STONE AGE.

LET us come closer to these British aborigines. They have no knowledge of letters. They had set out from their original homes before the invention of the alphabet. They have brought with them the implements of the shepherd and of the hunter, and in the foresight of danger they have provided themselves with some rude weapons of defence, such as the club and the stone hatchet, but they are wholly ignorant of the art of conversing with posterity, and of communicating to the ages to come a knowledge of what they were, and what they did. This parts them from our ken even more completely than the wild sea around their island sundered them from their contemporaries, and it may seem bootless, therefore, to pursue them into the thick darkness into which they have passed. And yet the labour of such inquiry will not be altogether thrown away. These ancient men have left behind them traces which enable us to reproduce, in outline, the manner of life which they led, much as the Arab of the desert can tell from the footprints of the traveller on the sand to what tribe he belonged, whether he carried a burden, and the days or weeks that have elapsed since he passed that way. The characters which we are now to essay to read are inscribed on no page of book, they are written on the soil of the country; nevertheless, they bear sure testimony regarding the men to whom they belong, and the study of them will disclose to us something, at least, of what went on in our dark land before history arrived with her torch to dispel its night.

We begin with the stone age. We know not when this age opened or when it closed, and it is bootless to enquire. Viewing the matter generally, the stone age was coeval with man. All around him were the stones of the field. They were his natural weapons, especially of attack, and he must have continued to make use of them till he came into possession of a better material for the fabrication of his implements and tools. This was not till the arrival of bronze, a date which it is impossible to fix. These great discoveries were made before history had begun to note the steps of human progress, and therefore we are here able to speak not of *time* but of *sequences*. We are not, however, to conclude that all nations began their career with the stone age. There was one family of mankind which retained the traditional knowledge of the metals, but the colateral branches of that family, when they wandered away from their original seat, lost the art of extracting and smelting the ore, and had to begin their upward career on the low level of the stone age. Let us hear what archeology has to say of our country on this head.

On yonder moor is a cairn. It was there at the dawn of history; how long before we do not know. It has seen, probably, as many centuries as have passed over the pyramids. Its simplicity of structure has fitted it even better to withstand the tear and wear of the elements than those mountainous masses which still rear their hoar forms in the valley of the Nile; and it has more sacredly guarded the treasures committed to its keeping than have the proud mausolea of the Pharaohs. Let us open it, and see whether it does not contain some record of a long forgotten past.

We dig down into it, and light upon a stone coffin. We open the lid of the rude sarcophagus. There, resting in the same grave in which weeping warriors laid him four thousand or more years ago, is the skeleton of one who was, doubtless, of note and rank in his day. We can imagine the blows that great arm-bone would deal when it was clothed with sinew and flesh, and the fate that would await the luckless antagonist who should encounter its owner on the battle-field. This ancient sleeper, whom we have so rudely disturbed in his dark chamber, may have surpassed in stature and strength the average Caledonian of his day,[1] but even granting this, he enables us to guess the physical endowments of a race which could send forth such stalwart, if exceptional, specimens to assist in clearing the forest or subduing the rugged globe, or fighting the battles of clan or of country.

We open this coffin as we would a book, and we scan its contents with the same engrossing interest with which we devour the printed volume which tells of some newly-discovered and far-off country. But we have not yet read all that is written in this ancient tome. We turn to its next page. The weapons of the warrior have been interred in the same rude cist with himself. Here, lying by his side, is his stone battle-axe. Its once tough wooden handle is now only a bit of rotten timber. On its stone head, however, time has been able to effect no change: it is compact and hard as when last carried into battle. This stone axe is a silent but significant witness touching the age in which its owner lived. No one would have gone into battle armed only with an implement of stone if he could have provided

---

[1] A cairn on the moor above Ardoch when opened was found to contain a cist in which was the skeleton of a man seven feet long. Sir John Sinclair, *Statistical Account of Scotland*, vol. viii. p. 497; Wilson, *Prehistoric Annals*, p. 64, Edin. 1851.

himself with a weapon of iron, or of other metal. But weapon of iron the occupant of this cist had none. He fought as best he could with such weapons as his age supplied him with, making strength of arm, doubtless, compensate for what was lacking in his weapon. The inference is clear. There was an age when iron was unknown in Scotland, and when implements of all kinds were made of stone.

There is a close resemblance betwixt the battle-axes dug out of the cairns and *tumuli* of our country and those fabricated by the savages of the South Sea Islands not longer ago than a little prior to the last age. It is not necessary that we should suppose that the latter worked upon the models furnished by our ancestors of savage times. The constructive powers of man in a savage state are always found working in the same rugged groove, and hence the resemblance between the two though parted by thousands of years. All his implements, peaceful and warlike, did man then fabricate of stone. With an axe of stone he cut down the oak; with an axe of stone he hollowed out the canoe; with an axe of stone he drove into the ground the stakes of his rude habitation; with an axe of stone he slaughtered the ox on which he was to feast; and with an axe of stone he laid low his enemy on the battle-field, or himself bit the dust by a blow from the same weapon. It was the STONE AGE, the first march on the road to civilization.

The harder stones were used in the fabrication of the heavier instruments. It was of no use going into battle with a weapon which would fly in splinters after dealing a few blows. The stone used in the manufacture of the battle-axe was that known as green-stone. But the lighter weapons, and in particular the projectiles, were fashioned out of flint. A mass of flint was split up in flakes, the flakes were chipped into the form of arrow-heads, and were fitted on to a cane, and made fast by a ribbon of skin. These flint arrow-heads proved rather formidable missiles. Shot by a strong hand from a well-strung bow, they brought down the roe as he bounded through the forest, or laid the warrior prostrate on the field. These flints were capable of receiving an edge of great sharpness. Flint knives were made use of by both the Hebrews and the Egyptians in their religious rites, in those especially where a clean incision had to be made, as in the process of embalming and other ceremonies. The hieroglyphics on the Egyptian obelisks are supposed to have been cut by flint knives. The granite in which the hieroglyphics were graven is too hard to have been operated upon by bronze or iron, and the Egyptians were not acquainted with steel.

These arrow-heads buried in the soil are often turned up at this day in dozens by the spade or the plough, showing how prevalent was their use in early times, and for a very considerable period. They suggest curious thoughts touching the artists that so deftly shaped them, and the men who turned them to so good account in the chase or in the fight. Were these ancient warriors to look up from their cairns and stone cists, how astonished would they be to mark the difference betwixt their simple missiles and the formidable projectiles—the breech-loaders, the guns, the mortars, and various artillery — with which the moderns decide their quarrels.

In some localities these flints are gathered in a heap, as if they had fallen in a shower, and lay as they fell till the plough uncovered them. This accumulation of weapons tells a tale of forgotten warfare. When we dig in the moor of Culloden, or in the field of Waterloo, and exhume the broken shells, the round shot, the swords, and other memorials of battle which so plentifully exist in these soils, we say, and would say, though no record existed of the carnage formerly enacted on the spot, here armies must have met, and here furious battle must have been waged. And so, when we gaze on these long-buried flints laid bare by the plough, we are forcibly carried back to a day in our country's unrecorded past, when uncouth warriors, with matted locks, painted limbs, and eyes gleaming with the fire of battle, gathered here to decide some weighty point of tribal dissension, and awaken the echoes of the lonely hills with their wild war-whoop, and the crash of their stone axes.

Let us look a moment with the eyes of these men, and view the world as it was seen by them. What a narrow horizon begirt them all round! History had never unrolled to their eye her storied page, and beyond the genealogy of their chief, which they had heard their senachies rehearse, they knew little of what had happened in the world till they themselves came into it. In front they were shut in by a near and thick darkness. The moor on which they dwelt was their world. The chase or the battle was the business of their lives; and to die at last by the side of their chieftain in some great tribal conflict, and have their bones inurned in the same sepulchral mound, was the supreme object of their ambition. Their range of knowledge and enjoyment was only a little less contracted than that of the beasts that perish. What a change when knowledge lit her lamp, and the barbarian, loosed from the handbreadth of earth to which he had been chained, could make the circuit of the globe, and the circuit of the centuries, and draw the elements of his happiness from all the realms of space, and from all the ages of time!

Let us ascend an eminence and take a survey of the

landscape of this age. It looks to the eye a vast shaggy wood, crossed by sedgy rivers, dotted by black tarns, and broken by rocky cliffs and ridges. Here and there a gleam of gold tells where a patch of grain is ripening, and the ascending wreath of blue smoke reveals the wattle-worked homestead that nestles in the forest. We visit one of these clearings. We find the hamlet within its staked enclosure. The inhabitants, some in linen, for they grow a little flax, others in skins, are variously occupied. Some are cutting wood with stone axes of wonderful sharpness, or sawing it with pieces of notched flint, or splitting it up by means of a stone wedge. Others are fabricating spear-shafts, arrow-heads, or scraping skins, or polishing celts, or carving implements out of bone and antler. Outside the huts the women are grinding the corn with pestle and mortar —for the hand quern has not yet been invented—and cooking the meal on the fire, or they are spinning thread with spindle and distaff, to be woven into cloth on a rude loom. Perchance some are engaged moulding with the hand vessels of clay. It is verily but the infancy of the arts, but we here behold the foundation on which have been built the mighty industries that now occupy our populations.

Outside the stockade that runs round the hamlet are flocks of sheep, herds of goats, troops of horses, and droves of short-horned cattle. Numerous hogs scour the clearing in search of roots, tended by swine herds and defended by large dogs against the bears, wolves, and foxes that infest the forest that forms the environment of the homestead.[1] Such is the picture the clearing presents.

[1] "Early Man in Britain," by W. Boyd Dawkins, p. 272, Lond. 1880.

CHAPTER V.

THE BRONZE AGE.

THE tall, fair-haired, round-headed Celt brought the knowledge of bronze with him into Britain. Man made a vast stride when he passed from stone to metal. With that transition came an instant and rapid advance all along the line of civilization. The art of war was the first to feel the quickening influence of the new instrument with which man was now armed. His weapons were no longer of stone but of bronze; and although this is every way an inferior metal to that by which it was to be succeeded, iron, to wit, it was immeasurably superior to stone, and accordingly victory remained with the warrior who entered the field armed with sword, and axe, and dagger, all of bronze. This wrought a revolution in the military art not unlike that which the invention of gunpowder in an after-age brought with it.

When we speak of the Celts, and the gift they conferred on the nations of the West, let us pause a moment to note their origin and career. They are known in history by three names—the *Celtæ*, the *Galatæ*, and the *Galli*. Their irruption from their primeval home in Central Asia was the terror of the age in which it took place. In the fourth century before Christ, after some considerable halt, they resumed their migration westwards in overwhelming numbers and resistless force. They scaled the barrier of the Alps, rushed down on Italy, gave the towns of Etruria to sack, defeated the Roman armies in battle, and pursued their victorious march to the gates of Rome, where they butchered the senators in the Capitol, and had well nigh strangled the Great Republic in its infancy. Another division of these slaughtering and marauding hordes took the direction of Greece, and threatened to overcloud with their barbarism that renowned seat of Philosophy and Art. It was with the utmost difficulty that they were repulsed, and Athens saved. The legions of the first Cæsar, after nine bloody campaigns, broke the strength of the Galli; but it was not till the days of the second Cæsar that all danger from them was past, and that Rome could breathe freely.

This is the first appearance of the Celts in history; but it is undoubted that long before this, at a period of unknown antiquity, they had begun to migrate from the East, and to mingle largely with the Cimmeric nations which had preceded them in their march westwards. The whole of Europe, from the border of Scythia to the Pillars of Hercules, was known to Herodotus as the *Land of the Celts*. Their sudden and furious descent on Italy and Greece was probably owing to the pressure of some other people, Scythic or Teutonic, that began to act upon them, putting them again in motion, and sending them surging over the great mountains that flanked their westward march. Their prolific swarms largely mixed themselves with the Iberians of Spain, the Cimri around the German Ocean, and the aborigines of Britain, and generally formed the great bulk of the population west of the Rhine and the Alps.

They were a pastoral people. To till the ground they held a mean occupation, and one that was below the dignity of a Celt. But if they disdained or neglected the plough, they knew how to wield the sword. They were fierce warriors. Even Sallust confesses that they bore off the prize from the

Romans themselves in feats of arms. Compared with the legions, they were but poorly equipped—an ill-tempered sword, a dagger, and a lance were their weapons—though they far excelled the Britons, whom they found, when they first came into contact with them, doing their fighting with weapons of stone. They delighted in garments of showy colours, which they not unfrequently threw off when they engaged in combat. The character of the Celts was strangely and most antithetically mixed. It presented a combination of the best and the worst qualities. They were eager to learn, they were quick of apprehension, they were very impressible, they were impulsive and impetuous, but they were unstable, lacking in perseverance, easily discouraged by reverses, and it was their ill fortune to mar their greatest enterprises by the discords and quarrels into which they were continually falling among themselves. The picture drawn of them by Cato the censor has been true of them in all ages of their history. "Gaul, for the most part," said he, "pursues two things most perseveringly—war and talking cleverly."[1]

Such were the people who brought the knowledge of bronze into Britain. Hewing their way through a population armed only with implements of stone, the intruders taught the Caledonian by dear experience to avail himself of the advantage offered by the new material. This was the first fruit that grew out of their invasion. But the Celts were destined to render, in an after-age, a far higher service to the nations of the West than any we see them performing on occasion of their first appearance in Europe. But they had first to undergo other vicissitudes and migrations. They had to be dislodged from great part of that vast European area of which they had held for a while exclusive possession.

[1] Smith, *Ancient History*, iii. 259-270. Lond. 1868.

They must flee before the sword with which they had chased others: they must be parted into separate bodies, shifted about and driven into corners; they must, in particular, mingle their blood with that of the Caledonian and the Scot, imparting to these races something of their own fire, and receiving back something of the strength and resoluteness of these other. The faith which they had left behind them in their Aryan home, then only in the simplicity of its early dawn, will break upon them in the West, in the full, clear light of Christianity; this will open to them new channels for their activities and energies, and then they will crown themselves with nobler victories than they have won heretofore. Instead of unsettling kingdoms by the sword, it will now be their only ambition to build them up by diffusing amongst them the light of knowledge, the benefits of art, and the blessings of Christianity. There awaits the Celts in the future, as we shall see at a subsequent stage of our history, the glorious task of leading in the evangelisation of the West.

But this is an event as yet far distant, and we return to our task of tracing, as dimly recorded in our sepulchral barrows and cairns, the changes in our national life consequent on the introduction of bronze. The first of man's pursuits to feel the influence of the new metal was war, as we have said. And, accordingly, when we open the cists and cairns of that ancient world, there is the sword, and there are the other instruments of battle, all of bronze. But in its evolutions and applications, bronze was found to benefit the arts of peace even more than it quickened the work of human slaughter. The art of shipbuilding took a stride. From earliest time man had sailed the seas, at least he had crept along their shores, but in how humble a craft! a boat of wicker work, covered with skin, or a canoe hollowed, by means of fire or a stone hatchet, out of a single trunk; but now he begins to cross frith and loch in a boat built of plank. His vessels, though still diminutive, are now more sea-worthy. He can more safely extend his voyages. He can cross the narrow seas around his island, carrying with him, mayhap, a few of the products of his soil, which perchance his neighbours may need, and which he exchanges in barter for such things as his own country does not produce. Thus the tides of commerce begin to circulate, though as yet their pulse is feeble and slow.

There is an advance, too, in the art of house-building. A chamber in the earth, or a hut of turf and twigs above ground, had heretofore contented the Caledonian, who bravely met with hardihood and endurance the inclemencies which he knew not otherwise to master. But now, in the bronze age, he erects for himself a dwelling of stone. His habitation as yet can boast of no architectural grace, for his tools are still imperfect, and his masonry is of the rudest type; but his ingenuity and labour make up for what is lacking in his art or in his implements, and now his hut of wattles is forsaken for a stone house, and his stronghold underneath the ground is exchanged for strengths, or castles of dry stone, exceedingly sombre in their exterior, but cunningly planned within, which now begin to dot the face of the country.

A farther consequence of the introduction of bronze was the development of a taste for personal ornament. The love of finery is an instinct operative even in the savage. Our ancestors of unrecorded time were not without this passion, or the means of gratifying it. The beauties of those days rejoiced in their bead necklaces and bracelets. These were formed of various materials—bone, horn, jet, the finer sort of stones, and frequently of sea-shells, perforated, and strung upon a sinew or vegetable fibre. Beads of glass have in some instances been discovered in the cists and tumuli of the stone period, the importation probably of some wandering trader, from the far-off shore of Phœnicia. But when we come to the cists of the bronze age, we find them more amply replenished with articles of personal ornament than those of the foregoing period. These, moreover, are of costlier material, and, as we should expect, they are more elegant in form, and more skilful in workmanship. As among the ancients so with the primitive Britons, neck-ornaments seem to have been the most highly prized; for collars abound among the treasures of the cist. The other members of the body had their due share, however. There were pendants for the ears, clasps for the arms, rings for the finger, and anklets for the legs. Nor was this love of ornament confined to the females of the period. As is the case among all savage nations, it was hardly less strongly developed among the gentlemen of Caledonia than among the ladies. The archæologist finds not unfrequently in the cist of the chieftain and warrior, lying alongside his skeleton, the ornaments which graced his person, as well as the sword and spear that served him in the battle. Among female ornaments, necklaces have been discovered, consisting of alternate beads of jet and amber. The native origin of these articles is placed beyond doubt by the fact that they totally differ from the Anglo-Roman or classic remains, and that they are found in the earliest tombs, dug long ere foot of Roman had touched the soil.

A yet greater obligation did Scottish civilization owe to bronze when it introduced, as it now did, a superior and more serviceable class of domestic utensils. Hitherto culinary vessels and table-dishes had been of stone or clay rudely fashioned. These would fall into disuse on the advent of bronze. The natives had now access to a material of which to fashion vessels, possessing not only greater durability, but susceptible also of greater variety of form and greater grace of decoration. The articles of bronze—cups, tripods, kettles, and cauldrons—dug up from underneath our mosses, show that the Caledonian was not slow to appreciate the advantages which bronze put within his reach, that he set himself to acquire the art of working in it, and that he succeeded in producing utensils of greater utility and of superior beauty to any that he or his fathers had known. His table had a grace which had been absent from it till now. He felt a pardonable pride, doubtless, as he beheld it garnished with vessels of precious material and curious workmanship. A king might sit at his board. Nor did the matter end there. The art refined the artificer. The Caledonian workman came under the humanising influence of a sense of beauty. As time went on his genius expanded, and the deftness of his hand increased. Every new creation of symmetry or of grace as it unfolded itself under his eye gave him a new inspiration, and not only prompted the desire, but imparted the ability to surpass all his former efforts by something better still—some yet rarer pattern, some yet lovelier form. Thus grew up the Celtic art. The time of its efflorescence was not yet come—was far distant. But when at length that period arrives, and Celtic art is perfected, it is found to challenge a place all its own among the arts of the world. From the simplest elements it evolved effects of the most exquisite grace and beauty. It was unique. Celtic hands only knew to create it, and on none but Celtic soil did it flourish.

It is natural to suppose that for some time after the introduction of bronze the supply of the metal was limited, and its cost correspondingly high. In these circumstances vessels of stone and clay would continue some little time in use, along with those of the new manufacture. The *finds* in the bogs and cists of our country verify this conjecture. The two kinds of vessels are found in bogs and pits in miscellaneous heaps, showing that the worker in clay and stone was not instantaneously superseded by the worker in bronze. Not only did his occupation continue, but from this time his art was vastly improved. He profited, doubtless, by the metallic patterns to which he had now access, and he learned to impart to his stone arts and implements something of the symmetry and grace which characterised the new creations in bronze. It is now that we come on traces of the potter's wheel; as later on of the turning lathe. The clay vessels of the period are no longer moulded rudely by the hand, they have a regularity and elegance of shape which the hand could not bestow, and which must have been given them by machinery. This is particularly the case as regards the cinery vases, which are found in the cists and cairns of the bronze period: many of them are specially graceful. The appearance of urns containing the ashes of the dead in this age, and not till this age, is significant as betokening the entrance of a new race and of new customs, if not of new beliefs. The inhumation of the body was, beyond doubt, the earliest mode of sepulture in our country. Its first inhabitants had brought this custom with them from their eastern home, and continued to practise it, and, accordingly, in the very oldest cairns and cists the skeleton is found laid out at its full length, and one consequence of its long entombment is that on the opening of the cist, and the admission of air, the bones fall in dust and the skeleton disappears under the gaze. But in the bronze age there is a change: this most ancient and patriarchal method of burial is discontinued. The presence of the cinery vase in the grave shows that the body was first burned, and then the ashes were collected and put into an urn. This treatment of the dead has classic example to recommend it. Every one knows that the Greeks and Romans placed the bodies of their departed warriors and philosophers on the funeral pyre. Homer has grandly sung the burning of the bodies of Hector and Patroclus on the plain of Troy: the kindling of the pile over-night, the quenching of the flames at dawn with libations of wine, and the raising over the inurned ashes of the deceased heroes that mighty tumulus that still attracts the gaze of the traveller as he voyages along that shore. But despite the halo which these high classic examples throw around the funeral pyre, we revolt from it. It shocks the reverence which clings even to the bodies of those whom we have revered and loved while they were alive. From these grand obsequies on the Trojan plain we turn with a feeling of relief to the simple yet dignified scene in the Palestinian vale, where the Hebrew Patriarch is seen following his dead to hide it out of his sight in the chambers of the earth. This mode of sepulture, that is, by incremation, would seem to have been only temporary. When we come later down the cinery urns disappear from the graves, and we are permitted to conclude that the Caledonians ceased to light the funeral pyre, and reverted in their disposal of their dead to the more ancient and certainly more seemly rite of laying them in the earth.[1]

With bronze, too, came a marked improvement on the dress of the natives. Their clothing hitherto had alternated betwixt a coat of fur, which was worn in winter, and a garment of linen, which formed their summer attire. The former cost them little trouble, save what it took to hunt

[1] Wilson, *Pre-historic Annals of Scotland*, Chap. v., vi., vii. Edin. 1851.

the boar or other beast of prey and compel him to give up his skin for the use of his captor. The latter they wove from the little flax which they had learned to cultivate. But they needed a stuff more suitable for clothing in a moist and variable climate than either the hide of ox or the light fabric of linen. A woollen garment was what they wanted as intermediate betwixt one of fur and one of flax. But in the stone age it does not appear that they knew to weave wool into cloth. Probably their implements were at fault. But the arrival of bronze got them over the difficulty. It supplied them with finer tools, and now an advance takes place in the arts of spinning and weaving. They had now less need to rob the bear of his skin, or slaughter the ox for his hide. The wool of their flocks would furnish a garment more suitable for most purposes than even these. Accordingly, woollen cloth now begins to make its appearance. And from this time we can imagine the Caledonian, when he went a-field, wrapping himself in his woollen plaid, or donning his woollen cloak and cap, while his legs are encased in leather, and his feet are thrust into sandals of skin.

But it is in the agriculture of the country that the main change that followed the introduction of bronze is seen. The stone axe, with its edge so easily blunted, made the process of clearing the forest a slow and laborious one. The oaks and firs that covered Scotland yielded to the axe only after long and painful blows, and it was with immense toil that a small patch was redeemed for pasture, or for growing a little grain. In truth, the clearances were mostly effected by the agency of fire. But when bronze made its appearance the Caledonian became master of the great forests that environed and hemmed him in. His pasturages stretched out wider and wider; the golden grain was seen where the dark wood had waved. The beasts of prey decreased, their covert being cut down. If the hunter had now less scope for the exercise of the chase, and his venison began in consequence to grow scarce, he could make up for the lack of that food in which he delights by a freer use of the flesh of his flocks and herds. There came to be no lack of corn and milk; and the morasses beginning to be drained, not only was the face of the country beautified, but the air above it became drier and more salubrious. Such is the evidence furnished by the contents of the refuse-heaps of the bronze age, found in caves, in barrows, in lake-dwellings, and in ancient burial-places.[1]

It is the admixture of tin with copper that gives us bronze. Copper is one of the most abundant of the higher metals, but it is also one of the softest, but when alloyed with tin in the proportion of from a tenth to a twelfth per cent., copper acquires the hardness requisite to fit it for all the purposes to which bronze was put. And as this is the proportion found in the bronze relics which have been dug up in the various countries, it is thence inferred that bronze was diffused from one centre, and that centre in Asia Minor. Brass is a later and different metal. It is the admixture of zinc with copper, and is not found in use till we come down to the rise of the Roman empire.[2] The invention of bronze carries us back to an unknown antiquity.

[1] See Dawkin's "Early Man in Britain," chap. xxi., for the works from which the above facts are gleaned, and on which the deductions stated in the text are founded.
[2] Anderson's "Scotland in the Pagan Times and the Iron Age," p. 223.

CHAPTER VI.

THE IRON AGE.

The iron age is a sort of twilight between the utter night of the stone and bronze periods and the morning of history. Of all the metals iron is by far the most useful. This superiority it owes to its greater hardness, which permits, especially when converted into steel, tools to be made of it which are equally adapted for the most delicate operations and the roughest labours. With iron we can trace the finest line on the precious stone, or hew a pathway into the bowels of the mountain. When man came into possession of this metal, he wielded that one of all the material instrumentalities which was the fittest to give him the mastery of the globe. Man could now till the earth, quarry the rock, dig into the mine, clear the forest, build cities, and enclose them within impregnable ramparts. But what, perhaps, most pleased the Caledonian of that age was that he could now ride forth to battle in his war chariot, brandishing his flashing weapons, and blazing in a coat of mail.

But if the first result of the introduction of iron, as in the case of bronze, was the dismal one of increased battle-carnage, aftertimes were to bring a compensation for this initial evil in the indefinite multiplication of the resources of art. The half-trained savage, as he busies himself smelting the ore and hammering the metal to forge therewith an instrument of slaughter, little dreams that he is in reality a pioneer of peace. And yet it is so. He is making proof of a substance whose many unrivalled properties need only to be known to convince man that he now holds in his hand an instrument of such potency that compared with it Thor's famous hammer was but a reed. When the qualities of iron shall have been tested and ascertained, man will be able to harness and set working in his service the mighty forces of steam and electricity. And when this has come to pass, the savage shall have grown into a sovereign with not an element in earth, in sea, or in air, which is not his willing subject and servant. The mountain will part asunder to give him passage, the billows of the Atlantic will support his steps, and the lightnings will run on his errands to the ends of the earth.

In Asia, it is probable, was the discovery made that iron-stone is an ore, and can be smelted and wrought like the more ductile bronze. At all events, it is in that quarter of the world that we come upon the first historic traces of this metal. The Homeric heroes are seen fighting with weapons of bronze and of iron. The dream of Nebuchadnezzar makes it undoubted that iron was known in Chaldea in his day. This metal formed an important part of the colossal figure that stood before the king in his sleep.[1] From the ancient centres—Egypt, Assyria, and Phœnicia—iron slowly made its way westward. Hesiod (B.C. 850) tells us that in his day it had superseded bronze among the Greeks. The

---

[1] It is curious to mark that the order in which the four metals are arranged in the image of Nebuchadnezzar is the same with that, generally speaking, of their discovery and prevalent use in the world. In the image the head of gold came first; next the breast and arms of silver; then the belly and thighs of brass; and fourth, the legs of iron. In the earliest days gold was the most plentiful metal, though, from its great softness, of little practical use. It is found frequently with the bronze in our cists, and recent explorations in the plain of Troy attest its great abundance in that age. Next comes silver, though scarce, and repre-

Aryan races, which were the first to settle in Europe, were ignorant of metals. Not so the Celtæ which succeeded them. They excelled in the metallurgic arts, and if not the first teachers of the Romans in them, they greatly advanced their knowledge and proficiency. The Norici, a Celtic tribe, inhabiting near the Danube, and to whom is ascribed the art of converting iron into steel, are believed to have supplied the Romans with iron weapons in their life and death struggle with Carthage. In the days of Augustus, a Noric sword was as famous at Rome as a "Damascus blade" or an "Andrew Ferrara" in after times. From the Mediterranean iron travelled into northern Europe by the ordinary channels of commerce, and finally made its appearance in Britain. The Caledonians were, doubtless, at first dependent on the southern nations for their supply, but only for a time, for their country abounds in iron ore; and from the day that they learned the art of smelting, they were wholly independent of their neighbours for their supply of this useful metal. In the days of Cæsar the native mines yielded, we know, enough for the needs of the inhabitants. Their implements and weapons were now of iron; their personal ornaments were formed of the same metal, along with bronze, which, though now dismissed from the service of the arts, was still retained in the business of personal ornamentation.

The change which iron brought with it in the arts and uses of life, was neither so sudden nor so radical as that which was attendant on the introduction of bronze. It was not to be expected that it would. The transition from

sented by the short-lived kingdom of Medo-Persia. Third comes the period of bronze and brass, as exemplified in the powerful brazen-coated Greeks. And fourth comes the iron kingdom of Rome. These four metals came into use and dominancy in the same order in which they are seen in the image. The historic eras are, the golden, the silvern, the brazen, the iron.

bronze to iron was not by any means so great as that from stone to bronze. The change now effected was simply a change from an inferior metal to a higher. Many of the purposes served by iron had been served by bronze, though not so well. Custom and prejudice were on the side of the older metal. The savage would be slow to discard the tools which had served him aforetime, or to cast aside the ornaments in which he had taken no little pride, and which he might even deem more fitting than those, so lacking in glitter, as ornaments of iron. Besides, iron at first was doubtless the more costly. Though the most abundant of all the metals, its ore is the most difficult to smelt. It fuses only under an intense heat. But its greater utility at last carried the day and brought it into general use, first of all on the field of battle. Self-preservation being the first law of nature, man will always make choice of the best material within his reach for the weapons with which he defends himself. The bronze sword was adapted only for attack. The warrior who was armed with it could deal a thrust, but he could not parry the return blow. His sword of cast bronze was apt to shiver like glass. It was useless as a weapon of fence. This revolutionised the battle-field; and we begin to find the record of that revolution in the cists and cairns. The leaf-shaped bronze sword disappears, and the iron brand comes in its room. The shape of the weapon, too, is different. The sword has now a guarded handle. It is clear that the warrior used it to parry the blow of his antagonist as well as deal a thrust, and this necessitated some contrivance for guarding his sword-hand.[1]

From the battle-field, and the dreadful work there required of it, iron passed into the kindlier and lovelier uses of social and domestic life. And for some of the uses to

[1] Wilson, *Pre-historic Annals;* Dawkins, *Early Man.*

which it was now put, iron would seem to be but little adapted, as, for instance, that of personal adornment. The modern beauty would think iron a poor substitute for gold in the matter of jewellery, and would feel nothing but horror in the prospect of appearing at the concert or in the ballroom as the horse appears in the battle, harnessed in iron. But not so her sisters of two or three thousand years ago. They deemed that their charms had not justice done them unless they were set off in iron bracelets, iron anklets, and other trinkets of the same unlovely metal. Even their lords, who were hardly less enamoured of personal ornaments than their ladies, wore, Herodian tells us, their iron neck-collars and iron girdles as proudly as Roman his insignia of the finest gold; another proof, by the way, of the adage that there is no disputing about matters of taste. This much, however, can be said for the Caledonian, even that the metal was novel, that it was probably rare and costly, and therefore was deemed precious. Nor was the Caledonian done with these things when he died. He took them with him to the grave, that he might appear in a manner befitting his rank in the spirit world. He would wear them in Odin's Hall.

Iron, too, was used in the coinage of our country. The current money of our island in those days consisted in good part of iron coined into small rings. So Cæsar informs us. Iron money has this advantage over gold, it better resists the tear and wear of use; and this may have recommended it to the Caledonians. We can imagine our ancestors going a-marketing provided with a score or two of these little iron rings. The Caledonian wishes to provide himself with a skin coat, or a plaid of the newest pattern and brightest colours, or a hand-guarded iron sword, for flint arrow-heads and bronze-tipped spears are now antiquated; or he would like to grace his table with a drinking-cup, or a bowl, or other utensil turned on the wheel; or he aspires to present his better-half with a bracelet or a finger-ring, and having counted the cost and found that he is master of the requisite number of iron rings, he sets off to effect the purchase. The seller hands over the goods and takes the rings in payment; they are current money with the merchant. We moderns like to combine the beautiful with the useful even in these every-day matters. It gratifies our loyalty as well as our taste to see the image of our sovereign, bright and gracious, every time we handle her coin. The Caledonian did not understand such subtle sentimentalities. The iron rings he traded with bore neither image nor superscription. They did his turn in the market nevertheless, and he was therewith content.

A gold coinage appears to have been not altogether unknown even then. "Little doubt is now entertained by our best numismatists," says Wilson, "that the coins of Comius, and others of an earlier date than Cunobeline, or the first Roman invasion, include native British mintage. There is no question at any rate that they circulated as freely in Britain as in Gaul, and have been found in considerable quantities in many parts of the island. The iron or bronze or copper ring money of the first century must therefore be presumed as only analogous to our modern copper coinage, and not as the sole barbarous substitute for a minted circulating medium."

These rings, in some cases, at least, were interred with the dead, despite the saying of Scripture that we bring nothing with us into the world and shall carry nothing out of it. The departing in these ages carried with them the money with which they had traded in the markets of earth,

[1] Wilson, *Pre-historic Annals*, pp. 353, 354.

or what portion of it their friends judged necessary. Here it is beside them in their graves, doubtless, in the idea that in some way or other it would be serviceable in the world beyond. The porter at the gate of Valhalla might be the more quick to open if he had the prospect of a gratuity. And the man to whom he gave admission—unless, indeed, this new world was altogether unlike the one from which he had come—would be all the more welcome that he was known to be not without assets, and might help his friends at a pinch. But not to dogmatise about the theory that underlay these burial ceremonies, the fact is undoubted that these little rings are found in the graves and cists of that ancient time lying alongside the skeleton of their former owner. The discovery, however, makes us little the wiser. The great enemy of iron is rust. The hardest of all the metals, it more quickly succumbs to corrosion than any of the others. The ring money found in the old graves cannot be described, because it cannot be handled and examined. It is found, on the opening of the tomb, to be nothing but a circlet of brown rust. The thin gold ornaments dug up at Mycenæ, and now in the museum at Athens, are as old, at least, as our ring money, and yet they can be seen and handled at this day. Not so the iron coinage of our forefathers. Not unfrequently does it happen, when their graves are opened, that the small rings remain visible for a few minutes, and then, along with their companion skeleton, dissolve in ashes.

The cists and graves testify to the new face that began to appear on our northern and barbarous country on the coming of iron. With it the streaks of the historic dawn begin to be seen on the horizon. The isolation of the land is now well nigh at an end. The Britons in the south are seen crossing and recrossing the channel in frequent intercourse with their neighbours and kinsfolk the Belgæ. The arts draw them together. They understand one another's speech. The coinage of the two nations passes from hand to hand on both sides of the sea. The tides of commerce flow more freely. The pulse of trade is quickened. State necessities, too, draw them to each other, and tend to cement their friendship. Rome is advancing northward, and wherever she comes she imposes her yoke, and the Britons, desirous, no doubt, of keeping the danger from their own door, send secret assistance to the Belgæ in resisting the advances of their great enemy. The influences which this contact and commingling make operative in the south of the island extend into the north, bringing therewith a certain refinement to the Caledonian, and multiplying the resources of his art, of which we begin to find traces in that only writing he has left behind him—his cairns and cists, to wit. His art-designs are better defined, and also more graceful. He has better material to work with, and he does better work. He is gathering round him new appliances both for use and for ornament, and may now be said to stand on the level which the nations of Asia had reached five centuries before, or, it may be, earlier. His fighting equipage is now complete. He appears on the battlefield in his war-chariot; and when his battles come to an end, he takes it with him to the grave. For when we uncover his barrow, there are the iron wheels that were wont to career over the field, carrying dismay into the hostile ranks, resting in darkness—at peace, like the skeleton alongside. There, too, is his shield with its iron rim and studs, together with his sword, the prey, all of them, of the same devouring rust, but telling their tale, all the same, of bloody conflicts long since over. We have a glimpse, too, into the boudoirs of the period. We see the beauty performing her toilet with the help of a polished iron mirror; for when we open her cist, there, resting by her side, in the dark land, is the identical mirror in which she was wont to contemplate the image of her beauty when she lived beneath the sun; and there, too, are the trinkets of gold, of amber, and of other material which she wore above ground, and which she has taken with her as credentials of the rank she is entitled to claim in the world into which she has now passed.[1]

Of the thrifts and industries practised in the Scotland of those days, we have memorials not a few treasured up, unwittingly, long ago for our instruction in this latter age. Let us bestow a glance upon them. We have seen how the Caledonian could build, sagaciously planting his winter house far down in the warm earth, and his summer retreat of twigs hard by in the open air. Now that he is in possession of iron tools, many improvements, doubtless, take place in the accommodation and furnishings of his hut. But he knows also to weave. The loom of that age, like its plough, was of the simplest construction, existing only in its rudiments. It survives, however, in the cairns and cists—the great storehouse of pre-historic records—and with it specimens of the cloth woven upon it. Here is the long-handed, short-toothed comb with which the thread, having been passed through the warp, was driven home. This, and the beam to which the threads were fastened, formed the loom. In the tumuli are found portions of cloth of a quality far from contemptible, and sometimes of bright and even beautiful colours. To create such fabrics on so rude a loom, argues both deftness and taste on the part of the workman. To pass from the weaver of the iron age to the potter, we trace, too, an advance in his art. The cups

---

[1] Wilson, *Pre-historic Annals of Scotland*, ii. 146; Thurnam Davis, *Crania Britannica*, Part xii.; Greenwell, *Ancient British Barrows*, p. 450.

and vases dug up are more elegantly shaped, and by means of a few waving lines, have a simple but graceful decoration given them. The art of glazing pottery—the colour commonly being green—has now been found out. From the potter's wheel we come to an instrument of still greater importance in domestic life. The grain-stones are now laid aside, and the quern has come in their room. May we not infer from this that a greater breadth of corn has now began to be grown, and that the natives depend more on the field than on the chase for their subsistence, and may have regaled themselves on the same dish that may yet be seen on the breakfast tables of our own day. Nor are the cists silent respecting so humble an actor on the scene as the dog. The attendant of man in all stages of his career, we know that he followed the steps and looked up into the face of the Caledonian, savage though he was, for here the bones of dog and master lie together in the same grave. And when the Caledonian was no longer a savage, though still a barbarian, he had broken to his use, and attached to his person and service, a yet nobler animal—the horse, to wit. For here, in the same barrow, beside the bones of the warrior, lie those of the steed that bore him into the battle, and mayhap carried him safely out of it. He shares the honour as he shared the perils of his master.

Nor did beauty in those days, any more than in ours, neglect the labours or disdain the aids of the toilet. Here are the whalebone combs, the bone and iron pins, and the articles of gold and amber and jet, which were employed in the arranging of the hair and the adorning of the person. These remain, but—such is the irony of time—the charms they helped to set off have long since faded. The men of those days, too, made merry on occasion. Here are the drinking-cups, the goblets, and the vases that figured at their banquets, once bright and sparkling, but now encrusted with the rust of two thousand years and more. In vain we question these witnesses of the long past carousals touching the liquor that filled them, and the warriors and knights that sat round the board and quaffed it, while the song of bard or the tale of palmer mingled in the loud din of the banquetting-hall. The climate of Scotland did not favour then, any more than in our day, the cultivation of the vine; but when denied the juice of the grape, man has seldom been at a loss to find a substitute, and commonly a more potent one. Our ancestors, like the Germans, regaled themselves on a beverage brewed from a mixture of barley and honey, termed mead; and, though stronger than the simple wines of southern lands, it was greatly less so than the potent drinks with which the art of distillation has since supplied their descendants.

The cuisine of the Caledonians of that period was far from perfect. But, if their food was cooked in homely fashion, it was varied and nutritious, as the long preserved relics of their feasts testify. The museum at Bulak shows us on what luxuries the Egyptians of four thousand years ago regaled themselves. The buried hearthstones of our country show us the dainties on which the Scottish contemporaries of these old Egyptians were used to feed. The wheat-fields of Manitoba and Transylvania had not been opened to them. To the vineyards of Oporto and Burgundy they had no access. Of the tea and coffee plantations of China and Java they did not even dream. But their own island, little as had as yet been done to develop its resources, amply supplied their wants. They could furnish their boards from the cereals of their straths, the wild berries of their woods, the fish of their rivers, the milk and flesh of their herds, and the venison of their moors and mountains. There is not a broch in Orkney that does not contain the remains of the rein or red deer. The red deer does not exist in Orkney at this day; the animal continued down to about the twelfth century.

A marked feature in the Scottish landscape of those days was the broch. The broch was peculiar to Scotland; not a single instance of this sort of structure is to be found out of the country. The brochs were places of strength, and they tell of hostile visits to which Scotland was then liable, and which made it necessary for its inhabitants to provide for their safety. The brochs were built of dry stones; mark of tool is not to be seen upon them; nevertheless, their materials, though neither hewn nor embedded in mortar or lime, fit in perfectly, and make their walls compact and solid. When danger approached, we can imagine the whole inhabitants of a district leaving the open country and crowding into the broch with their goods, and finding complete protection within their strong enclosure. They were circular ramparts, in short, planted thick in some places—the districts, doubtless, most liable to incursion—and they must have given a fortified look to the land. Their average height was 50 feet, their diameter 40, and the thickness of their wall from 12 to 15 feet. Their door was on the ground level, but, for obvious reasons, unusually narrow and low. It was little over 3 feet in height and 2 in width. They were open to the sky within. Their thick wall was honey-combed with chambers, placed row above row, with a stair ascending within, and giving access to the circular chambers. Their windows looked into the area of the broch; their exteriors presented only an unbroken mass of building. In some instances they were provided with a well and a drain. There is not now one entire broch in Scotland, but their ruins are numerous. Not fewer than 370 have been traced in the country, mostly to the north of the Caledonian valley. More may have existed at one time, but their ruins have disappeared. The construction of these fabrics, so perfectly adapted to their purpose, argues a considerable amount of architectural skill on the part of their builders, and also a certain advance in civilization. The discovery of Roman coins, and the red glazed pottery of Roman manufacture in these brochs, indicate their existence and use down to the occupation of the southern part of Britain by the Romans.

There remains one point of great moment. What knowledge did the inhabitants of Scotland of that age possess of a Supreme Being and a future state? This is the inner principle of civilization, and, dissociated from it, no civilization is of much value, seeing it lacks the capability of being carried higher than a certain stage, or of lasting beyond a very brief period. What hold was this principle acquiring on our ancestors? We have only general considerations to guide us here.

Noah, before sending his sons forth to people his vast dominions, doubtless communicated to them, as we have said above, those Divine traditions which were their best inheritance, and which the posterity of Seth had carried down from Eden. He taught them the spirituality and unity of God; the institution of the Sabbath and marriage —the two foundation-stones of society; the fall of man, the promise of a Saviour, and the rite of sacrifice. These great doctrines they were to carry with them in their several dispersions, and teach to their sons. As one who had come up out of the waters of the deluge—the grave of a world— the words of Noah, spoken on the morrow of that tremendous catastrophe, would deeply impress themselves on the minds of his sons, and would remain for some considerable time, distinct and clear, in the memory and knowledge of their posterity. How long they did so we have no means of certainly knowing. Without a written record, and left solely to oral transmission, these doctrines, so simple and grand, and fully apprehended by Noah's immediate descendants, would gradually come to be corrupted by additions, and obscured by allegory and legend. We know it to have been so as a fact. Hence the world of heathen mythology which grew up, and grafted itself on the men and events recorded in early Scripture. When the tenth or twentieth generation of the men who had sat at the feet of the great Patriarch arrived on the shores of Britain, it is natural to suppose that parts of the primeval revelation were lost, and that what of it was preserved was greatly obscured. But in the darkest eras of our country, as we shall afterwards see, the rites of worship were publicly observed. And with worship there are necessarily associated two ideas—a Supreme Being, and a life to come.

There is one fact which throws a pleasing light on these remote times of our country—No idol or graven image has ever been dug up in our soil. The cists and cairns of our moors contain the implements of the hunter and of the warrior, but no traces of the image-maker—no gods of wood and stone. The museums of Egypt are stocked by the thousand with the gods her inhabitants worshipped in old time, and scarce can we cast up a shovelful of earth in Cyprus, but we find in it some memorial of pagan idolatry. In the lands of Italy, of Greece, of Assyria, and of India, long-buried deities are ever and anon cropping up and showing themselves in the light of day, but no such phenomenon has ever occurred on the soil of Scotland. Ancient Caledonia would seem, by some means or other, to have been preserved from a taint which had polluted almost every other land. Relics of all sorts have been found in our soil, but never idol of British manufacture; nor is one such to be seen in any of our museums. "The relics," says Wilson, "recovered from the sepulchral mounds of the great valley of the Mississippi, as well as in the regions of Mexico and Yucatan, display numerous indications of imitative skill. The same is observable in the arts of various tribes of Africa, Polynesia, and of other modern races in an equally primitive state. What is to be specially noted in connection with this is, that both in the ancient and modern examples the imitative arts accompany the existence of idols, and the abundant evidences of an idolatrous worship. So far as we know, the converse holds true in relation to the primitive British races, and as a marked importance is justly attached to the contrasting creeds and modes of worship and policy of the Allophylian and Aryan nations, I venture to throw out this suggestion as not unworthy of farther consideration."[1]

May we not infer from a circumstance so anomalous and striking that the ancient Briton had not lapsed into the gross polytheism to which the Greeks and Romans abandoned themselves. Lying off the highway of the world, and shut in by their four seas, they would seem to have been exempt, to a large extent, from the corrupting influences which acted so powerfully on the classic nations around the Mediterranean. They stood in "the old paths," while the latter, yielding to an idealistic and passionate temperament, plunged headlong into a devotion which at length crowded their cities with temples and altars, and covered their valleys and hills with gods and goddesses in stone.

We do not lay much stress—although some lay a great deal—upon the mode of burial practised by the ancient

[1] Wilson, *Pre-historic Annals*, pp. 341, 342.

Briton as a means of spelling out his creed. His weapons were interred along with the warrior. "Why?" it has been asked. "Because," it has been answered, "it was an article of his belief that he would need them in the spirit world." In times still later, the war horse of the chief, his favourite hound, his attendants in the chase, or his followers on the battlefield, were all interred in company, that all might together resume, in a future life, the occupations and amusements in which they had been wont to exercise themselves in this. With fleeter foot would they chase the roe and hunt the boar. With even keener delight would they mingle in the strife of battle, and as on earth, so again in the world beyond, they would forget the toil of the chase and the peril of the conflict in the *symposia* of the celestial halls.

It was not within the gates of Valhalla only that the departed warrior was permitted to taste these supreme joys. Between him and the world in which he had passed his former existence, there was fixed no impassable gulf, and he had it in his power to return for a space to earth, and vary the delights of the upper sky with occasional pastime under "the pale glimpses of the moon." Popular belief pictured the spectral warrior mounted on spectral steed, returning from the halls of Odin and entering his sepulchral barrow and becoming for a while its inhabitant. There, joined by those with whom he had fought, and hunted, and revelled, and whose bones lay in the same funereal chamber with his own, he would renew those carousals with which it had been his wont to close a day of battle or of chase during the period of his mortal life. The tumulus or barrow was sacred to his memory. His spirit was believed to haunt it, and might on occasion hold fellowship with surviving relations and friends who chose to visit him in it. The wife would enter it and lie down by the side of her dead lord, in the idea of having communion with him, or she would bring meat and drink to regale him, which she would place in little cups provided for the purpose. Helge, one of the heroes of the Edda, returned from the hall of Odin on horseback, and entered his tumulus accompanied by a troop of horsemen. There his wife visited him, and for some time kept him company in his grave. This superstitious idea protected these barrows from demolition, and to it is owing the preservation of so many of them, forming as they do the only contemporaneous and authentic record we possess of the age to which they belong. On the advent of Christianity, burial with "grave-goods" ceased.

It is one of the lessons of history that unaided man, whatever his stage of civilization, always paints the life to come in colours borrowed from the life that now is. His heaven is the picture of earth. It is a freshened, brightened, glorified life which he promises himself, but still, in its essentials and substance, an earthly life. The thinking of the mightiest among the Greeks on the question of the life that is to come, moved, after all, in the same low groove with that of our early forefathers. The philosopher of Athens, when dying, fancied himself departing to another Academe, where the same subtle speculations, and the same intellectual combats, which had ministered so much pleasurable excitement to him in the Porch or in the Grove, would be resumed, with this difference, that there his powers would be immensely refined and invigorated, and consequently should have attendant on their exercise a far higher and purer happiness than he had ever tasted here. The idea of a *new nature*, with occupations and pleasures fitted to that *new nature*, was an idea unknown alike to the Greek and to the barbarian. It is a doctrine revealed in the Bible alone.

CHAPTER VII.

THE DRUIDS—THE SUN WORSHIP OF ASIA AND CALEDONIA.

WE have travelled back thirty or forty centuries, and dug up the early Scottish world which, all the while, was lying entombed in our barrows and cairns. The historian of a former day never thought of looking into these ancient repositories, and hearing what they had to tell respecting the doings of a long past time. He obeyed, as he thought, a high authority, when he refused to entertain the hope of finding "knowledge or device in the grave." He knew of no record save a written one, and so turning to ancient chronicles, he accepted the picture which some pious father had painted in the twilight of his monastery, as the true and genuine image of the ancient world. He was all the while unaware that what he was in quest of was lying close at hand—in fact, under his feet. In yonder barrow, which he had passed and repassed an hundred times, but never once paused to inspect, was that same old world embalmed, and waiting through the long centuries to come forth and reveal the secrets of ancient time to the men of a later and more civilized age.

It is to this record we have turned. It is hardly possible that there should be deception or mistake in the picture. In truth it is no picture, it is the thing itself. It is that veritable world in all its barbarism: its battles, its boar hunts, its rude handicrafts, its earth-dug dwellings, its huts of wattled osiers plastered with mud, its feasts, its burials —in short, the men with all the scenery of their lives around them. It is not tradition speaking to us through the fallible voice of a hundred or more generations; the information comes direct, we receive it at first hand. For while the centuries have been revolving, and outside that tumulus races have been changing, and dynasties passing away, changes there have been none on the world within that tumulus, the ages have there stood still, and as regards the validity and certainty of the evidence it furnishes, it is all the same, as if we had opened that barrow on the morrow immediately succeeding the day on which it was raised and closed in.

From the barrow and the cist, where the history of the Caledonian is written in the weapons with which he fought and the tools with which he worked, we turn to another chapter in his history, one partly written and partly monumental. We have seen the Caledonian on his battlefields in the first age slaughtering or being slaughtered with his stone axe; in the next, plunging at his foe with his bronze sword; in the third, riding into battle in his iron chariot, and hewing down his foes with a sword of the same metal. We have seen him essaying the more profitable labours of art; first moulding the clay with his hand, not caring how unshapely his vessel if it served its purpose, then turning it on the wheel, and taking a pride in the symmetry and beauty of the cup out of which he drank. We have traced, too, his progress in dress: at first he is content to envelope himself in fur of fox or skin of deer, but by and by he aspires to be differently clad from the animals he pursues in the chase. With a stone whorle and spindle he converts flax into thread; and when the metals come to the assistance of his art, he spins wool, and clothes himself with a garment of that texture. Probably some visitor from the Phœnician shore, where the art is well understood, initiates him into the process of dyeing, and now his moors are illumined by the bright and glowing colours of the Caledonian tartan. We have seen his banquets and his funeral arrangements: but there is one chapter of his history we have not yet opened. How did the Caledonian worship?

There must all the while have been growing up at the heart of that barbarous world a higher life. Human society, however debased and barbarous, is ever at the core moral. Feeble, exceedingly feeble, its pulse may be, so feeble as to be scarce perceptible, but that pulse never can totally cease. For the moral sense of society is no acquired quality, it was given it by the law of its creation. But how can its moral consciousness be developed, unless in some rite, or system of rites, by which it gives expression to its sense of a Being above itself? By what rite, or system of rites, did the early Caledonian indicate his knowledge—vague, shadowy, and undefined it may have been—of a Supreme Being? Let us observe him as he worships, we shall have a truer knowledge of him, not of his art or his bravery merely, but of himself, his thoughts and feelings, than when we see him chipping arrow heads, or tipping the spear with stone or bronze for the chase or the battle.

We have abundant evidence, both monumental and historic, that the Caledonian worshipped, and not only so, but that his worship was purer than that of most early nations, and purer even than that of some contemporary nations who were far higher in the scale of civilization. Fetichism appears never to have defiled our country. Our barrows and cists contain no such figures, grotesque, hideous and horrible, as are objects of worship to some savage nations in our own day. We find no trace that such deities or demons were ever adored or dreaded by our early ancestors. The bestial idolatry of Egypt had not reached them. Their religious level appears to have been higher even than that of the Greeks and Romans. For, as we have said, by the side of the skeleton that three thousand years ago was a living man, there lies no image or god graven in stone, or in silver, or in bronze. Had such been in use by the men who sleep in these ancient cists, they would infallibly have been found in their graves. Around the dead man we discover that entire order of things amid which he lived: his battle-weapons, the trophies of the chase, the cups, clay or bronze, that graced his table, and brimed at his banquets; the trinkets of stone or of jet that he wore on his person, all are around him in the grave; but one thing is lacking, and, curious enough, it is that one thing which we should beforehand have made ourselves most sure of finding there, and which, had it formed part of the system amid which he lived, would infallibly have been there—the objects of his worship even. That the dead should sleep with their stone axe or their bronze sword by their side, and yet not seek to hallow their cist and guard their rest by the image of their god, is strange indeed. Yet so it is. We are driven, therefore, to the conclusion that the early Caledonians had no notion of a Supreme Being, in short, were atheists, or that their conceptions of God were higher and more spiritual than those entertained by many contemporaneous peoples.

It is the latter conclusion which is undoubtedly the true one. The Caledonian saw a Being above himself, All-powerful and Eternal. He had brought this great idea with him from his Aryan home, or rather—for that idea is not astricted to locality, or found only where man first began his career—it is the corner-stone of his constitution, and equally indestructible, and accordingly he instituted rites in honour of that Being, and reared, with his barbarian hands, structures, rough, huge, majestic, in which to perform these rites. This is a point which recent archæological discoveries in many and far-sundered lands have placed beyond dispute, and it enables us to pass to a very important phase of our country's early history—the Druidic, to wit.

Among the vestiges of a remote time that linger on the face of our country, none are more remarkable than the tall upright stones, ranged in circle, and the broad, massy horizontal slabs, resting table-wise on supports, that are so frequently met with on our moors and hill-sides, and sometimes in the depth of our forests. To both learned and unlearned these unique and mysterious erections are objects of curiosity and interest. The questions they suggest are, In what age were they set up, and what purpose were they meant to serve? Immemorial tradition connects them with the religious rites of the earliest inhabitants of Scotland, and teaches us to see in them the first temples in which our fathers worshipped. Till lately, the universal belief regarding these singular erections was in accordance with the immemorial tradition. It was no more doubted that these great stones, ranged in solemn circle, filling the mind of the spectator with a vague awe, had been set up with a view to worship, than it was doubted that the stone hammer and axe, their contemporaries, had been fashioned with a view to battle. But in more recent times opinion on this point has shifted. The theory that referred these structures to a far-off time, and which saw in them the work of men unskilled in art but reverent of spirit, began, some half century ago, to be discredited. We were told that we were ascribing to them an antiquity far too high, and that we ought to seek for their origin in an age much nearer our own.

The period of the Vikings was fixed upon as that which first saw these monuments lift up their tall, uncouth, and solemn shapes on the moors of Scotland. The northern marauders reared them in honour of their god. So it has been said. Devout and pious men must these sea robbers have been, seeing they were intent on converting to the faith of Woden the men whose goods they harried and whose blood they spilt. We had not thought that their incursions partook so largely an evangelistic character. But there are difficulties neither few nor easily surmounted in the way of accepting this theory. How is it that the few centuries which have passed since their erection have been able to impart to these columns the appearance of so marvellous an age? We have monuments at least four thousand years old which are not so time-worn and hoary. Moreover, if their origin lies within historic times, why is there no record or reference to their setting up? Why do we not read that such and such a Viking, having won a glorious victory, constructed a magnificent ring of monoliths on the Caledonian moor in honour of the god by whose help his arms had triumphed? And why, in fine, do the surface of these columns bear no mark of hammer or chisel, seeing iron tools were not unknown in the age of the Vikings? But it is needless to combat an opinion which has no inherent probability, and which has now scarce a supporter. Our dolmens and stone circles were grey with age before keel of Northman had touched our shore, or Norwegian rover had dyed our soil with blood, whether ours or his own.

Yet another theory has been broached to account for the existence of monuments so unique in point of rugged grandeur, and so unlike any that are known certainly to belong to historic times. There are archaeologists of our day who will have it that they are graveyards. They are the mausolea of a barbarous age in which sleep the dead of a long-forgotten past: chieftains of note and warriors of renown, but whose names have gone into utter oblivion. This is a theory only a little less improbable than that on which we have been commenting. Where, we ask, are the signs and tokens that they are sepulchres? Are they placed near city, or seat of population, as we should expect a great cemetery to be? On the contrary, they are found in the solitudes and wildernesses of our land, in spots not then, nor ever likely to become, the scene of populous life. It may indeed be said that these remote and solitary spots were chosen on purpose, that prince and warrior might sleep apart in lonely grandeur amid silence undisturbed. Then, why were these supposed mausolea constructed on so vast a scale? A few feet of earth will suffice for the greatest monarch, and as regards a funeral pile to draw the eye to his resting-place, a cairn like those that rise on our northern moors, or a tumulus like that which towers on the plain of Troy, or a mountain of stone like that beneath which Cheops sleeps, will serve the purpose far better than an open ring of monoliths enclosing some hundred or so of acres. We must surely grant to the builders of these structures some reasonable sense of fitness. Or if it again be urged that these places were meant to afford burial not to a few men of note only, but to the multitude, then, we ask, Did the thinly-peopled Orkney require a graveyard on the scale of the circles of Bogar and Stennes? Or did the England of that day demand a necropolis of a size so vast as Stonehenge and Avebury?

And then, too, where are the memorials of the dead

supposed to have been interred in these ancient graveyards? When we dig into the barrow or the cairn, we are at no loss as to their character and design. Their contents make it clear that they were meant to be receptacles of the dead; for there to this day is the skeleton of the chieftain or warrior who was committed to its keeping, and along with their leader, it may be, the bones of the men who fell fighting around him, and now sleep in a common tomb. But when we search around the Cyclopean monoliths on the plain of Stonehenge, or the wilds of Stennes, we fail to discover relic or memorial of the dead. We light on nothing to show that bier of prince or of peasant was ever borne within their precincts; nothing, at least, to show that the dead of a nation, great and small, and not for one generation only, but for many, were brought hither and interred, as must have been the case, if they were national burying-places.

It is the fact, no doubt, that, in some instances, explorers have found the remains of mortality beneath or adjoining these stones. But this is just what we should expect. If these structures bore a sacred character, and were the scene of religious rites, as we believe them to have been, what so likely as that men of note should wish to lie within their hallowed enclosure, and that the wish, in some cases, should be acceded to. But these few solitary graves only strengthen our contention that these places were temples, not graveyards. For if these exceptional burials still attest themselves by the presence of stone cists with their mouldering contents, why should there not be traces also of that great multitude of burials which must have taken place here, if they were public receptacles for the dead? Why have the few been preserved, while the majority have disappeared? In fact, many of these stone circles and cromlechs stand on a bed of rock, where grave never could have been dug, or the dead interred.

Moreover, is it not a fact universally true of all early nations, that their first great monuments were reared not in memory of their dead, but in reverence of their deities? They honoured the departed warrior by piling over his remains a heap of stones, the height of the cairn corresponding to the rank of the deceased: their common dead they disposed of with less ceremony. In short, they did not need public graveyards; their earliest buildings were altars, or sacred towers. The tower on the plain of Shinar, the earliest monument of which we read, being an instance in point.[1] We may adduce, also, in corroboration of our assertion, the colossal temples of Egypt and India, and the less immense, but more beauteous, fanes of Greece and Italy. They were not mausolea, but shrines. The race started with the idea of the Deity strong in them, and it was their delight to expend the appliances of their labour and the resources of their skill in rearing structures that might be worthy of Him. The proudest of their edifices, those that challenged admiration the most by their size, or by their strength, or by their glory, rose not in honour of their dead, not even in honour of their kings, but in adoration of their gods. This

[1] The dwellers on the plains of the Tigris and Euphrates reared towers of from 500 to 700 feet in height for astro-theological uses. Some they dedicated to the sun, others to the moon, or to the seven planets. These towers were of brick, sun-dried or burned, and cemented with bitumen. The builders began by rearing a high and solid platform. On this basis they erected a series of receding towers, rising storey on storey to the height we have indicated. In the upper chamber was placed sometimes an image of the god for whose worship the tower was raised; at other times it was occupied by a priestess. The ruins of these earliest temples still remain in the mighty mounds that rise on that great plain, and which mark the site of its earliest cities. Our ancestors did the best they could to imitate these structures by piling up an altar of huge blocks, and drawing round it a grand circle of tall, shaggy columns.—See Smith and Syce's *Babylonia;* Rawlinson's *Ancient Monarchies*, vol. i.

fact, so universal as to amount to a law, authenticates the tradition which connects the grandest of our early fabrics with the service of our early worship.

The oldest of our monuments are stones set on end, and standing singly, or in groups. All savage nations are seen rearing such memorials; they are their first attempts to communicate with posterity. Some event has happened deemed by them of importance, and which they wish, therefore, should be known to those who are to come after them. How shall they hand it down to posterity? They have not yet acquired the art of committing transactions to writing: they know not to engrave or to paint: but they have simpler and readier methods. They set up a tall stone on the spot where the occurrence took place. Father tells to son the story of the pillar. It is a public and perpetual memorial of the fact; for should the tempest throw it down, pious hands will set it up again, that the event committed to its keeping may not fall into oblivion.

In the pages of the Bible, especially in its earlier pages, we meet with numerous traces of this custom. It was thus the patriarchs marked whatever was most eventful and memorable in their lives. Jacob sealed the vow which he made to the august Being who was seen by him in his dream, by setting up a stone on the spot when the morning broke, and anointing it with oil. The covenant betwixt the same patriarch and Laban, made on the summit of Gilead, instead of being written and attested by the signatures of the contracting parties, had, as its sole record, a cairn on the top of the mount. Twelve stones, rough as when taken from the bed of the river, rose on the banks of the Jordan as the perpetual witnesses of that miraculous act which opened to the Tribes the gates of the Land of Promise. At times the column of stone rose as a trophy of victory, and at other times as a symbol of personal or domestic sorrow. When Jacob laid his Rachel in the grave, he set up a pillar to mark the spot. By this simple act, the stricken man signified his desire that his descendants in days to come should mourn with him in a sorrow, the shadow of which was destined to hang around him till he reached the grave. And well, as we know, did that pillar fulfil its trust; for there was not an Israelite but knew where Rachel slept, nor ever passed her tomb without rehearsing the touching story of her death.

Simple blocks of unhewn stone were the earliest altars. Such were the altars, doubtless, which Abraham, and after him his son and grandson, built on the scene of their successive encampments as they journeyed through Palestine. Man in the earliest ages had no tools with which to quarry the rock; but the agencies of nature came to his assistance. The tempest, or the lightning, or the shock of earthquake, or simply the winter's frosts, tore up the strata, and made it ready for his use, whatever the purpose to which he meant to devote it, whether the record of a vow, or the seal of a covenant, or the trophy of a victory, or the symbol of grief. But of all uses to which stones were put in the early ages, none was more common than the religious one. They were shrines at which worship was performed. In the instances that have already come before us, the pillar simply indicated the spot hallowed by some special appearance, and henceforth set apart as the place where the family or the tribe was to assemble, at stated times, to worship Jehovah. When the knowledge of the true God waxed dim, the Sun was installed as his Vicar,[1] and worshipped

[1] Grivet quotes an Accadean (the earliest race) liturgy, in which Merodach is called, "I am he who walks before Ea—I am the warrior, the eldest son of Ea—the messenger." This is strikingly like the language of one who claims to stand before God in the way of being His vicegerent

as the Power who daily called the world out of darkness, and yearly awoke the vitalities and powers of nature. Towers or temples now rose to the sun and his goodly train of secondary gods, the moon, and the seven planets, or "seven lights of the world." The more civilized nations embellished the centres of their idol worship with great magnificence of art, but ruder nations, having neither the skill nor the materials for the construction of such splendid temples, were content to rear humbler shrines. They took a tall stone, unhewn and uncouth, as the tempest or the earthquake had torn it from the strata, and setting it on end, and consecrating it as the representative of the sun, or of some deified hero, they made it the rallying point and centre of their worship. Descending yet a stage lower, the stone so set up was no longer a mere stone like its fellows in the quarry, having neither more nor less virtue than they; it was now a consecrated pillar, and, as such, was filled with the spirit and potency, to some degree at least, of the god whom it represented. Worship *at* the stone passed easily, naturally, and speedily into worship *of* the stone. Lower still, and now it was believed that these stones were inhabited by a race of genii, or inferior gods, to whom had been given power over the destinies of men, and whom, therefore, it was the interest of man to propitiate by offerings and sacrifices. And thus it is that we find the worship of stones one of the earliest forms of idolatry, and one of the most widely-spread and universally practised. Palestine bristled throughout with these demon-stones when the Israelites entered it. Hardly a hill-top without its cluster of monoliths, or grove without its altar of unhewn, massy

or vicar. This would seem to indicate that idolatry crept in at first, not by a direct denial of the true God, but by a claim on the part of a class, or more probably a single usurper, to wield the power of God, and to act in His room.

block, on which fires burned in honour of the Sun or Bel, or human victims bled in propitiation of the deity who was believed to haunt the place. Hence the command to the Israelites to break down and utterly destroy these hateful and horrible objects, and to cleanse their land by sweeping from off its surface the last vestiges of an idolatry so foul and bloody. The specification of these idolatrous objects is very minute, and might equally apply to the Druidic shrines of Caledonia. It includes the *menhir*, or single stone pillar, and the altar-dolmen, as well as the graven image. Over both the Divine injunction suspended the same doom—entire and utter demolition.[1] Their stone pillars were to be demolished, their graven images of gold were to be battered and broken with the hammer, their wooden deities hewn with the axe, their sacrificial dolmens overturned, and the groves in which these demon-altars had stood were to be burned with fire. It is the very picture of Scotland some thousand years later; and hence the fallen menhirs, the broken and ragged stone circles, and the overturned and moss-grown dolmens that strew the face of our country,—the ruins which a once flourishing superstition has left behind it to attest its former prevalence and dominancy in our island.

This form of worship came to Scotland from the far east. We trace it by the footprints it leaves behind it as it journeys westward. It accompanied, probably, not the first, but the second great wave of immigration which poured itself forth from the great birthplace of nations in Central Asia. East and west we behold this mighty system extending its dark shadow, and enveloping all lands. For though it has now passed away, at least in the names and rites it then sanctioned and made obligatory, it has left

[1] See Lev. xxvi. 1.

its roots in the supposed mystic virtue of rites, images, and holy places, as well as in the rude Cyclopean monuments which it set up, and which, after enduring the shock of the tempest and the violence of thousands of years, still show their gigantic fragments cumbering the soil of almost all countries. Yonder, in the far east, on the mountains of India, we descry the menhir, the ancestor of the obelisk. Tribes that knew no other art knew to rear the stone column in honour of the sun. Rude stone monuments are found in the hills of the Ganges, and in the heart of Africa; on the plains of Persia, and amid the mountains of Spain; in the countries bordering on the Dead Sea, and on the shores of the Euxine and the Baltic. They are found in Tuscany and in Orkney. We lose trace of them among the negro races. Their builders, it is supposed, were sprung of an early Asiatic stock, which preceded the Aryan and Semitic races, and flourished in the pre-historic stone and bronze ages, and whose migration westward into Europe can be traced by etymological as well as monumental proofs.[1]

The Land of Moab bristles from valley to mountain-top with menhirs, stone circles, and cromlechs, offering at this day the very spectacle which some of our moors present. The Phœnician plain afforded a magnificent theatre for this worship where it was fed by the riches of an opulent commerce, and embellished by the skill of a consummate art. Westward along either shore of the Mediterranean these idol-altars flamed. Travelling beyond the Pillars of Hercules, this system turned northwards, and extending along the western shores of Europe—then the farthest known West—it ultimately reached our island. Here grafting itself upon an earlier and purer system, it reared, with barbarous strength and rude pomp, its great cromlechs, and

[1] Conder, *Heth. and Moab*, p. 196. Lond., 1883.

its circles of tall, shaggy columns, and taught to the men of Caledonia the names of new deities, and the practice of new rites.

We have thought it necessary thus to trace at some length the early rise and eastern origin of this form of worship, because it throws light on the history of our country, and on its oldest existing monuments. It enables us to guess at the time when these monuments were erected, and it leaves hardly a doubt as regards their character and use. They were reared for worship. They form a part of that great system of sun-worship which sprung up soon after the flood, and which, with essential unity, but great variety of names and forms, travelled over the earth, and set up its altars, and taught the practice of its foul and cruel rites in every land and to every people.

CHAPTER VIII.

THE DRUIDS—THEIR RELIGION, DEITIES, HIERARCHY, DOCTRINES.

It is delightful to watch the first buddings of art and the first kindlings of patriotism, and see in these the great imperishable elements in man—in even savage man—asserting themselves, and fighting their way upward through the darkness of savage life into the light of civilisation. But there is a power which is still more potential as regards the development of society than either art or liberty, for it is the nurse of both. Its divine touch awakens them into life, and not only puts them in motion, but guides them along the road that leads to their supreme goal. To watch the expanding sphere and the growing influence of this power is a truly delightful and profitable study. Religion is the glory of man and the crown of the State. This can be said, however, of but one religion, that even which, having its origin neither in man nor on the world on which he dwells, but descending from a sphere infinitely above both, sits apart, and refuses to own either equality or kindred with the crowd of spurious faiths that surround it. These others, though classed in the category of religions, may blast rather than bless society. Their power in this respect will depend on the degree in which they retain the essential elements of that one religion which is divine. Had the Caledonians a religion, and what was it? A history of Scotland with this great question left out would be a husk with the kernel lacking—a skeleton of dry facts but with no soul under "the cold ribs of death."

We have already said that the Caledonians had a religion, and that that religion was Druidism. It must, however, be acknowledged that the religion of early Caledonia is a point on which all are not agreed. Some go the length of maintaining that the Caledonian had no religion at all: that altar he never set up, and that god he never worshipped, but all life long went onward, never once lifting his eye to heaven, in a night of black atheism. A dismal past, truly! but happily we are under no necessity to accept it as the actual past of our country. To maintain, as some have done, that the Druids are an entirely fabulous class of men, like the Fairies, Kelpies, and similar beings with which superstition peopled our moors and lochs, is a bold position in the presence of the numerous and palpable footprints which the Druid has left behind him. In truth, the Druidic age is as plainly written on the face of Scotland as the stone age, and the bronze age, and the iron age. Our cairns and cists do not furnish more convincing evidence as to the tools with which the Caledonian worked, and the weapons with which he fought, than the stone fanes, the ruins of which dot the moors and hills of our country, testify to a time when the creed of the Druid was dominant in our land, and the Caledonian worshipped accordingly. Besides the names attached to numerous localities clearly connecting them with the Druidic religion, the traces of its ancient rites still lingering in the social customs of the people, and keeping their place though all knowledge of their origin and meaning has been lost, present us with indisputable proofs of the former existence of a powerful but now fallen Druidic hierarchy. These footprints of the Druid will come more fully under our notice at a subsequent stage.

But farther, we hold, on the fundamental principles of man's nature, that the profession of downright atheism is impossible to a savage or barbarous people. Such a thing can only take place in a nation that has made certain advances in what it deems enlightenment, and has so far cultivated the faculty of reason as to be able to make this woful abuse of it. One must have eyes before he can be subject to the illusion of the mirage, and in like manner one must have considerable practice in the science of sophistry before he can be able to reason himself into a position so irrational as that there is no God. Atheists are not born, but made.

Did Druidism spring up on the soil of Scotland, or was it imported from some other and remote region? This is the first question. We have already more than hinted our belief that Druidism—we mean the system, not the name—arose in a very early age, and had its birth in the primeval seat of mankind. Druidism is a more venerable system than the paganism of Italy, or the polytheism of Greece. It had a less gross admixture of nature worship, and it was more abstract and spiritual. Druidism was an elder branch of sun-worship which arose in Chaldea. Leaving its eastern birthplace at an early period, and travelling northward, where for ages it occupied an isolated position, it had no opportunity of studying the newest fashions of sun-worship, and it consequently retained till a late period its comparative simplicity and purity. Such is our idea, and that idea has of late received strong corroboration from the inscribed tablets and hieroglyphic records which have been dug up in the buried cities of Assyria and Chaldea. And to the same conclusion do all the recent philosophical investigations which have been made into this creed tend. Reynaud, in France maintains that "the ancient Druids were the first clearly to teach the doctrine of the soul's immortality, and that they had originally as high conceptions of the Deity as the Jews themselves. If they afterwards encouraged the worship of subordinate deities, it was," he says, "for the purpose of reconciling Druidism to that class of uneducated minds for which the cultus of demi-gods and angels has more attraction than the worship of the Unseen One." [1]

The countryman of Reynaud, M. Amédée Thierry, who has subjected the religions of ancient Gaul to analytical and philosophical enquiry, comes to substantially the same conclusion. He finds traces of two distinct religions in ancient Gaul. One resembled the polytheism of the Greeks. The other was a kind of metaphysical pantheism, resembling the religions of some eastern nations. The latter appeared to him to be the foundation of Druidism, and had been brought into the country by the Cymric Gauls when they entered it under their leader Hu or Hesus, deified after his death.[2] In other words, this writer, with whom agrees the historian Martin, finds, as the result of his enquiries, that Druidism comes from the East, that in its earlier stages it was a comparatively abstract and spiritual system, but in its later days became mixed in the West with the nature worship of the Greeks, its votaries adoring deified heroes as representing the sun, as also storms, groves, fountains, and streams; taking these natural agencies for the action of the invisible spirits that resided in them. Pinkerton, though he wrote before the polytheisms had been tracked to their original birthplace, could not help being struck with the oriental

---

[1] Reynaud, *L'Esprit de la Gaule; Encyclopædia Britannica*. vol. vii., 9th Ed., article "Druidism."

[2] Amédée Thierry, *Histoire des Gaulois. Ency. Brit.*, vol. vii., article "Druidism."

features borne by Druidism, and ascribed to it an eastern origin. He says briefly but emphatically, "Druidism was palpably Phœnician."[1] Had he gone farther east he would have come still nearer the truth.

BEL (sun-worship) was, in sooth, the prodigal son who left his father's house and travelled into far countries, under various disguises and amid great diversity of fortune. The wanderer changed his name and his garb to suit the genius of every people, and aspired to be accepted as the true son of the Great Father over all the earth. As he passed from land to land, he accommodated himself to the predominating tastes and passions of the peoples among whom he successively found a home. Idolatry was philosophical and abstract among the Orientals. It was darkly mysterious, but boundlessly voluptuous among the Egyptians. It came to the Greeks in the garb of poetry and beauty. Among the warlike Romans it marched at the head of their armies, delighting in the clash of arms and the shout of them that overcome. Among the Caledonians it affected a severe simplicity and majesty, as befitted the people and the cloud-capped mountains which were their dwelling. It was the real Proteus who assumed a new name and a new shape in each new land. And as the consequence of these endless transformations, its votaries in one country strove with its votaries in another for the supremacy of their several deities, blindly mistaking for rivals those who all the while were in truth but one. "Religion," says James, "assumed almost in every country a different name, in consequence of the difference of language which everywhere prevailed. Among the ancient Hindoos it was called 'Brachmanism,' and its ministers 'Brachmans'; among the Chaldeans 'Wisdom,' and its ministers 'wise men'; among the Per-

---

[1] Pinkerton. *Enquiry into the History of Scotland*, i. 17.

sians 'Magism,' and its ministers 'Magi'; among the Greeks 'Priesthood,' and its ministers 'priests'; among the ancient Gauls and Britons 'Druidism,' and its ministers 'Druids':—all synonymous terms, implying 'wisdom and wise men, priesthood and priests.'"[1] This was the link which united the Scotland of those ages with the far-off Chaldea, this overshadowing idolatry, to wit, which made its deities, though under different names, be adored all round the earth—in the temples of Babylon and the fanes of Egypt, in the shrines of Greece and the Pantheon of Rome, in the woods of Germany and the oak forests of Scotland.

This essential oneness of the false religions accounts for the fact, otherwise inexplicable, that in all of them we find more than mere naturalism. The idolatries are not, out and out, the institution of man, they all embody conceptions above man, and, like man himself, exhibit amid the ruins of their fall some of the grand uneffaced features of their glorious original. They all contain, though to no real practical purpose, the ideas of sin, of expiation, of forgiveness, and of

---

[1] James' *Patriarchal Religion of Britain*, p. 34. Lond., 1836.

As regards the etymology of the word Druid, the author, instead of offering any opinion of his own, is glad to be able to quote the high authority of Don. Mackinnon, Esq., Professor of Celtic Languages, History, and Literature in the University of Edinburgh. That gentleman has favoured the author with a note on the subject, which it gives him much pleasure to insert here:—

"I think there is no doubt that 'Druid' is connected with and derived from the root that gives δρυς, δενδρον, δορυ, in Greek; *drus*, 'wood,' in Sanskrit; *tree* in English; *doire*, a 'grove,' and *darach*, 'oak,' in Gaelic.

"That the word came, perhaps after the fall of the system, to mean a 'wise man' is undoubted. Jannes and Jambres (2 Tim. iii. 8) are called 'Druids' in an Irish gloss of the 8th century; in an old hymn our Saviour is called a Druid; in the early translation of the Scriptures the 'wise men' are Druids (Matt. ii. 1).

"In our modern language 'Druidheachd,' *i.e.*, 'Druidism,' is magic, sorcery, witchcraft. Instead of saying 'Druid' means 'wise man,' I would say the word is derived from the word for 'an oak,' which, as you point out, figured so largely in their worship. It came in Celtic literature to mean a 'wise man,' a 'magus,' a 'sorcerer.'"

purification. This is owing to no unanimous consent or happy coincidence of thought on the part of widely dispersed tribes: the fact is soluble only on the theory of the origination of all the idolatries in a common source, and their propagation from a common centre. These doctrines could no ways have grown up in the field of naturalism; they are, as history and etymology attest, the traces, sadly obscured, of what was once more clearly seen, and more firmly grasped by the race. They are at once the twilight lights of a departing day; and are the morning tints of a coming one.

Were the gods of Druidism one or many? This is the next question, and the answer to it must depend upon the stage of Druidism to which it applies. In the course of its existence of from one to two thousand years, Druidism must have undergone not a few modifications, and all of them for the worse. In its early stage it had but one Deity, doubtless, whom, however, it worshipped through the Sun as His symbol, or through Baal, the Chaldean representative of the Sun. In its latter stages it aspired to be like the nations with whom it had now begun to mingle. Cæsar, the first to describe the Druids, paints their pantheon in a way that makes it bear no distant resemblance to the Olympus of the Greeks. The Druidic gods, it is true, have other names than those under which the Greek deities were known, but they have the same attributes and functions, and we have but little difficulty in recognising the same deity under his Celtic appellative, who figures in the Greek pantheon under a more classic cognomen. In the Teutates of the Druids Cæsar found Mercury, the god of letters and eloquence. In Belenus or Bel he saw a likeness to Apollo, the god of the sun. In Taranis, which is Celtic for thunder, he found Jupiter the thunderer. And in Hu or Hesus he thought he could detect Mars.[1] The Cale-

[1] Cæsar, *Bell. Gall.* vi. 17.

donians had no Olympus, lifting its head above the clouds, on which to enthrone their deities; they could offer them only their bare moors, and their dark oak forests. There they built them temples of unhewn stone, and bowed down in adoration unto them.

The hierarchy of the Druids formed a numerous and powerful body. The priests were divided, Cæsar tells us, into three classes. There was, first, the Chroniclers, who registered events and, in especial, gave attention to the king, that his worthy acts might be handed down with lustre unimpaired to the ages to come. There was, second, the Bards, who celebrated in verse the exploits of the battlefield, and sang in fitting strains the praises of heroes. Then, third, came the Priests, the most numerous and influential of the Druidic body. They presided over the sacrifices, but to this main function they added a host of multifarious pursuits and duties.[1] They were the depositories of letters and learning, and had a great reputation for vast and profound knowledge. The estimate of that age, however, our own may not be prepared to accept, unless with very considerable modification. They were students of science, more especially of astronomy and geometry, in which they were said to have been deeply versed. The astronomy of those days was mainly judicial astrology: though there can be no question that the early Chaldeans made great attainments in pure astronomy, and recent discoveries in Babylonia have given back to the Chaldean astronomers an honour which has hitherto been assigned to the Egyptians, that, even, of determining and naming the constellations of

---

[1] These three orders are said to have been distinguished by the different colours of their dresses: the chroniclers wore blue, the bards green, and the priests white—none but a priest durst appear in white. See Myrick's *Costumes of the Ancient Britons;* Dr Giles's *History of the Ancient Britons;* Wood's *Ancient British Church.*

the zodiac. In geometry the Druids were so greatly skilled as to be able, it is said, to measure the magnitude of the earth. At least they had enough geometry to settle disputes touching the boundaries of properties. They searched into the virtues of herbs, and by this useful study qualified themselves for the practice of the healing art. They were the interpreters of omens—a branch of knowledge so seductive that their class in no land has been able to refrain from meddling with it. Their divination was founded mainly on their sacrifices. They narrowly watched the victim, sometimes a human one, as he received the blow from the sacrificial knife, and drew their auguries from the direction in which he fell, to the right or to the left, the squirting of his blood, and the contortions of his limbs.

At the head of the priesthood was an arch-Druid.[1] The post was one of high dignity and great authority. Being an object of ambition and of emolument, the office was eagerly sought after. It was decided by a plurality of votes, and the person chosen to fill it held it for life. The rivalships and quarrels to which the election to this great post gave rise were sometimes so violent and furious that the sword had to be called in before the priest on whom the choice had fallen could mount the Druidic throne. The official dress of the arch-Druid was of special magnificence and splendour. "He was clothed in a stole of virgin-white, over a closer robe of the same fastened by a girdle on which appeared the crystal of augury cased in gold. Round his neck was the breastplate of judgment. Below the breastplate was suspended the Glain Neidr, or serpent's jewel. On his head he had a tiara of gold. On each of two fingers of his right hand he wore a ring; one plain, and the other the chain ring of divination."[2]

[1] Cæsar, *Bell. Gall.*, vi. 14.
[2] Nash, *Taliesin: the Bards and Druids of Britain*, p. 15. Lond., 1858.

The Druids acted as judges. By this union of the judicial and the sacerdotal offices they vastly increased their influence and authority. A tumulus, closely adjoining their stone circle, or even within it, served for their tribunal. At other times they would erect their judgment seat beneath the boughs of some great oak, and when the people came up to sacrifice, or gathered to the festivals, they had the farther privilege, if so they wished, of having their causes heard and decided. The Druids were also, to a large extent, the legislators of the nation. Their position, their character, and, above all, their superior intelligence, enabled them easily to monopolise the direction of public affairs, and to become the virtual rulers of the country. No great measure could be undertaken without their approval. They were the counsellors of the king. With their advice he made peace or he made war. If he chose to act contrary to their counsel it was at his own peril. It behoved him to be wary in all his dealings with a class of men who enjoyed such consideration in the eyes of the vulgar, and whose power was believed to stretch into the supernatural sphere, and might, if their pride was wounded or their interests touched, visit the country with plague, or tempest, or famine, or other calamity. So powerful was the control which the Druids wielded, Cæsar informs us, that they would arrest armies on their march to the battlefield. Nay, even when rank stood confronting rank with levelled spears and swords unsheathed, if the Druids stepped in betwixt the hostile lines, and commanded peace, the combatants, though burning to engage, instantly sheathed their weapons and left the field.

The Druids held an annual general assembly for the regulation of their affairs. This convocation, Cæsar informs us, was held in the territory of the Carnutes in Gaul, by which Dreux, north of the Loire, is most probably meant. Their places of rendezvous was a consecrated grove. Whether delegates attended from Caledonia we are not informed. It is not likely that they did, seeing the Scottish Druids regarded themselves as an earlier and purer branch of the great Druidic family, and were not likely to own submission to a body meeting beyond seas. They had their own convocation doubtless on their own soil, and framed their own laws for the guidance of their affairs. The convention at Dreux, besides enacting general decrees binding on all their confraternities throughout Gaul, gave audience to any who had private suits and controversies to prosecute before them. It was understood that all who submitted their quarrels to their arbitrament bound themselves to bow to their decision. The court was armed with terrible powers for enforcing its judgment. If any resisted he was smitten with excommunication. This penalty stript the man of everything. It placed him beyond the pale of all natural and social as well as ecclesiastical rights. No one durst speak to him or render him the least help, even to the extent of giving him a morsel of bread, or a cup of water, or even a light. His extremity was dire, and alternative he had none, save to submit to Druidic authority, or be crushed by Druidic vengeance.

This powerful class enjoyed, moreover, large and special immunities. Whether a national provision was made for them does not appear. They hardly needed such, considering the wealth which must have flowed in upon them from a variety of sources. "Their endowment," says Yeowell,[1] "was five free acres of land," without making it clear whether it was each individual Druid or each fraternity that was so endowed. They are said to have imposed a tax on each plough in the parish in which they officiated as priests.[2]

[1] Yeowell, *Chronicles of the British Church*, London, 1847.
[2] *Ibid.*

They were the judges, physicians, and teachers of their nation, besides being the dispensers of the sacred rites; and it is not easy to believe that all these functions were void of emolument. The Druids enjoyed, besides, other and very special privileges. Their persons were held inviolable. They could pass through the territories of hostile tribes without dreading or receiving harm. His white robe was protection enough to the Druid. When he journeyed he was welcomed at every table, and when night fell he could enter any door and sleep under any roof. He was exempt from land tax. He was never required to gird himself with sword or risk life on the battlefield. He was not obliged to toil at the plough, or the spade, or the loom. He left these necessary labours to others. "They contributed," says Toland, though the sentence, after what we have said, will be felt to be too sweeping — "They contributed nothing to the State but *charms.*"

It is a question not less important than any of the preceding, What were the doctrines that formed the creed of Druidism? We can answer only doubtfully. Not a scrap of writing has come down to us from hand of Druid; and in the absence of all information at first hand touching their tenets, we are compelled to be content with the fragmentary notices which Cæsar and Pliny and Tacitus and Pomponius Mela and others have been pleased to give us. These are not exactly the pens from which we would expect a full and accurate account of Druidic theology. These writers but pause in the midst of weightier matters to bestow a glance on what they deemed a curious if not barbarous subject. With every disposition to be accurate, we may well doubt their ability to be so. But we must accept their statements or confess that we know nothing of the creed of Druidism. On the more prominent doctrines—especially those discussed in the schools of their own country—these writers could hardly be mistaken, and with their hints we may venture on an attempt to reconstruct the framework, or rather, we ought to say, exhume the skeleton of Druidic theology from its grave of two thousand years.

Philosophy begins at MAN; the starting point of theology is GOD. What were the notions of the Druids respecting the first and highest of all Beings? From all we can gather, they cherished worthier and more exalted ideas of the Supreme than the other peoples of their day. They brought with them from the East, and would seem to have long preserved, the great idea of one Supreme Being, infinite, eternal, and omnipotent, the maker of all things, and the disposer of all events, who might be conceived of by the mind, but of whom no likeness could be fashioned by the hand. Such is the account transmitted to us by Pliny,[1] and his statement is corroborated by Tacitus, who says, that "they do not confine their deities within buildings, nor represent them by any likeness to the human form. They merely consecrate bowers and groves, and designate by the names of gods that mysterious essence which they behold only in the spirit of adoration."[2] It is farther authenticated by the negative testimony of our cairns and cists. In these, as we have already said, no image of God, no likeness of the Invisible has hitherto been found. This fact is striking, especially when the state of things in Egypt and Greece is taken into account, and is explicable only on the supposition that the Caledonians abstained from making images of the object of their worship, and clung to the nobler and more spiritual conceptions of their early ancestors.

Some doubt is thrown on this, however, by the statement

[1] Plinii, *Nat. Hist.*, lib. xvi. cap. 44.
[2] Tac. Trib. Ger. c. 9.

of Cæsar already quoted, that the Druids worshipped a plurality of gods. His words were spoken with an immediate reference to the Druids in Gaul. The Druidism of Britain, he admits, was not exactly of the same type; it was purer. Nor does it follow from Cæsar's statement that the British Druids made images of their gods, even granting that they had now come to worship the Supreme under a variety of names. In Cæsar's day the more abstract and spiritual Druidism of an early time had come to be mixed and debased both in Gaul and Britain with the polytheistic notions of the Greeks. The light of primeval revelation which the first immigrants brought with them, imperfect from the first, had faded age after age, as was inevitable where there was no written record, and where the memorials of the primitive faith were committed solely to tradition. And though preserved longer in a state of purity in Britain than anywhere else, those who now inhabited our island cherished less worthy notions of the Deity, and were more polytheistic in their worship than the men whom the first transport fleet of canoes had carried across to its shore.

That they believed in the immortality of the soul, and consequently in a state of existence beyond the grave, we have the explicit testimony of Pomponius Mela. And he assigns the motive which led the priests to inculcate this doctrine on the people, the hope even that it would inspire them with courage on the battlefield. His words are, "There is one thing they teach their disciples, which also has been disclosed to the common people, in order to render them more brave and fearless; even that the soul is immortal, and that there is another life after death."[1] The testimony

---

[1] Unum ex iis quæ præcipiunt, in vulgus effluxit, videlicet ut forent ad bella meliores, æternas esse animas, vitamque alteram ad manes. Pomponii Melæ, De Situ Orbis, Libri Tres, cap. 2, Ludg. Batav., 1696.

of Cæsar on the point is to the same effect. The soul's immortality, and a life to come, in which every worthy and valorous deed shall receive reward, forms, he tells us, part of the teaching of the Druids. And he notes, too, its salutary influence in heightening the courage of the warriors by removing the fear of death as the end of existence. There was no such certain belief on this point in the country of the great Roman, and the teaching of the Athenian sages was, too, less clear and definite touching a life after death. But a doctrine unknown, or but dimly seen in the noon of Greek and Roman civilization, was fully apprehended in the barbaric night of the remote Britain. To this extent the Druidism of Caledonia surpassed the paganisms of classic lands, and to the extent in which it excelled them did it approximate primeval revelation.

The Pythagorean doctrine of the transmigration of souls has been attributed to the Druids, but on no sufficient evidence. Transplanted from the hot valley of the Nile to the scarcely less genial air of Athens, that tenet might flourish in Greece, but hardly in the bleak climate of Caledonia. In fact, the doctrine of the future life as a scene of rewards and punishments, and the doctrine of the transmigration of souls, are hardly compatible, and could scarce be received as articles of belief by the same people. If in the life to come the hero was to receive honour and the coward to meet merited disgrace, was it not essential that both should retain their identity? If they should change their shapes and become, or appear to become, other beings, might not some confusion arise in the allotment of rewards? What was to hinder the coward running off with the honours of the hero, and the hero being subjected to the stigma of the coward? Besides Pomponius Mela, in his few pregnant sentences on the Druids, communicates a piece of information touching a curious burial custom of theirs, which is certainly at variance with the belief that souls, after death, migrate into other forms with a total forgetfulness of all that passed in their previous state of existence. He tells us that when they inurned the ashes of their dead they buried along with them their books of account and the hand notes of the moneys they had lent when alive, but which had not been repaid them by their debtors, that they might have the means of prosecuting their claim in the world beyond the grave.[1] They were clearly not of opinion that death pays all debts. But if they accepted the doctrine of transmigration as a truth, it was idle to take with them to the grave the accounts of their undischarged acceptances; for, amongst the multitude of shapes into any one of which the debtor might chance to be metamorphosed, how was it possible for the creditor to discover and identify him, so as to compel him to discharge the obligations which he had shirked in the upper world? On the theory of transmigration the thing was hopeless.

This is all that we can with certainty make out as regards the religious beliefs of the Druid. And, granting that all this is true, how little, after all, does it amount to! He is sure of but two things, a Being, eternal and omnipotent, and an existence beyond the grave, also eternal. But these two awful truths bring crowding into his mind a thousand anxious enquiries, not one of which he can answer. He has no means of knowing with what dispositions the great Being above him regards him, and so he cannot tell what his own eternal lot and destiny shall be. The two lights in his sky are enough, and only enough, to show him the fathomless

[1] Itaque cum mortuis cremant ac defodiunt apta viventibus olim. Negotiorum ratio etiam et exactio crediti deferebatur ad inferos erantque qui se in rogos suorum, velut una victuri, libenter immitterent. Pom. Mel., lib. iii. cap. 2.

night that encompasses him on all sides, but not his way through it. Travel in thought, or strain his vision as he may through the appalling succession of ages, eternity rising behind eternity, it is still night, black night, and he never comes to streak of morning, or to golden gleam as from the half opened gates of a world beyond these ages of darkness. Such was Druidism in its best days.

In what an air of mystery and wisdom did the Druid wrap up the little that he knew! He abstained from putting his system into writing, and communicated it only orally to select disciples, whom he withdrew into caves and the solitude of dark forests; and there, only after long years of study, in the course of which their minds were prepared for the sublime revelation to be imparted to them, did he initiate them into the highest mysteries of his system.[1] This retreat and secrecy he affected, doubtless, not only to guard his sacred tenets from the knowledge of the vulgar, but to aid the imagination in representing to itself how awful and sublime a thing Druidism was, when its last and profoundest doctrines could be whispered only in the bowels of the earth, or the deepest shades of the forest, and to none save to minds trained, purified, and strengthened for the final disclosure, and so conducted step by step to those sublime heights which it might have been dangerous and impious to approach more quickly. Had the Druid made the experiment of reducing his system to writing, and stating it in plain words and definite propositions, he would have seen, and others too would have seen, that his vaunted knowledge might have been contained within narrow limits indeed—compressed into a nut shell.

When the intercourse between our island and Phœnicia

---

[1] Docent multa nobilissimos gentis clam et diu vicennis annis in specu, ut in abditis saltibus. Pom. Mel., lib. iii. cap. 2.

and Greece sprang up and became more frequent, the golden age of British Druidism began to decline. It was natural that the eastern trader should bring with him the newest fashions from these noted theatres of paganism, and should strive to teach the unsophisticated islanders a more æsthetic ritual. And yet there is no evidence that the change effected was great. The British Druid fought shy of these foreign novelties, and continued to walk in the "old paths;" and Cæsar, long after, found the system flourishing here in a purity and perfection unknown to it in other lands, which made it be looked upon as a product peculiar to Britain, and forming a model and standard for Druidism everywhere else. Those in Gaul who wished to be more perfectly initiated into its mysteries than was possible in their own country, crossed the sea to what they believed to be its birthplace, and there "drank at the well of Druidism undefiled."[1]

[1] *De Bello Gallico*, lib. vi. cap. 14.

CHAPTER IX.

THE DRUID'S EGG—THE MISTLETOE—THE DRUID'S SACRIFICE.

We have essayed to reproduce the theology of the Druids so far as we can glean it from the fragmentary notices of the classic writers. Had these writers been of the number of its inner disciples, and sat at the feet of Druid in dark cave or in gloom of oak forest, we should have known more of the tenets of those venerable teachers who might be seen in former ages traversing, in long white robes, the same fields and highways which are now trodden by ourselves. Instead of a meagre outline we might have had a full body of Druidic divinity transmitted to us. And yet it might not have been so. We shrewdly suspect that we are in possession of all the truths which Druidism contained, and that what we lack is only the shadowy sublimities in which they were wrapped up, and which, by removing them beyond the sphere of clear and definite comprehension, made them imposing.

From the theology of Druidism we pass to its worship and rites. Some of these rites were curious, others were picturesque, and others were repulsive and horrible. Of the first, the curious, but not less credulous than curious, was the Druid's egg. This egg appears to have been an object of some interest to the ancients, seeing they speak of it, and some of them aver having actually seen and handled it.

Of the number who have specially described it is Pliny. If half of what is related of this egg be true, it must be to us, as it was to the ancients, an object of no little wonder. It was formed of the scum of serpents. As the snakes twisted and writhed in a tangled knot, the egg, produced in some mysterious way, was seen to emerge from the foaming mass of vipers, and float upward into the air.[1] It was caught by the priests while in the act of falling. The Druid who found himself the fortunate possessor of this invaluable treasure took instant measures to prevent being stript of it almost as soon as he had secured it. Throwing himself upon a horse that was kept waiting for him, he galloped off, pursued by the snakes, nor halted till he had got on the other side of the first running water to which his flight brought him. His pursuers were stopped by the stream; they had power to follow him no farther. The egg was his. It was an inexhaustible magazine of virtues, a storehouse of mighty forces, all of them at his command, and endowing its happy possessor with the enviable but somewhat dangerous attribute, so liable to be abused, one should think, of obtaining almost all he might desire, and of doing nearly all that he pleased. Of those who have testified to having seen this egg, we do not know one who was witness to its birth, or was prepared to speak to the extraordinary circumstances said to accompany its production, or the wonderful deeds performed, or that might have been performed, by the Druid who was so fortunate as to get it into his keeping.

The story of the mistletoe is less curious but more credible. The mistletoe grew upon the oak, the sacred tree of the Druids. The mighty parent trunk, its tender offshoot clinging to it, with its ever-green leaves and its bunches of yellow flowers, was a thing of beauty. But what made it

[1] Plinii, *Nat. Hist.*, lib. iii. c. 12, xvi. 44.

so pleasing in the eyes of Druid was not its loveliness, but its significance. The mistletoe was the emblem of one of the more recondite mysteries of his creed. Its finding was an occasion of great joy, and the ceremony of gathering it wore the sunny air of poetry, reminding one of some of the festivals of ancient Greece, of which it had the gaiety but not the voluptuousness. The mistletoe—the child of his sacred tree—the Druid held in high veneration, and the severing of it from the parent oak was gone about with much solemnity. It was gathered on the sixth day of the moon. A procession was formed, and walked slowly to the oak on which the mistletoe grew : a priest in white robes climbed the tree, and cutting away the plant with a golden sickle, he let it drop into a white sheet held underneath, for it might not touch the ground without losing its virtue. The sacrifice of two milk-white bulls concluded the ceremony.

The reverence in which the Druids held the mistletoe, and the ceremonies connected with it, have led to the formation of some very extravagant theories respecting this system, as if it was almost, if not altogether, an evangelical one. While some will have it that the night of the ancient Caledonia was unbroken by a single ray from the great source of Divine revelation, there are others who are equally confident that Caledonia was nearly as brightly illuminated as Judea itself, and place the priesthood of the Druids only a little way below the priesthood of the Hebrews.[1] These last find in the ritual of the mistletoe an amount of Christian doctrine and evangelical sentiment which we are very far from being able to see in it, and which we believe the Druids themselves did not see in it. Their views, however,

---

[1] *Religion of Ancient Britain historically considered.* London, 1846; Yeowell, *Chronicles of the Ancient British Church.* London, 1847 ; Nash, *Taliesin,* pp. 12, 13. London, 1858.

have been set forth with great plausibility, and it may be right, therefore, that we give a few moments to the statement of them.

The Druids named the mistletoe the "Heal-All;" and they made it, according to the theory of which we speak, the emblem of the Great Healer who was to appear on the earth at a later day, and by his sovereign interposition cure all our ills. The oak, out of which the mistletoe sprang, was held to represent the Almighty Father, eternal, self-existent, defying all assaults, and living through all time. From him was to come the "Branch" foretold by the prophets of Israel, and sung of also by the poets of classic antiquity. Virgil, speaking of this plant, calls it the "golden branch," and says, that "by its efficacious powers alone could we return from the realms below." Homer, too, makes mention of the "golden rod or branch." Above these doubtful utterances, a far greater voice is heard predicting the advent of the Messiah, and saluting him as the "branch," "the rod from the stem of Jesse," the "plant of renown." The Druids, catching up and prolonging the strain of the inspired prophet, hail the coming deliverer, and adopt the mistletoe as his symbol: they see in this plant, as it clings to the great oak, the figure of one who was to spring from an eternal stock, and who was to grow up as a tender plant, full of heavenly virtue, the desired of all nations, and by whose efficacious death man was to return from the realms of the grave. Such is the evangelical garb the system of Druidism has been made to wear.

Most pleasing would it be to be able to put a little Bible light into these dark mysteries. Most pleasing assuredly would it be to think that our fathers heard in these legends the voices of the prophets, and saw in these rites the day of a coming Saviour. A new and more touching interest would gather round their sleeping places on moor and hill-side. But we cannot conceal from ourselves that these notions lack footing in historic fact; and neither do they receive countenance from a critical analysis of the system. Without the key of the prophets we should not have so unlocked the arcana of Druidism, and without the lamp of the apostles we should never have seen such evangelical things in it. The fact is, we bring these evangelical meanings to Druidism, we do not find them in it. Druidism was the worship of the fire—the worship of Baal. Still it was better for Scotland that Druidism should be, than that it should not be. It was a link between man and the world above him. It kept the conscience from falling into the sleep of death; it maintained alive a feeble sense of guilt and the need of expiation, and to that extent it prepared the way for a better system, and a more sovereign remedy for the many maladies of the human soul than ever grew on oak of Druid.

As the great symbol in Druidism was the mistletoe, so the central act in its worship was sacrifice. Here, again, we approximate in point of form the divinely appointed worship of the Hebrews. In common with the whole heathen world, the Druids connected the idea of expiation with their sacrifices. They offered them to propitiate the Deity. Nevertheless their sacrifices were *pagan* not *evangelical*. The victim on the altar of the Druid was itself the propitiation; the victim on the Jewish altar was the type, and nothing but the type, of that propitiation. The Hebrew looked beyond his sacrifice to the divine victim typefied and promised by it, and whose blood alone could expiate and cleanse. Of this divine victim we have no proof that the Druid knew anything, beyond sharing, it may be, in the vague and uncertain expectation which then filled the world of the coming of a Great One who was to introduce a new and happier age, which should make that "golden morning" of which the poets sang, be forgotten in the greater splendour of the world's noon. Beyond these vague hopes, the priests of Druidism had no settled beliefs or opinions, and to their own sacrifices did they attribute exclusively that power to propitiate, which, of all the sacrifices of all the ages belonged to but one sacrifice, and that a sacrifice as yet in the distance.

It is long since the baleful fires of Druid were seen on our hill-tops. A purer light has since arisen in the sky of Scotland. But we are able to recall the scene which for ages continued to be witnessed in our land. Like all false religions, the spirit of Druidism was terror, and we can imagine the awe it inspired in the minds of men over whom it had been its pleasure for ages to hang the threefold cloud of ignorance, superstition, and serfdom.

The festival has come round, and this day the fires are to be lighted, and the sacrifice is to be offered on the "high place." The procession has been marshalled. At its head walks the high-priest, a venerable and imposing figure, in his long-flowing robes of white.[1] His train is swelled by other priests, also attired in white, who follow, leading the animal destined for sacrifice. It is the best and choicest of its kind; for only such is it fit to lay upon the altar. It is a bullock, or a sheep, or a goat, or, it may be, other animal. It has been previously examined with the greatest care, lest, peradventure, there should be about it defect, or maim, or fault of any sort. It has been found "without blemish," we shall suppose, and now it is crowned with flowers, and led away to be slain. As the procession moves onward, songs are sung by the attendant bards. The multitudes that throng round the priests and the victim perform dances as the pro-

[1] Toland, *Hist. of the Druids*, p. 69. Lond. 1726.

cession, with slow and solemn steps, climbs the sacred mount. The height has been gained, and priests and victim and worshippers sweep in at the open portal of the stone circle, and gather round the massy block in the centre, on which "no tool of iron has been lift up," and on which the sacrifice is to be immolated. The more solemn rites are now to proceed; let us mark them.

The priest, in his robes of snowy whiteness, takes his stand at the altar. He lays his hand solemnly upon the head of the animal which he is about to offer in sacrifice. In this posture—his hand on the sacrifice—he prays. In his prayer he makes a confession of sin, his own, and that of all who claim a part in the sacrifice. These transgressions he lays—such is his intention—on the victim, on whose flower-crowned head his hand is rested. It is now separated —devoted—for even the Druid feels that with sin is bound up doom, and that on whomsoever the one is laid the other lies also. Wine and frankincense are freely used in the ceremony of devotement. Set free from human ownership, the animal is now given to the deity. In what way? Is it dismissed to range the mountains as no man's property? No: bound with cords, it is laid on the altar; its blood is poured on the earth, its flesh is given to the fire, its life is offered to God.

Such was the worship of the Druid. It consisted of three great acts. First, the laying of his offence on the victim. Second, the offering up of the life of that victim. Third, the expiation, as he believed, thereby effected. The three principles which underlie these three acts look out upon us with unequivocal and unmistakeable distinctness. We can neither misunderstand nor misinterpret them. We do not say that the three principles were full and clear to the eye of Druid in his deep darkness. But though he had become unable to read them, that no more proves that they were void of significance and taught no truth, than the inability of the barbarian to understand a foreign tongue or a dead language proves that its writings express no intelligible ideas, and that it never could have been the vehicle of thought. We leave its meaning to be interpreted by the men to whom it was a living language. So in respect to these rites, we look at them in the light of their first institution, and we place ourselves in the position of those to whom they were, so to speak, a living language, and when we do so the three doctrines that shine out upon us from the sacrificial rites of the Druid are the doctrine of the Fall, the doctrine of a substitutionary Victim, and the doctrine of Expiation and Forgiveness. Such is the testimony borne by the altars of the Druid to the three earliest facts in human history, and the three fundamental doctrines of revealed religion.

How came the Druids to worship by sacrifice? No philosophy is sounder than that which, following up these traces, arrives at the conclusion of an original revelation, of which this is the remote and dim reflection. Sacrifice is no mere Druidic rite, transacted nowhere save in the oak forests of Scotland. A consensus of all nations had adopted sacrifice as the method of worship, and wherever we go, backward into history, or abroad over the earth, to ages the most remote, and to lands the farthest removed from each other, we find the altar set up and the victim bleeding upon it. Strange and amazing it is that the nations of the earth, the most polished as well as the most barbarous, the Greek with his passionate love of beauty, and the untutored and realistic Goth, should with one consent unite in a worship, the main characteristics of which are BLOOD and DEATH. Who told man that the Almighty delights to "eat the flesh of bulls and drink the blood of goats"? Left to the promptings of his own instincts, this method of worship is the last which man would have chosen. From what he knew of the Creator from nature, he would have judged that of all modes of worship this would prove the most unacceptable, and would even be abhorrent. "What!" he would have reasoned, "shall He who has spread loveliness with so lavish a hand over all creation ; who has taught the morning to break in silvery beauty and the evening to set in golden glory; who clothes the mountain in purple, dyes the clouds in vermillion, and strews the earth with flowers—shall He take pleasure in a sanctuary hung in gloom, nay, filled with horrors, or delight in an altar loaded with ghastly carcases and streaming with the blood of slaughtered victims ?" So did the first-born of men reason ; and in accordance with what he judged fit and right in the matter, he brought no bleeding lamb, he laid upon the altar instead an offering of new-gathered flowers and fruits. And so would the race have worshipped to this day but for some early and decisive check which crossed their inclinations and taught them that it was not only idle but even perilous to come before the Diety, save with blood, and to offer to Him ought but *life*.

Apart from the idea of an original divine appointment, there is no fact of history, and no phenomenon of the human mind more inexplicable than this consensus of the nations in the rite of sacrifice. A problem so strange did not escape the observation of the wise men of the heathen world; but their efforts to solve it were utterly abortive. To those of the moderns who refuse to look at the inspired explanation of this phenomenon, it remains as abstruse and dark as it was to the ancients.

These red prints—these altars and victims—which we trace down the ages, and all round the earth, what are they ? They are the foot-prints which have been left by the soul of man. They are like the etymological and archæological traces, which the early races have left on the countries which they inhabited, and which so surely attest the fact of their presence at a former era in the regions where these traces occur. So of these moral traces. They could no more have imprinted themselves upon the mind of the species apart from causes adequate to their production, than the etymological and archæological ones could have written themselves upon the soil of a country, without its previous occupation by certain races. These moral vestiges lay a foundation for philosophical deduction, quite as solid as that which the other lay for historic and ethnical conclusions. They form a chain by which we ascend to the fountain-head of history. We have in them the most indubitable attestation of the great fact of the fall. We have its historic imprint made visible to us in the sense of guilt, so deep, so inextinguishable, and so universal, which that primal act of transgression has left on the conscience of the world, and which has transformed worship, in every age, and among every people, from an act of thanksgiving into an act of propitiation. This is the world's confession that it has sinned: it is the cry of the human soul for pardon.

We have DEATH in the worship of man; we have GUILT in the conscience of man: and these two facts compel us to infer the existence of a third great fact, without which the first two are inexplicable, even SIN in the history of man. No other solution can even philosophy accept.

CHAPTER X.

THE TEMPLES OR STONE CIRCLES OF THE DRUID.

From the worship of Druidism we pass to the structures in which it was performed. These were so unlike the temples of later ages that we hesitate to apply to them the same name, or to rank them in the same class of edifices. The whole idea of their construction was borrowed from eastern lands and from patriarchal times. The models on which they were reared had come into existence before architecture had grown into a science, or had taught men to build walls of solid masonry, or hang the lofty roof on tall massy column. In the temple of the Druid no richly coloured light streamed in through mullioned oriel, and no pillared and sculptured portico, or gate of brass, gave entrance to the long train of white-robed priests, as they swept in, leading to the altar the flower-crowned sacrifice. But if these graces were lacking in Druidic structures, they possessed others in some respects even more in harmony with their character as religious edifices. They had a rough, unadorned grandeur which made them more truly imposing than many a fane which boasts the glory of Byzantine grace or of Gothic majesty. If the simplest, they were notwithstanding among the strongest of all the fabrics of man's rearing. They have outlasted races and empires, nay, the very deities in whose honour they were set up. And while the pyramids, which it cost millions of money and millions of lives to build, are bowing to the earth, or have wholly vanished from it, these simple stones still stand erect on field and moor, and link us in these western parts with the world's morning and the first races of men.

We have three examples of these, the earliest of British fanes, in a state of tolerable preservation: Stennes, Stonehenge, and Avebury. All these are partially in ruins, but enough remains to show us the mode of their construction and to give us an idea of their magnitude and grandeur when they were entire, while the fact that they have survived, though only in fragmentary condition, to our day, sufficiently attests their amazing and unsurpassed strength. Nothing could be simpler than the plan of their construction. They consisted of single stones, rough and shaggy, as when dug out of the earth, or when taken from the quarry, set on end, and ranged in a circle, each stone a little way apart from the other. The area which they enclosed was consecrated ground, and in the centre of it was the altar, an enormous block of stone.[1] The chisel had not approached those great blocks; ornament and grace their builders knew not and indeed cared not to give them. We look in vain for carving or inscription upon them. They were the work of an illiterate age. They possess but one quality, but that is the quality which of all others the barbarian most appreciates—size, colossal size.

The description of these structures belongs to the archæologist, and hardly falls within the province of the historian. The latter has to do with them only as they shed light on the social and religious condition of the people, among whom and by whom they were reared. At Stennes, in Ork-

[1] In Craigmaddie, Stirlingshire, is an enormous Druidical altar or dolman; the top-stone is eighteen feet in length, and three or four feet in thickness. It rests on two perpendicular stones placed triangularly to one another. It is believed to be the largest in Scotland.

ney there are two circles, the larger, called Brogar, consisting originally, it is believed, of sixty stones, of which only thirteen remain erect, and ten lie overturned; the smaller being a half circle. The greater circle was a temple to Baal, or the sun-god, while the smaller was dedicated to the moon. Others see in the smaller a court of judicature. The Druids, adding the office of judges to their functions as priests, generally set up their courts hard by their temples. The Norse rovers of the ninth century found these circles standing when they took possession of the island, for the spot is referred to under the name of Steinsness by Olaf Trygresson, when recording the slaughter of Earl Havard (970). Designating the spot by its most remarkable feature, the Norsemen called it, in their own language, the Stiensness—that is, the Ness of the Stones—the Stones' ness.

Stonehenge[1] is the second greatest stone circle that remains to us. It stands on the open plain of Salisbury, with no bulky object near it to mar its effect by dwarfing its apparent size. It must be visited before its weird splendour can be truly judged. The length of the tallest stone is 21 feet; the number of stones still erect is 140; and the diameter of the circle which they form is 106 feet. The circle appears to have had a coping, or corona, of headstones, but nearly all of these are now displaced. Henry of Huntingdon, writing in the twelfth century, calls Stonehenge one of the four wonders of England. It was old even in his

---

[1] An Anglo-Saxon name, borrowed from one of the features of the monument, the imposts, or "hanging stones" which are denoted by *henge*. "The ancient or Cymric name," says, Gidley, "appears to have been *Gwaith Emrys*, divine, or immortal." An ancient coin of Tyre has on it two stone pillars with the inscription, "Ambrosiæ petræ," ambrosial stones. Stukeley quotes Camden as speaking of a remarkable stone near Penzance, Cornwall, called Main Ambre, or the ambrosial stone. It was destroyed by Cromwell's soldiers. The ancient name of Stonehenge is preserved probably in the neighbouring town of Amesbury.

day, for he confesses that he knew nothing of its origin, or of the means by which such stupendous columns had been set up.

Diodorus Siculus quotes a passage from Hecatæus of Abdera, who lived B.C. 300, and wrote a history of the Hyperboreans, or people of the farthest north. Speaking of an island the size of Sicily, lying opposite the coast of Gaul, and which he characterises as grassy and fertile, Hecatæus says, "The men of the island are, as it were, priests of Apollo, daily singing his hymns and praises, and highly honouring him. They say, moreover, that in it there is a great forest, and a goodly temple of Apollo, which is round and beautified with many rich gifts and ornaments."[1] Mr Davies, author of the "Celtic Researches," reasonably concludes that the island here spoken of is Britain, and the temple in which harpers sang daily the praises of Apollo is Stonehenge and the Druids. If so, Stonehenge was in existence B.C. 300. And this supposition is strengthened by Pindar, the Greek lyric poet, who speaks of "the Assembly met to view public games of the Hyperboreans."[2] It was the custom of the ancients to celebrate games and races on the high festivals of their gods; and that they did so at Stonehenge when the people assembled for sacrifice is rendered almost certain by the discovery of Dr Stukeley (1723) of a "cursus," or hippodrome, half a mile north of Stonehenge, about 10,000 feet in length, and 350 feet in width. It runs east and west, and is lined by two parallel ditches. At the west end is a curve for the chariots to turn, and on the east a mound where the principal men might view the contest, and the judge award the prizes to the victors.

These stones have a weird spell to which the imagination not unwillingly surrenders itself. Standing on the bare,

---

[1] Diod. Sic., lib. iii. c. 13. [2] Pind. Pyth. x. 30.

solitary plain, they suggest the idea of a Parliament of Cyclops met to discuss some knotty point of the stone age: for with that age, doubtless, are they coeval. As the centuries flow past, new races and new arts spring up at their feet, still they keep their place and form part of the British world of to-day. They saw the Celtæ arrive and bring with them the bronze age. They were standing here when Cæsar and his legions stepped upon our shore. Their tall forms were seen on that plain when One greater than Cæsar walked our earth. They saw the Romans depart, and the Angles and Saxons rush in and redden the land with cruel slaughter. They heard the great shout of the Gothic nations when Rome was overturned. They saw the sceptre of England handed over from the Saxon to the Norman. They have waited here, fixed and changeless, while a long line of great kings—the Johns, the Edwards, the Henrys, of our history—have been mounting the throne in succession and guiding the destinies of Britain. And now they behold the little isle in which they first lifted up their heads become the centre of a world-wide empire, and the sceptre of its august ruler—the daughter of a hundred monarchs—stretched over realms which extend from the rising to the setting sun, and far to the south under skies which are nightly lighted up with the glories of the Southern Cross. Such are some of the mighty memories which cluster round these old stones. To see them morning by morning, freshening their rugged forms in the radiance of the opening day, and to watch them at eve solemnly and majestically withdrawing themselves into the dusk and cloud of night, is to feel something of the awe with which they inspired our forefathers of three thousand years ago.[1]

---

[1] "Stonehenge itself is enclosed by a double mound or ditch, circular in form; and there is an avenue or approach leading from the north-east;

But wonderful as Stonehenge is, it is eclipsed by the grandeur of Avebury. According to the remark of Aubrey two hundred years ago, and quoted by Sir Richard Colt Hoare, "Avebury does as much exceed in greatness the so-renowned Stonehenge as cathedral does a parish church."

A vast earthen rampart or mound sweeps round the site of this rude but majestic fane. Inside this mound is a fosse or ditch, and the perpendicular height in some places from the bottom of the fosse to the top of the mound is 80 feet. Half-way up the mound, on its inner side, is a broad ledge, running round the entire circle, on which the spectators could seat themselves by hundreds of thousands and witness the rites which were celebrated on the level floor, 28 acres in extent, which the vallum and rampart enclosed and overlooked. Just within the fosse was a second rampart of great stones, set on end, and sweeping round the entire area, stone parted from stone by an average interval of 27 feet. The row consisted of an hundred stones of from 17 to

and bounded on each side by a similar mound or ditch. The outer mound is 15 feet high, the ditch nearly 30 feet broad, the whole 1009 feet in circumference, and the avenue 594 yards long. The whole fabric consists of 2 circles and 2 ovals. The outer circle is about 108 feet in diameter, consisting, when entire, of 60 stones, 30 uprights, and 30 imposts, of which remain only 24 uprights, 17 standing and 7 down, 3½ feet asunder, and 8 imposts. The smaller circle is somewhat more than 8 feet from the inside of the outer one, and consisted of about 30 smaller stones, of which only 19 remain, and 11 standing. The walk between these two circles is 300 feet in circumference. At the upper end of the adytum is the altar, a large slab of blue coarse marble, 20 inches thick, 16 feet long, and 4 broad: pressed down by the weight of the vast stones that have fallen upon it. The whole number of stones when the structure was complete is calculated to have been about 140. The heads of oxen, deer, and other beasts have been found on digging in and about Stonehenge, and human bodies have also been discovered in the circumjacent barrows."—*Encyclopædia Britannica*, vol. xx. p. 709, eighth edition, Edin., 1860. "At the summer solstice the sun would be seen by one standing on the altar stone to rise over the summit of the bowing stone."—Stonehenge, Rev. L. Gidley, p. 49, Lond., 1873.

20 feet in height, not one of which had known chisel or hammer. To give them firm hold of the earth they were sunk to a depth of 10 feet, making the actual length of the stone about 30 feet. There are remains of an inner row, showing that this encompassing circle of grand monoliths was double. The diameter of the area enclosed by the fosse is 1200 feet, and of that enclosed by the great outer mound 1400 feet.[1]

In the centre of the area rises a beautiful little artificial hill of which we shall presently speak. On each side of this mount, and equally distant from it, stood a double concentric stone circle, formed of the same columnar masses as the great outer ring, presenting us with two small fanes enclosed within the great fane. The outer ring of these two little fanes contains thirty, and the inner twelve pillars, and the diameters of the rings were respectively 270 feet and 166 feet.

The conical mount in the centre is 125 feet high. Seldom disturbed by foot it has a covering of the freshest and loveliest verdure. It is wholly composed of earth, with an area at the top of 100 feet, and 500 at the base. Dr Stukeley says that in his time (1740) its height was 170 feet. It was ringed with stone pillars at the base. What its use was, whether an altar or a judgment-seat, it is now impossible to say.

This grand temple, with its fourfold circumvallation and its inner sanctuaries, is approached by two grand pathways which sweep on with a slight curve (the one from the north-east and the other from the north-west) for upwards of a mile. These approaches are spacious, thousands might journey along them without jostling, their breadth being not less than 45 feet, and they are lined throughout with a grand balustrade of pillars. They remind one of those grand

[1] *Rust.*, p. 116.

avenues of sphinxes that lead up to the great temples of ancient Egypt; and doubtless the impression they made on the Druidic worshipper as he drew nigh the grand shrine, was not less solemn than that which the marvels of Edfou made on the mind of the Coptic devotee; for what impresses the barbarian most is not artistic grace, but colossal size. It was when the Romans had passed the climax of their civilisation, and begun to decline once more towards barbarism, that, despising the Athenian models, they began to rear piles remarkable mainly for their stupendous magnitude.

All round the level plain on which these monuments occur swell up the ridges or low heights of Avebury. These little hills are dotted thickly over with sepulchral tumuli. If the great temple which is enclosed by this zone of graves be one of our earliest cathedrals, as in a sort it no doubt is, may we not, in the well-nigh obliterated sepulchres around it, see one of the earliest graveyards of our country? Here king and priest, warrior and bard mingle their dust, and sleep together. They have gone down into a land of "deep forgetfulness," for even Tradition has grown weary of her task, and has long since ceased to repeat their names and tell the story of the exploits which doubtless made these names, however forgotten now, famous in their day.

In comparison with these cyclopean structures, which it required only strength, not art, to rear, the grandest temples of Greece and Italy, on which science had lavished her skill, and wealth her treasures, were but as toys. The special charm of the Greek temple was beauty: majesty was the more commanding attribute of the Druidic fane. The snow-white marble, the fluted column, with its graceful volutes and sculptured pediment, the airy grace which clothed it like sun-light, was a thing to fascinate and delight, but in proportion as it did so it conflicted with the spirit of devotion, and lessened the reverence of the worshipper. The stone circle of the Druid, severe, sombre, vast, its roof the open heavens, was a thing to engender awe, and concentrate, not distract the mind. In our judgment our barbarian forefathers had a truer apprehension of the sort of structure in which to worship the Maker of the earth and heavens than the Greeks and Romans had.

We have already stated our deliberate and settled conviction that these monuments were reared for a religious purpose, in short are the earliest fanes ever set up on Scottish or British soil. But the recent discovery of a grand dolmen-centre in the land of Moab offers new and, we think, conclusive proof in support of our opinion. This discovery, moreover, sheds a new and most interesting light on the early history of Scotland, and corroborates the account we have given touching its first settlers, as coming from Eastern lands, and bringing with them this earliest of the forms of worship, while yet in a state of comparative purity.

No reader of the Old Testament needs to be told of the interest that invests Mount Nebo, or to have recalled to his mind the memorable occasion on which that hill was engirdled with altars and seen to blaze with sacrificial fires. Recent discoveries in that locality vividly recall the whole scene as depicted on the sacred page. The scholars of the "Palestine Exploration," enjoying a leisure for investigation which ordinary travellers cannot command, have discovered not fewer than 700 dolmens, standing or overturned, in the territory east of the Jordan. With these were mingled the remains of stone circles. This multitude of ruined shrines in one territory may well astonish us, and yet it is probable that these are only a few out of that great host of similar monuments with which that whole region bristled in former days. One shudders when he thinks of the abyss in which the inhabitants were sunk, as attested by these relics of a worship at once lewd and bloody. These monuments appear to have been equally numerous on the west of the Jordan before the entrance of the Israelites into Palestine, and if their ruins are there more rarely met with it is owing to the Divine injunction laid on Joshua to utterly destroy these erections and cleanse the land from the fearfully demoralising and debasing practices to which they gave birth.

Mount Nebo, in the land of Moab, was an object of special interest for examination on the part of the members of the "Palestine Exploration" expedition. "Close beside the knob of the mountain they saw," says Captain Conder, "a dolmen standing perfect and unshaken." They found other dolmens on the southern slope of the mountain; and on the west side of Nebo, yet another a little way below the "field of Zophim." This latter lies overturned. There is, moreover, a rude stone circle on the southern slope of the mountain.[1] Around this very hill-top did Balak rear seven altars, thrice told; may not these be their remains? Here stood "Balaam with the king and princes of Moab beside him," and while the smoke of the sacrifices ascended into heaven, and the dolmen tables ran red with the blood of the slain bullocks, the "son of Beor" looked down on the city of black tents in the gorge at his feet, and obeying an impulse by which his own inclination and wishes were overborne, he broke out into a lofty strain of prophetic blessing where he had hoped to pour forth a torrent of scathing maledictions.

This is the holy place of Moab, and these are the altars of Baal. But in shape, in size, in the method of their construction, in short, in every particular, they are the exact resemblances of the Druidic remains of Scotland. There are races

[1] Conder, *Heth and Moab*, pp. 147, 149.

which even at this day raise such structures in connection with religious uses. The tribes of the Khassia hills, the remains of the pre-Aryan inhabitants of India, still continue to erect menhirs.[1] The Arabs worshipped stones before the days of Mohammed: and no traveller can pass through Palestine without having his attention arrested by fields dotted all over with little pyramids of stones, the humble imitations of those statelier monuments which former ages reared for a sacred purpose. The Khonds of Eastern India, the remains of the Dravidians, still employ circles in connection with their worship of the rising sun. They offer at times human sacrifices. This was a common though horrible practice of the Baal worshipper of ancient days. He deemed his altar specially honoured when he laid upon it a human victim. Above the blood of bullock his diety delighted, he believed, in the blood of man.

The Druids were of opinion that the higher the victim the greater its power to make expiation. On this theory the sacrifice of a human victim was of all others the most efficacious and the most acceptable to the deity. They therefore on occasion offered such, as Cæsar and others assure us. It is easy to see what a fearful effect this would have in hardening the heart, and leading to waste and destruction of human life. Lucan tells us that in the forests the stone altars of the Druids were so thick, and the sacrifices so numerous, that the oaks were crimson with the blood. When a great man made atonement it was often with a human victim. Such, however, was generally selected from condemned criminals; but when these were not to be had, a victim was procured for the altar by purchase, or other means. Moloch turned the hearts of his worshippers to stone. In Caledonia, as in Judea, the mother shed no tear

[1] Conder, *Heth and Moab*, p. 200.

when she threw her babe upon the burning pile, nor did the father utter groan when he offered his son to the knife of the Druid. Sigh or tear would have tarnished the glory of the sacrifice.[1]

Nor was a single victim enough for the Druid's altar. He constructed, on occasion, castles of wicker-work, and filling their niches with young children, whose shrieks he drowned in the noise of his musical instruments, he kindled the pile, and offered up all in one mournful and dreadful hetacomb. But human sacrifices are not the reproach of barbarous races to the exclusion of civilized peoples. It was not the Moabite and Druidic altar only that flowed with the blood of man. These ghastly holocausts were seen among the Greeks and Romans, and that, too, in their most enlightened age. The same city that was the centre of ancient commerce was also the theatre of human sacrifices. The altars of Phœnicia—whence Greece borrowed her letters and arts—smoked with the bodies of infants immolated to Moloch. At Carthage a child was yearly offered in sacrifice, and the custom was continued down to the days of the pro-consul Tiberias, who hanged the priests on the trees of their own sacred grove. The rite of human sacrifice was not abolished at Rome, according to Pliny, till B.C. 87. Idolatry at the core is the same in all ages and among every people. It is a thing of untameable malignity, and unsatiable bloodthirstiness. Despite of arts and letters, and conquest, and all counteracting influences, it hardens the heart, that fountain of life and death, and slowly but inevitably barbarises society. What a difference betwixt the circle of unhewn stones on the Caledonian moor and the marble

---

[1] Speaking of the sacrifices of the Druids, Cæsar says, "Quod pro vita hominis nisi vita hominis reddatur." And Tacitus says that the first care of the Romans in Britain was "to destroy those groves and woods which the Druids had polluted with so many human victims."

temples of Greece! what a difference betwixt the unadorned ritual performed in the one, and the graceful and gorgeous ceremonial exhibited in the other! but whatever the people, whether painted barbarians or lettered Greeks, and whatever the shrine, whether a fane of unchiselled blocks, or a temple of snow-white marble, idolatry, refusing to be modified, was the same malignant, cruel, and murderous thing in the one as in the other. It was invincibly and eternally at war with the pure affections and the upward aspirations of man. It converted its priests into man-slayers, and made the mother the murderess of her own offspring.

Of the old pre-historic stones that linger on moor or in forest of our country, we do not affirm that all are remains of religious or Druidic structures. Some may mark the site of battles, others may signalise the spot where a warrior or chief was interred, and others may have been set up to commemorate some important event in the history of a clan or of a family. These are like the memorial-stones of the Patriarchal and Jewish history. But whatever the original use and purpose of these venerable monuments, they have now become, all of them, in very deed, "stones of remembrance," and the sight of them may well move us to thankfulness that the "day-spring" has risen on the night of our country, and that the advent of Christianity, by revealing the "one great sacrifice," has abolished for ever the sacrifice of the Druid.

CHAPTER XI.

THE "ALTEINS" OR STONES OF FIRE—BELTINE OR MAY-DAY AND MIDSUMMER FESTIVALS.[1]

THE names which the first settlers of a country give to the particular localities which they occupy, are not mere *brands*, they are significant appellatives. Such were the names of the ancient Palestine. They expressed some quality or incident connected with the town or valley or mountain which bore them, and despite the many masters into whose possession that land has since passed, and the diverse races that have successively peopled it, the aboriginal names still cling to its cities and villages though now in ruins. It is the same with Scotland. Its first inhabitants gave names in their vernacular to the localities where they reared their

---

[1] We have no intention of constructing a genealogical tree of the gods. Pagan mythology is a truly labyrinthic subject. What is the use of expending time and labour in tracing the genealogy and relationships of a class of beings that never existed, and which are the pure invention of the priests and poets of pagan times? It is true, doubtless, that these deities never existed, but the *belief* of their existence exercised for ages a powerful and fearfully demoralising influence on almost all the nations of the earth. Their ceremonies, moreover, were interwoven with the life and history of the nations, and so furnish light, not unfrequently, by which we are able to explain the past, and to account for the present. Not unworthily, therefore, nor uselessly, have some great scholars devoted their life to researches into this subject. To give even the briefest summary of what they have written on the gods and goddesses of antiquity is here impossible. We mention only a few leading facts—the bare outline of the mythological tree—to enable the reader to understand the allusions in the text. It is agreed on all hands that the first form of idolatry was the worship of the sun and moon. These were adored as the types of the

wattled dwellings or dug their underground abodes. There have since come new peoples to mix with the ancient population of the land, and new tongues to displace the original speech of its inhabitants, nevertheless the names given to hamlet and village in olden times are, in numerous instances, the names by which they continue to be known at this day; and these names carry in them the key which unlocks the early history of the place to which they are affixed. Some of these names are simply the footprints of the Druid.

Of these footprints one of the most noted is the term *clachan*. Clachan is a Gaelic word signifying *stones*. From this, which is its primary meaning, it came to denote, secondarily, a stone erection, and, in especial, a stone erection for religious observances. Gaelic lexicographers define "Clachan" to be "a village or hamlet in which a parish church is situate."[1] Before a hamlet could be promoted to the dignity of a clachan it was required of it that it should possess two things—a stone fabric and a place of public worship. But the curious thing is that in many of these *clachans* there is not now, nor ever was, a parish church or place of Christian worship of any sort. And farther, these

power and attributes of the Supreme Being. The first seat of this worship was Chaldea. In process of time the Sun came to have his type or representative on earth, to whom divine honours were paid. This was the founder or monarch of Babylon, who was worshipped under the title of Bel or Baal, which signifies the supreme lord. Baal became the supreme god to all the pagan nations, but under a different name in the various countries. He was worshipped as Baal by all the Semitic nations —the Assyrians, Arabians, Hittites, Phœnicians, &c. By the Greeks he was adored as Zeus, and by the Romans as *Jupiter*, Apollo, Saturn; that these are names of the same god has been shown by Selden, "De Dis Syriis," cap. i. p. 123. The wife of Baal was named Beltis, which is the feminine form of the word. She was the Rhea of the Assyrians, the Istar of the Persians, the Astarte and Ashtaroth of the Syrians and Phœnicians, the Venus of the Greeks and Romans. Her worship was widely prevalent. The Jews at times offered cakes to her as the "Queen of Heaven."

[1] Drs M'Leod and Dewar. Dict. of Gael. Lang. Word "Clachan." Glasgow, 1831.

hamlets have held the rank of *clachan* from a date when there was not a stone house in them, and their inhabitants dwelt in mud huts, or in fabrics of wattles. How, then, came they by their name of *clachan* or "stones," when they had neither parish church nor stone house. Simply in this way, and only in this way can the name be accounted for, that they had a "stone circle," which was their parish church, inasmuch as they assembled in it for the celebration of the rites of Druidism. Hence to go to the "stones" and to go to worship came to mean the same thing. "Going to and from church," says Dr Jamieson, "and going to and from the clachan are phrases used synonymously."[1] Even till recently this was a usual form of speech in the Highlands, and is probably in use in some parts still. Thus has Druidism left its traces in the language of the people as in the names of localities.

Altein is another of these footprints. Altein is a name given to certain stones or rocks found in many districts of Scotland, and which are remarkable for their great size, and the reverence in which they are held by the populace, from the tradition that they played an important part in the mysteries transacted in former days. *Altein* is a compound word—*al*, a stone, and *teine*, fire, and so it signifies "the stone of fire." It is corrupted sometimes into Alten, Altens, and Hilton. One of these *alteins*, or "stones of fire," is found in the neighbourhood of Old Aberdeen. It is termed the "Hilton Stone," and stands a mile west of the cathedral, upon what have always been church lands. It is a truly magnificent column of granite, rhomboidal in form, each of its sides a yard in breadth, and measuring from base to top 10 feet. The religious use to which it was destined is certified by the near proximity of two stone circles, each thirty

[1] Jamieson, *Hist. of the Culdees*, p. 27.

yards in diameter, and having, when entire, eighteen granite columns. The eastern circle remained untouched till 1830. Spared so long by tempests and other and worse agents of destruction, it was demolished in the year just named, and its monoliths broken up and utilised as building materials. The western circle, too, has all but vanished. It is represented at this day by but two stones, standing, doubtless, in the position in which Druid placed them long ages ago. When entire, these two granite circles, with the grand rhomboidal "stone of fire" standing betwixt them, would form a tolerably complete Druidic establishment; and thence, not improbably, was borrowed the name of the neighbouring cathedral city, which is often spoken of as the Altein-e-Aberdeen, or, to render the Gaelic appellatives into modern vernacular, *the stone of fire at the city on the mouth of the black river*.[1] Were the dead of seventy generations ago, which sleep in the neighbouring churchyards, to look up, they would describe for us the scenes that were wont to be enacted here, and in which they bore their part. They would paint the eager upturned faces of the crowd that pressed around this "altein" expectant of the fire which, as they believed, was to fall upon it out of heaven. And not less vividly would they picture the yet greater crowds, that, on high festival days, gathered round these "stone circles," and looked on in silent awe, while the white-robed Druid was going through his rites at the central dolmen. Victim after victim is led forward and slain—mayhap in the number is babe of some poor mother in the crowd, who seeks by this cruel and horrid deed to expiate her sin—and now the

---

[1] Not auld town of Aberdeen, but altein-e-Aberdeen. "We never," says Mr Rust (*Druidism Exhumed*, pp. 50-57), "say Altein-e-Edinburgh, or even Aulton o' Edinburgh, but auld town o' Edinburgh. The two words *auld* and *town* are never abbreviated into the compound *altein* or *aulton*."

altar streams with blood, besmeared are hands and robe of officiating priest, and gory prints speckle the grassy plot which the granite monoliths enclose. The sound of the rude instruments waxes yet louder, till at last their noise drowns the cries of the victim, and the smoke of the sacrifices rises into the sky and hangs its murky wreaths like a black canopy above the landscape.

Alteins are met with in various parts of Scotland. Every locality to which such name is affixed, is marked by its great rock-like stone, on which the fire of Druid was wont to blaze in days long past. Here Druid no longer kindles his fire, but the stone remains as if to bear its testimony to the beliefs and usages of old times. There is the *lia-teine*, or stone of fire, in the parish of Belhelvie, corrupted into Leyton. A few miles to the west of Edinburgh is the parish of Liston. The name has a similar derivation and has undergone a similar corruption as Leyton and Alton. Liston is at once the compound and the corruption of *Lias-teine*, and being rendered from the Gaelic into the vernacular, signifies the "stone of firebrands." Thus translated, the name opens a vista into far back ages. It recalls the ceremonies of that eventful night, October 30th, on which, as Druidic ordinance enjoined, the fire of every hearth in Scotland, without one exception, had to be extinguished, and the inhabitants of its various districts were to repair to their several "stone of firebrands," at which, on payment of a certain specified sum, they would receive from the hands of officiating Druid a torch kindled at his sacred fire, to carry back to their homes, and therewith rekindle their extinguished hearths.

The stone of Liston,[1] at which this ceremony was wont to

---

[1] The term *ton* (town) may have been added to *lis* or *lios* by the Scotch when the Gaelic meaning of the word was forgotten.

be enacted, is nine feet and a half in height. It is to be seen in a field a little to the east of the mansion-house of old Liston, not far from the stone circle and dyke which surround the mound called "Huly Hill." Other and more exciting scenes has this quiet neighbourhood witnessed than the ordinary rural occupations that engross its inhabitants in our day. Here Druid has left the print of his foot, and it is not difficult, and it may not be unprofitable, to recall the scenes in which he was here pleased to display the extent of his power and the mysteries of his craft, year after year, through long centuries.

The day has again come round. It draws towards evening, the last gleam of sunlight has faded on the summits of the Pentlands, and the shadows begin to lengthen and thicken on the plain at their feet. The gloom is deepened by reason of the absence of those numerous lights which are wont, on other evenings, to flicker out from dwelling and casement on the departure of the day. No lamp must this night burn, no hearth must this night blaze: for so has Druid commanded. And that command has been faithfully obeyed. In every house the inmates have extinguished the brands on their hearth and carefully trodden out the last embers. But it is not in the parish of Liston only that every fire has been extinguished in obedience to Druidic authority. The command is obligatory on every house in Scotland. Not a hearth in all the land is there that is not this night cold and black; nor dare it be rekindled till first the Druid, by his powerful intercessions, has brought fire from heaven. Then only may the kindly glow again brighten hearth and dwelling.

And now comes the more solemn part of the proceedings. From all the hamlets and dwellings around the inhabitants sally forth and wend their way in the dusk of the evening, across meadow and stubble-field, or along rural lane, towards that part of the plain where stands the "altein," or stone of firebrands. They carry torches in their hands, if so be, by favour of Druid, they may return with them lighted. They gather round the sacred stone, and await in awe the mysteries that are about to be enacted. A little knot of Druids have preceded them thither, and stand close around the "pillar of firebrands." All is dark,—dark around the stone as throughout the whole region. Anon the silence in the crowd is broken by a voice which is heard rising in prayer. It is that of a priest who beseeches Baal to show his acceptance of his worshippers by sending down fire to kindle anew their hearths. He cries yet louder, all the priests joining in the supplication, and lo! suddenly, a bright and mysterious light is seen to shoot up from the "altein." The flame has come down from heaven: so do the priests assure the awe-struck crowd. Their god is propitious: he has answered by fire. The multitude hail the omen with shouts and rejoicings.

And now the people press forward around the "altein," and holding out their torches, kindle them at the sacred flame, and bear them in triumph to their several homes. Long lines of twinkling lights may be seen in the darkness moving in the direction of the various villages and cottages, and in a little space every hearth is again ablaze. From every casement the cheerful ray streams out upon the night, and the whole region is once more lighted up with the new holy fire.

These "stones of fire" form a connecting link between the early Caledonia and the ancient Phœnicia. Of this latter country, the pioneer, and to a large extent the instructress of the ancient Caledonians in the mysteries of fire-worship, the capital, Tyre, was as distinguished for its idolatry as for its commerce; and if it transmitted the alphabetic letters invented in Chaldea and Egypt to the western world, it transmitted not less to the Westerns the deities of Asia. These were but second-hand gods, though set forth by the Phœnicians as if they had been the divine aborigines of their famous coast; for the gods and goddesses of paganism start up in different countries with other names. Here Ashtaroth was born rising on her shell from the blue deep. Here her star or thunderbolt fell on the island, which afterwards became the seat of Tyre, and that city never forgot what it owed to her who had given so miraculous a consecration to its soil. Here Hercules, a local Adonis, reigned supreme. His dog it was that fished up the first *murex* from the sea, its mouth purpled with the dye. Here Adonis, killed by the wild boar as he hunted in the Lebanon glen, was mourned by Ashtaroth, the Phœnician Venus; and here rejoicings were yearly held in honour of the awakening of Adonis, the Phœnician Tammuz. These festivals of mourning and rejoicing were not restricted to the Phœnician shore, they crept into the nighbouring country of Judea; hence the women whom Ezekiel saw in the temple "weeping for Tammuz." And here, too, as we have said, rose the *altein*.

The fire-pillars that blazed at the foot of Lebanon burned in honour of the same gods as those that lighted up the straths of Caledonia. Ezekiel speaks of the "stones of fire" of Tyre, and his description enables us to trace the same ceremonies at the Phœnician *alteins* as we find enacted at the Scottish ones.

When kindled, on the 30th of October, the Druid kept his "altein" alive all the year through till the 30th October again came round. It was then extinguished for a brief space, in order that a new gift of fire might be bestowed by his god. And as was the custom of the Scottish Druid, so, too, was that of the Phœnician Magus. His fires were kept burning, night and day, all the year round. Ezekiel depicts Tyre as "walking up and down in the midst of the stones of fire." For what purpose? To trim them and keep them alive, lest should they be suffered to go out, the gods in whose honour they burned might take offence, and visit the State with calamity. They were guardian fires, and, while they shone, the glory of Tyre was safe, and her rich merchandise, spread over many seas, was guarded from tempest and shipwreck. Compassed about by these guardian fires, her invincible defence as she deemed them, Tyre believed herself secure against overthrow; but the prophet foretold that destruction would find entrance nevertheless, and the crowning feature in the prophecy—so full of magnificence and terror—of her fall, is the extinction of these "alteins," or fires [1]—"I will destroy thee, O covering cherub, from the midst of the stones of fire." [2]

The words of Ezekiel throw light on what was done in old time on the moors of Scotland. They pierce the darkness of long past time, and show us the ceremonies enacted at the "alteins" and "stone circles" of Caledonia by our fore-

---

[1] Ezekiel, xxviii. 14, 16.

[2] Phœnicia was a chief seat of fire-worship. The Phœnicians came direct from the primitive seat of this worship, and made their new country a second Chaldea. Herodotus says that they passed over from the Persian Gulf to the shore of the Mediterranean. The Kaft, says Conder, which are known from the bilingual decree of Canopus to be the Phœnicians, appear on the Egyptian monuments as the neighbours of the Hittites, as early as the 14th century B.C. The term Phœnicians means Lowlanders. They were so named in contrast to the Giblites, who occupied the mountain, and were spoken of as mountaineers. They were the founders of Carthage, Cadiz, Marseilles. The fishers on Lake Menzalch, Port Said, and the Neapolitans are believed to be descended from them.

fathers of three thousand years ago. Hardly can a doubt remain that the "alteins" of early Scotland, and the "fire-stones" of Phœnicia, were identical as regards their character and use. We behold the same priests standing by them, and the same rites performed at them. Both were altars to Baal, or Moloch, or the Sun-god. In both countries their ruins still remain, though the baleful fires that so often blazed upon them have been long extinct. In Scotland a better light has arisen in their room. On the Phœnician shore the night, alas! still holds sway; and though there Astarte is no longer worshipped, she has bequeathed her "crescent" as the symbol of a new faith equally false, and even more barbarous.

The great days, or holy seasons of the Druid, still retain their place in our almanacs, and have a shadowy celebration in the observances of our peasantry, at least in some parts of the country. The 1st of May was wont to be known as Beltane, and to this day figures in our almanacs under this name. It is a festival of Druidic times, and its observance has not wholly ceased even yet. In the neighbourhood of Crieff there are the remains of a Druidic stone-circle, where a number of men and women were wont to assemble every year on the 1st of May. "They light a fire in the centre," says a witness and narrator of the ceremonies; "each person puts a bit of oat cake in a shepherd's bonnet: they all sit down, and draw blindfold a piece from the bonnet. One piece has been previously blackened, and whoever gets that piece has to jump through the fire in the centre of the circle, and pay a forfeit. This is in fact a part of the ancient worship of Baal. Formerly the person on whom the lot fell was burned as a sacrifice. Now, passing through the fire represents the burning, and the payment of a forfeit redeems the victim."[1]

The rites of this festival, as practised in the district of Callander in the end of last century, have been described to us in yet fuller detail by the Rev. John Robertson, minister of that parish.

"Upon the first day of May," says Mr Robertson, " which is called *Beltan*, or Bal-tein day, all the boys in a township or hamlet meet on the moors. They cut a table in the green sod, of a round figure, by casting a trench in the ground of such circumference as to hold the whole company. They kindle a fire, and dress a repast of eggs and milk in the consistence of a custard. They knead a cake of oatmeal, which is toasted at the embers against a stone. After the custard is eaten up, they divide the cake into so many portions, as similar as possible to one another in size and shape as there are persons in the company. They daub one of these portions all over with charcoal, until it be perfectly black. They put all the bits of the cake into a bonnet. Every one, blindfold, draws out a portion. He who holds the bonnet is entitled to the last bit. Whoever draws the black bit, is the *devoted* person who is to be sacrificed to *Baal*, whose favour they mean to implore, in rendering the year productive in sustenance for man and beast. There is little doubt of these inhuman sacrifices having been once offered in this country, as well as in the east, although they now pass from the act of sacrificing, and

---

[1] So did Lady Baird, on whose property stood the circle, assure the late Lord John Scott, from whom the Rev. Alex. Hislop of Arbroath had the anecdote. See "The Two Babylons," by Rev. A. Hislop, p. 148, Edin., 1862. When we mention this work, we do it no more than justice to say that it is one of vast erudition on the subject it discusses. It merits the study of all who wish to understand the structure and genius of pagan mythology with reference to Papal worship.

only compel the *devoted* person to leap three times through the flames, with which the ceremonies of this festival are closed." Mr Robertson adds other facts in which we can clearly trace the rites of sun-worship. "When," says he, "a highlander goes to bathe, or to drink waters out of a consecrated fountain, he must always approach by going round the place, from *east to west on the south side*, in imitation of the apparent diurnal motion of the sun. When the dead are laid in the earth, the grave is approached by going round in the same manner. The bride is conducted to her future spouse in the presence of the minister, and the glass goes round a company in the course of the sun. This is called, in Gaelic, going round the right or the *lucky way*."[1]

Next comes Midsummer. Then again the Druid lighted his fires. Alike on the Chaldean plain and on the moorlands of Caledonia, the summer solstice was a notable and sacred season. In Assyria the midsummer fires blazed in honour of the return from the dead of Adonis or Tammuz.[2]

---

[1] *Statistical Account of Scotland*, vol. xi., pp. 620, 621. Edin. 1794.

Beltane. We are happy to be able to insert the following note kindly sent us by the accomplished Professor of "Celtic Languages and Literature" in the University of Edinburgh :—

"Beltain—beltane (Bealltainn in modern Gaelic). The attribution to Baal, whether scientific or not, is very old.

"The earliest explanation of the meaning of the word known to me is that given in Cormac's Glossary (edited by O'Donovan & Stokes, Calcutta, 1868) (Cormac, 831-903, was prince and bishop of Cashel)—'Belltaine, *i.e.* bil-tene, *i.e.* lucky fire, *i.e.* two fires which Druids used to make with great incantations, and they used to bring cattle [as a safeguard] against the diseases of each year to those fires.'"

[2] There are some who find the *basis* of the whole of the pagan mythology in the early history of the race as recorded in the first pages of the Bible. The deities of paganism, they hold, are the patriarchs and fathers of mankind exalted to gods, and worshipped under other names (see Bochart), and the traditions, allegories, and mythical narrations respecting them, are disguised or veiled accounts of the services they rendered to their descendants. They hold, too, that the Creation,

In Scotland this festival was celebrated with more immediate reference to the harvest, which Baal the sun-god was invoked to bless and ripen. "These midsummer fires and sacrifices," says Toland, "were to obtain a blessing on the fruits of the earth, now becoming ready for gathering, and the last day of October as a thanksgiving for the harvest. . . . It was customary for the lord of the place, or his son, or some other person of distinction, to take the entrails of the sacrificed animals in his hands, and walking barefoot over the coals thrice, after the flames had ceased, to carry them straight to the Druid, who waited in a whole skin at the altar. If the nobleman escaped harmless it was reckoned a good omen, welcomed with loud acclamations; but if he received any hurt, it was deemed unlucky, both to the community and himself." "Thus have I seen," adds Toland, "the people running and leaping through the St John's fires in Ireland—the same midsummer festival—and not only proud of passing unsinged, but, as if it were some kind of *lustration*, thinking themselves in an especial manner blest by the ceremony."[1] It is not in the cities of Phœnicia, nor in the Valley of the Son of Hinnom only, that we see men

---

the Fall, the Deluge, the promise of a Redeemer, and even His death and resurrection, are all set forth and exhibited under the mythical veils which priests and poets have woven around these doctrines and facts. Ingenious and elaborate interpretations have been given of the heathen mythology on these lines. The recent discoveries in Assyria, which show that the early post-diluvian races had a fragmentary traditionary knowledge of the creation, the fall, and the deluge agreeing in substance with the Bible, lends some countenance to this theory, and shows that pagan mythology may not be wholly the product of the craft of priests, and the fancy of poets. But if these things be mythical representations of the great facts of inspired history, and the great doctrines of revelation, they are exhibitions which mystify, invert, desecrate, and utterly darken the facts and doctrines exhibited, and not only do they frustrate the end for which these doctrines were given, but they are charged with a meaning and spirit which make them work out the very opposite end.

[1] Toland, *The Druids*, pp. 107, 112.

passing through the fire to Baal; we behold the same ordeal undergone on the soil of our own country, and doubtless in the same belief, even, that in these fires resided a divine efficacy, and that those who passed through them were purified and made holy.

Chambers informs us, in his *Picture of Scotland*,[1] that a fair is held regularly at Peebles on the first Wednesday of May, called *the Beltaine Fair*. It has come in the room of *the feast of the sun*. "To this hour," says Toland (1720), "the 1st of May is by the original Irish called *La Bealtine*, or the day of Belan's fair."[2] "These last," May and Midsummer eve, says Owen (1743), "are still continued in Wales without knowing why, but that they found it the custom of their ancestors;" as are those on Midsummer eve "by the Roman Catholics of Ireland," says Toland, "making them in all their grounds, and carrying flaming brands about their cornfields." "This they do," adds he, "likewise all over France, and in some of the Scottish isles."[3] The custom of *passing through the fire* was also observed in these countries. "Two fires," says Toland, "were kindled on May eve in every village of the nation, as well as throughout all Gaul, as well as in Britain, Ireland, and the adjoining lesser islands, between which fires the men and the beasts to be sacrificed were to pass. One of the fires was on the carn, another on the ground. Hence the proverb amongst the people, when speaking of being in a strait betwixt two, of their being *between Bel's* two fires."[4] "The more ignorant Irish," says Ledwich, "still drive their cattle through these fires as an effectual means of preserving them from future accidents." The identity of these rites with those practised in Phœnicia, and in Judea in its degenerate age, and in lands lying still farther to the east, cannot be mistaken.

[1] Vol. i. 178. Edin., 1827. [2] Toland, pp. 101, 103.
[3] Ibid, p. 107. [4] Ibid, p. 104.

As the midsummer festival was one of the more important of the Druidic observances, care was taken that it should be kept punctually as to time. Outside the stone circle it was usual to set up a single upright pillar. This was termed the pointer, and its design was to indicate the arrival of the summer solstice. It stood on the north-east of the circle, and to one standing in the centre of the ring, and looking along the line of the pointer its top would appear to touch that point in the horizon where the sun would be seen to rise on the 22nd of June. When this happened the Druid knew that the moment was come to kindle his midsummer fires. At Avebury the pointer still remains. So, too, at Stennes in Orkney. In Upper Galilee, as we have already said, the white top of Hermon indicates the point of sunrise at midsummer to one standing in the centre of the stone-circles to the west of Tel-el-Kady, the ancient Dan. These stones were the clocks of the Druid : they measured for him the march of the seasons, and enabled him to observe as great exactitude in the kindling of his fires and the celebration of his festivals as the sun—the god in whose honour his sacrifices were offered — in his annual march along the pathway of the zodiac.

CHAPTER XII.

VITRIFIED FORTS—ROCKING-STONES—DRUID'S CIRCLE—
NO MAN'S LAND — DIVINATION — GALLOW-HILLS — A
YOKE BROKEN.

In our vitrified forts, too, it is possible that we behold a relic of the times and observances of Druidism. This is the likeliest solution of a problem which, after many attempts, still remains unsolved. We know that on a certain night of the year immense bonfires were kindled on the more conspicuous of our hill tops, and the whole country from one end to the other, was lit up with the blaze of these pyres. The intense heat of such immense masses of wood as were consumed on these sites year by year through a series of centuries, must, in process of time have converted the stones and rocks on which they were kindled into a vitrified mass. The idea that these vitrifactions were forts is barely admissible. They occur, with a few exceptions, on mountains which possess no strategical quality, and which were not likely to have been selected in any great plan of national fortification, supposing the natives capable of forming such a scheme of military defence. The undoubted hill-fortresses of Scotland may be traced by hundreds in their still existing remains, but these are of a character wholly different from the antiquities of which we are now speaking. The site selected for their erection was some hill of moderate height, standing forward from the chain of mountains that swept along behind it and which overlooked the wide plains and far-extending straths which lay spread out in front. The builders of these strengths, whoever they were, did not seek to fuse the materials with which they worked into a solid mass, they were content to draw around the mountain-tops, which they fortified, a series of concentric walls, broad and strong, constructed of loose stones, with ample space betwixt each circular rampart for the troops to manœuvre. The vitrifactions, on the other hand, are scattered over our mountainous districts, with no strategical link binding them together, and in the absence of any conceivable use to be served by them, which would compensate for the toil of dragging up their materials to the elevated sites where they are found, the annual occurrence of a religious observance which, year by year, during a very lengthened period, rekindled on the same spot immense bonfires, presents us with by much the likeliest solution of their origin.

Other vestiges of this early and now fallen superstition are scattered over the face of the country, and a glance at these may help to bring back the image of the time, and strengthen the proof, if it needs further strengthening, that Druidism once dominated in Scotland. Among the more prominent of these are the rocking stones, so termed because the slightest application of force sufficed to set them a vibrating. They were huge unhewn rocks, weighing from thirty to fifty tons, hoisted up and placed on the top of another rock, equal to the burden, and so nicely poised as to move at the touch of the finger.

The rocking-stone is not a megalithic curiosity known only to Scotland. It is met with in England and Ireland, and in countries lying far beyond the British seas. When we travel back in time we find mention made of it by writers who flourished twenty centuries ago. Camden speaks of one in

Pembrokeshire, Wales, on a sea-cliff, within half a mile of St David's. It is so large, that, says Owen, his informant, "I presume it may exceed the draught of an hundred oxen." It is "mounted upon divers other stones, about a yard in height; it is so equally poised that a man may shake it with one finger."[1] Perhaps the most remarkable is that in Cornwall, called "the Logan Stone," at Treryn Castle, in the parish of St Levan. It is supposed to weigh ninety tons, yet is so balanced on an immense pile of rocks that "one individual, by placing his back to it, can move it to and fro easily."[2] Rocking-stones are found in Ireland as well as in Cornwall and Wales. Toland regards them as part of the mechanism of Druidism, and so do almost all who have occasion to speak of them whether in ancient or in modern times.

"It was usual," says Bryant, "among the Egyptians to place one vast stone above another for a religious memorial, so equally poised, that the least external force, nay, a breath of wind, would sometimes make them vibrate."[3] Nor did these stones escape the notice of Pliny. "Near Harpasa, a town of Asia," says he, "there stands a dreadful rock, moveable with one finger, the same immoveable with the whole body." The motion of so large a body on the application of so slight a force, Photius in his life of Isidore, tells us, formed the subject of some curious discussions. Some attributed the vibrations of the stone to divine power, but others saw in them only the workings of a demon.[4] It does not surprise us to find a class of men so astute as the priests of Druidism quick to perceive the use

---

[1] Camden's *Britannia*, vol. ii. p. 520, Lond. 1789.
[2] Stockdale's *Excursions in Cornwall*, p. 69.
[3] Bryant, *Anal. Mythol.*, vol. iii., apud Moore, *Hist. of Ireland*, p. 39, Lond. 1835.
[4] Vita Isidori, apud Photium, in Moore's Ireland, p. 39.

to which these stones might be turned in the way of supporting their system. The man conscious of guilt when he saw the ponderous mass begin to quiver and tremble the moment he laid his finger upon it, mistaking the mechanical principle, of which he was ignorant, for the presence of the deity to whom his crime was known, would feel constrained to confess his sin.

These stones were termed also Judgment Stones. They were, in fact, the Urim and Thummim of the Druid. They could not be worn on the breast like the oracle of the Jewish priesthood, they were set up in the glen or on the moor and were had recourse to for a divine decision in matters too hard for the determination of a human judge. If one was suspected of treason, or other crime, and there were neither witnesses nor proof to convict him, he was led into the presence of this dumb, awful judge, in whose breast of adamant was locked up the secret of his innocence or his guilt, and according to the response of the oracle, so was the award of doom. If the stone moved when the suspect touched it, he was declared innocent; if it remained obdurately fixed and motionless, alas! for the unhappy man, his guilt was held to be indubitably established. A judge with neither eyes to see, nor ears to hear, but in whom dwelt a divinity from which no secrets were hidden, had condemned him. From that verdict there was no appeal; as was wont to be said of another judge, whose decisions were received as the emanations of divine and infallible knowledge, so was it said of the Druidic Infallibility.

"Peter has spoken, the cause is decided."

"Behold you huge
And unhewn sphere of living adamant
Which, poised by magic, rests its central weight
On yonder pointed rock; firm as it seems,
Such is its strange and virtuous property,

> It moves obsequious to the gentlest touch
> Of him whose breast is pure; but to a traitor,
> Tho' even a giant's prowess nerved his arm,
> It stands as fixed as Snowdon."

A rocking-stone was a quarry in itself, and such stones were dealt with as such in process of time; that is, they were broken up, and dwelling-houses and farm-steadings were built out of the materials which they so abundantly supplied, and hence, though anciently these rocking-stones were common they are now rare. There was a "rocking" or "judgment" stone at Ardiffery near Boddam. Half a century ago it still existed, and called up images of unhappy persons standing before it, awaiting, in trembling and terror, their doom. It has now vanished, doubtless under the forehammer of the builder. It lives only in the pages of a local antiquary, who describes it as he saw it sixty years ago. "In walking up this solitary glen (Boddam) you come in contact with a very large stone of unhewn granite, and whose dimensions are (as measured in May 1819), 37 feet in circumference and 27 feet over it. ... It is placed upon several small blocks of granite, so as to free it entirely from the ground, which must evidently have been done by the hands of men. As there are evident marks of fire close by it, I have every reason to believe it to have been accounted sacred, and a place of worship of the ancient Druids."[1]

By what means these great stones were placed in the position in which we find them is a problem which remains to this day a mystery. The combined strength of a whole parish would hardly have sufficed, one should think, to accomplish such a feat. It is plain that the Druids knew the art of the engineer as well as the science of the astronomer, and possessed appliances for combining, ac-

[1] *Buchan*, Annals of Peterhead, p. 42.

cumulating, and applying force in the transportation of heavy bodies far beyond what we commonly credit them with. They knew the uses before they knew the principles of the mechanical powers, and hence such machines as pulleys, cranes, and inclined planes have been in practice from time immemorial. They could yoke hundreds of oxen, or thousands of men to the car on which these immense masses were conveyed from the spot where they were dug up to the spot where they were to stand; but having dragged them thither, how were these enormous blocks to be lifted into the air? hung, as it were, on a needle's point, and so evenly balanced as to vibrate at the gentlest touch? This would have taxed the resources, and it might be baffled the skill of the mechanist of the present day. And yet, the natives of Scotland could accomplish this feat three thousand years ago! When one thinks of this one is tempted to half believe that the builders of these mighty structures, which war, tempest, and time have not been able even yet utterly to demolish, did indeed possess the magical powers to which they laid claim. The only magic with which they wrought was knowledge; but is it wonderful that the untaught multitude mistook a skill and craft that were so far above their comprehension, and which they saw performing prodigies, for a knowledge wholly supernatural, and, in the awe and terror thus inspired, were willing to accept the manipulations of the Druid for the intimations of the Deity?

The Druid's favourite figure was the circle—another link between Scottish Druidism and the world-wide system of Sun worship. Two things have come down to us from the earliest ages as the most perfect of their kind, *seven* amongst numbers, and the *circle* amongst figures. A certain mystic potency was supposed to reside in both. When we turn to the all-prevalent system of sun worship we see at once how this belief arose. Bunsen tells us that the circle was the symbol of the sun.[1] It came thus to be the canonical and orthodox form of all buildings reared for his worship. Wherever we come on the remains of these structures, whether in Asia or Europe, they are seen to be circular. As the Magus performed his incantations within his circle, traced, it might be, on the ground with his staff, so the Druid, when he performed his worship, stood within his ring of cyclopean stones. The spell of the magician was more potent, and the worship of the Druid was more acceptable when done within this charmed enclosure. Nor was it their religious edifices only that were so constructed; almost all their erections were regulated as to shape by their belief that there was in the circle a sacred efficacy. From their barrows on the moor to their dwelling-houses, all were circular. The well-known Pict's house was a circle. And when these huts formed a brough or hamlet, they were so arranged as to form a series of circles. Of this a curious specimen is still to be seen in the north of England. On the slope of a hill in Northumberland, about six miles south of the Tweed, in a district abounding in stone remains of a Druidic character, is a little city in which no man has dwelt these long centuries. As it has been described to us by eye-witnesses, it is a congeries of circular huts, arranged in streets, all of which form circles having a common centre.

We have already spoken of the great days of the Druid, which even so late as the seventeenth century were observed with the old pagan honours by a large portion of the Scottish peasantry; nor has their observance wholly ceased even in our day. Fires were extinguished and rekindled, arts of divination were practised, and other ceremonies of Druidic times

[1] Bunsen's *Egypt*, vol. i., pp. 535, 537.

were performed, though in many cases all knowledge of the origin and design of these observances had been lost. "In many parts of the Scottish highlands," says Dr Maclachlan, "there are spots round which the dead are borne sunwise in their progress toward the place of sepulture; all these being relics not of a Christian but of a pagan age, and an age in which the sun was an object of worship." "There are places in Scotland where within the memory of living man the *teine eigin*, or 'forced fire,' was lighted once every year by the rubbing of two pieces of wood together, while every fire in the neighbourhood was extinguished in order that they might be lighted anew from this sacred source." [1]

It was accounted unlawful to yoke the plow or to engage in any of the duties of ordinary labour on these festival days; such seasons were passed in idleness, or were devoted to the practice of magical arts. There were, moreover, in various parts of the country, plots of land consecrated to the gods of Druidism, and sacredly guarded from all pollution of spade or plough. Such fields were termed, "the good man's land and the guid man's fauld." No one dared cultivate them for fear of incurring the wrath of the powerful and terribly vengeful imps of Druidism. They lay untilled from century to century, and were viewed with mysterious awe as the trysting-place of familiar spirits, who were supposed to be willing and able to disclose the secrets of futurity to anyone who had the courage to meet them on their own proper territory. So prevalent were these things that we find the General Assembly of the Church of Scotland of 1649 appointing a large Commission of their number to take steps for discouraging and suppressing these superstitious practices. We trace the action of the Commission in the consequent procedure of several of the Kirk Sessions.

[1] Rev. Dr Maclachlan, *Early Scottish Church*, pp. 33, 34, Edin. 1866.

These courts summoned delinquents before them and enjoined on them the cultivation of fields which had not been turned by the plow from immemorial time, and they required of farmers that they should yoke their carts on the sacred festival of Yule, and of housewives that they should keep their hearth-fire burning on Beltane as on other days.

Arrogance is an unfailing characteristic of all false priesthoods. To be able to open the human breast and read what is passing therein has not contented such pretenders: they have claimed to open the portals of the future and foretell events yet to come. Every idolatry has its Vatican or mount of divination. There is an instinctive and ineradicable belief in the race that He to whom the events of to-morrow and the events of a thousand years hence are alike clearly known, can, when great ends are to be served, make known to man what is to come to pass hereafter. It is a shallow philosophy that rejects the doctrine of prophecy in its predictive form. The second great Father of the world, before he died, gathered his children, then an undivided and unbroken family around him, and showed them what should befall them in the latter days. The race started on their path with this prophecy burning like a light, and carried it with them in their several dispersions. Their belief in it grew stronger as, age by age, they saw it fulfilling itself in their various fortunes; and though the divine gift, after the dispersion, remained only with the family of Seth—the worshippers of the true God—all nations laid claim to prophecy, and all priesthoods professed to exercise it. The Druids of Britain challenged this gift not less than the wise men of Chaldea, the Magi of Persia, and the priests of Greece. The earliest of our writings, which are the archæological ones, attest the former prevalence in Scotland of this, as well as of all the other forms of divination and soothsaying.

By the help of these archaeological lights we can still identify many of those "high places" to which the Druid went up, that there he might have the future unveiled to himself, and be able to unveil it to others. The "Laws" and "Gallow-hills" scattered here and there all over our country attest by the name they bear that here were the divining places of the priests of the Scottish Baal. The name comes from a Gaelic word, *gea-lia*, which signifies "The Sorcery Stone,"[1] now corrupted into *gallow*. The Gaelic words *gea* (sorcery), and *lia* (a stone) enter into a variety of combinations, and appear in many altered forms, but wherever we light upon them as the names of places we there behold the Druidic brand still uneffaced, though affixed so long ago, and most surely indicating that we are treading on what was once holy ground, and in times remote witnessed the vigils of the astrologer and the incantations of the soothsayer. It must be noted as confirmatory of this etymological interpretation, that these *laws* and *gallow-hills* have the common accompaniment of a neighbourhood abounding in Druidic remains—pillar-stones or remains of circles.

The popular belief regarding these *laws* and *gallow-hills* is that in other days they were places of judgment and of execution,—in short, that here stood the gallows. But this is to mistake the etymological meaning of the name. The term is not gallows-hill and gallows-gate, but gallow-hill and gallow-gate. It is the Celtic *gea-lia*, and not the English vernacular, *gallows*, which is but of yesterday, compared with the olden and venerable word which has been corrupted into a sound so like that it has been mistaken for it. The name was affixed to these places long before the gallows had come into use as an instrument of capital punishment, and sentence of death was carried out on the crim-

[1] Rust, *Druidism Exhumed*, p. 63.

inal by the stone weapon, or by the yet more dreadful agency of fire.

In no land, if ancient writers are to be believed, did divination more flourish than in the Britain of the Druid. No, not in Chaldea, where this unholy art arose; nor in Egypt, where it had a second youth; nor in Greece, where stood the world-renowned oracle of Delphi, nor even at Rome where flourished the college of augurs. The sooth-sayers of Britain were had in not less honour, their oaks were deemed not less sacred, and their oracles were listened to with not less reverence than were the utterances of the same powerful fraternity in classic countries. Nay, it would seem that nowhere did their credit stand so high as in Britain. The testimony of Pliny is very explicit. Speaking of Magism, by which the ancients meant a knowledge of the future, he says, "In Britain at this day it is highly honoured, where the people are so wholly devoted to it, with all reverence and religious observance of ceremonies, that one would think the Persians first learned all their magic from them."[1] So great was the fame of the British diviners that the Roman emperors sometimes consulted them. They rivalled, if they did not eclipse the Greek Pythoness, and the Roman augur, at least in the homage that waited on them in their own country, and the respect and submission which they extorted from all who visited the island.

The rites which they practised to compel the future to disclose itself to their eye, were similar to those which their brethren abroad—partners in the same dark craft—employed for the same end. They watched the sacrifices, and from the appearance of the entrails divined the good or ill fortune of the offerer. They drew auguries from the flight of birds, from the cry of fowls, from the appearance of plants, as also

[1] Plin. Nat. His., lib. xxx. c. i.

from the drawing of lots, and the observation of omens, such as tempests and comets. To these comparatively harmless methods they are said to have added one horrible rite. They took a man, most commonly a criminal, and dealing him a blow above the diaphragm, they slew him at a single stroke, and drew their vaticinations from the posture in which he fell, and the convulsions he underwent in dying. So does Diodorus Siculus relate.[1] To these arts they added, it is probable, a little sleight of hand; and, moreover, possessing considerable skill in medicine, in mechanics, and in astronomy, it is reasonable to suppose that they made use of their superior knowledge to do things, which to the uninstructed and credulous would appear possible only by the aid of supernatural power. His unbounded pretensions being met by the unbounded credence of his votaries, the Druid foretold the issue of battles, the defeat or triumph of heroes, the calamities or blessings that awaited nations—in short, the good or ill success of whatever enterprise of a private or of a public kind, might happen to be on hand.

A truly formidable power it was with which the art of divination armed the Druid. The people among whom he practised his auguries, and who accorded him the most unbounded faith as the possessor of the terrible attributes to which he laid claim, could never very clearly distinguish, we may well believe, between the power to foretell the future, and the power to fix the complexion and character of the future. The prediction of flood, or tempest, or earthquake, or other dire elemental convulsion, and the power to evoke and direct these terrible chastisements, were, doubtless, in their imagination, very much mixed up together. They had no clear conceptions of the limits of this mysterious power; or whether indeed, it had boundaries at all. He

---

[1] *Dio. Siculus*, lib. v. c. 35.

who could read the stars, for aught they knew, might be able to stay them in their courses, and compel them to do his pleasure. If he should command the ocean to leave its bed and drown their dwellings, would not its waters obey him? If he should summon the tempest, would it not awake at his call? Or if he should lift up his voice to the clouds, would they not straightway rain their hailstones and hurl their thunderbolts upon the disobedient? They saw the Druid, with all the forces, visible and invisible, of nature ready to be marshalled at his bidding against all who should dare to disobey or offend him. What a miserable vassalage! and from that vassalage there was no escape. The earth was but a wide prison, peopled throughout with invisible agents, countless in number, and malign in spirit, whose only employment and delight were to torment the race of man. Nature itself groaned "travailing in pain" under the bondage of this corruption, and waited in "earnest expectation," for the coming of Christianity that it might be brought into the liberty of a purer system. And when at length the Gospel came, and broke the divining rod of the Druid, and purged out the gross defilement of those vengeful deities with which he had peopled earth and air, sea and sky, and tumbled their dark empire—to believer in Druidism no imaginary one—into ruin, what a glorious and blessed emancipation!—not to man only, but also to the earth on which he dwelt. If, as some historians say, wailings were heard to issue from the shrines and oracles of paganism, when the cry went forth and resounded along the shores of every island and continent, "great Pan is dead," well might songs and shoutings arise from the Britons when they felt their ancient yoke falling from off their neck, and the thick gloom in which they had so long sat, giving place to the morning light of a better day.

CHAPTER XIII.

SCOTLAND AS SEEN BY AGRICOLA AND DESCRIBED BY TACITUS AND HERODIAN.

AFTER long ages—how many we do not know, for they reach back into the primeval night, and offer us nothing to guide our hesitating steps but the dubious memorials which the poor barbarian has left behind him in cairn and cist—we gladly welcome the rising of the light of history. It is a Roman hand that carries the torch that first illumines our sky, and reveals the face of our country to us. Time has not yet come to its "fulness," nor has the world's grand epoch taken place, yet here on the coast of England is the Roman fleet searching along the shores of Kent for a place of anchorage and disembarkation. The invasion is led by the great Julius in person. That remarkable man, uniting letters with arms, touches no spot of earth on which he does not shed light; alas! also inflict devastation. He has just set foot on a new shore, and he feels the curiosity of the discoverer as well as the lust of the invader and conqueror. We see him, on the evening after the battle, retiring to his tent, or to his ship, and noting down, in traces rapid and brief, but destined to be ineffaceable, whatever had fallen under his own observation, or had been reported to him by others, respecting the appearance of the country, and the manners, opinions, and condition of the barbarians on whose shore he had just hurled his legions.

It is verily no pleasant or flattering picture to which the pen of Cæsar introduces us. And the darkness of that picture is deepened by the sharp contrast which so strongly suggests itself betwixt the country of the writer, then just touching the acme of its literary and warlike glory, and the poor country which his pen seeks to pourtray. That contrast has since that day been most strikingly reversed. But if civilisation and empire have transferred their seat from the country of the polished writer and invincible conqueror to that of the skin-clothed man, on whose neck we see Rome now imposing her yoke, we behold in this no proof, though some might regard it as such, of the fickleness of fortune, and the instability of power and grandeur.

This change of place on the part of the two countries, looked at below the surface, is, on the contrary, a conspicuous monument of the stedfast and unchangeable working of those laws and forces that determine whether a nation is to go forward or to fall back—forward to empire or backward into slavery. Nations may win battles, or achieve great triumphs in art, but there is a mightier power in the world than either arms or arts, though the Roman knew it not, and statesmen still make but small account of it; and in the stupendous revolution of which we have spoken we trace simply the working of this Power : a power compared with which the strength of the Roman legions was but as weakness : a power, moreover, that crowns itself with far other victories than those which the mistress of the ancient world was wont to celebrate with such magnificence of pomp and haughtiness of spirit, on her Capitol.

It is England rather than Scotland which the invasion of Cæsar brings into view. No foot of Roman soldier, so far as is known, had yet been set down on Scottish soil. Slowly the Roman eagle made its way northward into Caledonia, as if it feared to approach those great mountains, dark with tempests, which nature had placed there as if to form the last impregnable defence of a liberty which Rome was devouring. It was in the year 55 B.C. that Julius Cæsar invaded Britain ; but it was not till about one hundred and thirty-five years after this, that is, in the year 80 of our era, that Agricola, leading his legions across the Tweed, brought Scotland for the first time into contact with Rome. All England by this time was comprehended within the limits of the empire, and had become a Roman province. It was dotted with Roman camps, and studded with Roman cities, in which both foreigners and natives were living the life of Italy under a northern sky. England, in a word, was already very thoroughly permeated by those refining but emasculating influences of which Rome was the centre, and which she studied to diffuse in all her provinces as a means of reconciling to her yoke, and of retaining under her sceptre, those countries which her sword had subjugated. But as yet Scotland was untouched by these insidious and enfeebling influences. Roman luxury had not relaxed its barbaric vigour, nor had Roman power tamed its spirit, or curtailed its wild independence. But now its subjugation was begun.

The task of conquering it, however, Agricola found a difficult one. Scotland was not to be so speedily subdued, nor so securely retained, as the level country of England. The forests were more dense, the swamps more impenetrable, and the mountain strengths more formidable on the north of the Tweed than in the southern country. The natives, moreover, less readily accepted defeat, and though routed and dispersed in battle, they would again renew the attack with revived desperation and in augmented numbers. But Roman discipline and perseverance at last surmounted these obstacles, though neither wholly nor permanently. The legions hewed their way into the country, scattering or crushing every living thing that opposed their progress. Advancing from stream to stream, and from one mountain range to another, guarding the passes behind him with camps, erecting forts of observation and defence on the hill tops, throwing bridges across rivers, and laying down lines of roads through forest and moor, and ever presenting a stern front to the natives, who kept retreating before him, unless when at times surprised and slaughtered by his soldiers, Agricola held on his way till at last he stood on the shores of the Firth of Forth. Here, in sight of the north hills, the conqueror halted, and drawing a chain of forts across the country from the Forth to the Clyde to repel the attack, or shut out the irruption of the natives still numerous in the country beyond, the Roman general fixed here for the time the boundary of the now overgrown empire of Rome. His future progress northward, and the sanguinary battles it cost him to make good this advance, will fall to be narrated in subsequent chapters. Meanwhile let us pause and look around on the country and the people amid which the triumphs of Agricola have placed both him and us.

Happily for us, in the invasion of Scotland under Julius Agricola, as in the previous invasion of England under Julius Cæsar, letters and arms were once more conjoined. Not, however, as before, in the same person, although in the same expedition. Along with this Roman general came his son-in-law, Tacitus, the great historian.[1] While the soldier,

---

[1] The author has assumed that Tacitus accompanied his father-in-law to Britain. This impression, amounting to almost certainty, was produced by his perusal of the "Life of Agricola." In describing the country and its inhabitants, Tacitus takes the attitude of an eye-witness. When he speaks of those parts to which Agricola and the legions did not penetrate, he gives us the testimony of others, using the phrase, "they represent,"

with keen eye scrutinised the strategic points of the country, and determined the movement of the legions, the historian, equally alert, noted down the more prominent and remarkable characteristics of the new region into which they had come, and the peculiar qualities and appearance of the race among which they found themselves. The touches of a feebler pen, especially when engaged on a country so obscure as Scotland then was, would have speedily faded into utter oblivion. The picture produced by the genius of Tacitus, posterity has taken care to preserve. It is vivid, but not complete or full. To see Scotland as it disclosed itself to the eyes of the two great Romans, it is necessary to fill in the bold outline of the great master with the fragmentary and casual glimpses which we obtain from the pen of other writers, chiefly those which flourished subsequent to the time of Tacitus.

There is a time for countries as for men to be born. Till that time had come to Scotland, the country lay shrouded in night; but now the hour had arrived when the world had need of this land lying far off in the darkness and storms of the Northern Ocean. Jerusalem had newly fallen. The Seer of Patmos was closing the canon of Inspiration. The

but he drops the phrase when he has occasion to speak of what he himself must have seen, on the supposition that he accompanied the army into Scotland. Referring to former writers who had treated of Britain, he says, "I shall describe anew on the evidence of facts." Moreover, his sketches abound *in* minute and graphic traits, the picture of the battlefield at the foot of the Grampians, for instance, such as would linger in the memory and flow from the pen of only an eye-witness. Since forming this opinion, the author has been confirmed in it by discovering that Dr Leonard Schmitz had come to the same conclusion, and on much the same grounds. "In A.D. 78 he (Tacitus) married the daughter of Agricola," says he, "and as in the same year the latter proceeded to Britain, it is not unlikely that Tacitus may have accompanied him; for in some parts of the life of Agricola he shows a knowledge of the country which could scarcely have been acquired without seeing it."—*A History of Latin Literature*, by Leonard Schmitz, LL.D., p. 167, Lond. 1877.

light, which had been waxing in brightness ever since its first kindling in the morning of time, was now perfected as a revelation or system of truth. It needed to be placed where it could be seen, and where the nations might be able to walk in its radiance. Providence had notified by a terrible event that henceforth it was not to occupy its old site. The city where, till now, it had been enshrined, had been cast down with tragic horror, and the Jews, whose glory it had been that they were the keepers of the "holy oracles," were deposed from their great function, and scattered to the four quarters of heaven. The philosophy of Greece, after shedding a false brilliance over that fair land for centuries, had gone out in darkness, never more to be rekindled. And with the failure of Greek philosophy all the wisdom of the previous ages had failed as the true guide of men to happiness; for the schools of Chaldea, of Egypt, of Phœnicia, and of all the earth, had emptied their intellectual treasures into the schools of Greece, that, through Athens, as the embodiment of the world's wisdom, they might make trial to the utmost of what the wisdom of man could do. The answer was a people emasculated and sensuous, and a state enslaved and fallen. Rome, whose name filled the earth, and whose sword had subjugated it, was reeling under the number of her victories, and was fated to sink under the more enormous burden of her ambition and her crimes, and to pull down with her into the ruin of corruption a wisdom not of this world, so far as it had been committed to her keeping. It was at this hour of impending terrible revolution that a new country was summoned out of the darkness to be in Christian times what Judea had been in early days—a lamp of light to the world. Agricola had gone forth on the errand of Cæsar, as he believed. He sought only to illustrate the greatness of Rome by adding yet another country to her already too vast dominions. But in truth he was doing the bidding of a greater than Cæsar, who had commissioned him to search in the North Sea, far away from the pride of learning and the pomp of empire, for a savage land and a barbarous people, where Christianity might build up from its foundations an empire of more durable estate and truer glory than that which Rome had succeeded in rearing after ages of intrigue and toil and blood. Neither learning nor the sword could claim any share in the brilliant achievement now to be witnessed in our solitary and barbarous isle. The work would here be seen to be entirely the doing of Christianity, and would remain a monument of its power to the ages to come. With Agricola, we have said, comes the historian of the age, whose pen alone could do justice to the wild country, and draw such a picture of it as the world would keep for ever in its eye, and measure by it the transformation the country was about to undergo, and confess that only one power known to man was able to have effected a change so marvellously vast, brilliant, and beneficent.

Let us mark it well. The Scotland of the age of Tacitus rises on the sight ringed with breakers—"lashed," says the historian, " with the billows of a prodigious sea!" Here it is upheaved in great mountains, there it sinks into deep and far-retreating straths, and there it opens out into broad plains never turned by the plough, and where neither is sower to be seen in the molient spring, nor reaper in the mellow autumn. The clothing of the surface is various. Here it wears a covering of brown moor, there of shaggy wood. The places not covered by heath or forest lie drowned mostly in reedy swamps and sullen marshes. The sea enters the land by numerous creeks. Arms of ocean intersect the country, and run in silvery lines far into the interior, up dusky glen, and round the base of dark, rocky mountain, their bright gleam imparting a softening touch to the rugged scenery. The tides flow and ebb along these firths. The rushing floods poured along these narrow channels by the ocean's pressure, so unlike the gentle risings and fallings of the Mediterranean, are a source of wonder to the Romans, who speak, in rhetorical phrase, of the tossing and foaming waters as presenting the picture of a sea-tempest in the heart of the quiet country.[1]

The forests are of Nature's planting. To nature, too, has been committed the task of rearing them. They have grown wild from primeval time. Their trunks stand close together, their branches overlap and interweave, and the gloom underneath their matted and tangled boughs is almost like that of night. If any of these great trunks lie overturned, it is the winter's tempest, not the axe, that has laid them low; scarce a branch has been lopped off. In their dark recesses lodge bears, wolves, boars, and other beasts of prey, which find secure and peaceful hiding in their labyrinths and mazes, which even the barbarian hardly knows or dares to track.

To the rivers has been extended the same exemption from man's control which the forests so amply enjoy. The torrents wander at will in the channels which nature has dug for them. No embankment regulates their current or restrains their overflow; and when the skies of winter let fall their contents, the brooks are converted into raging cataracts and the rivers expand into lakes. The devastation they work where they burst their bounds gives but small concern to the natives, for hardly are there any cornfields to drown, although it may happen now and then that a herd of cattle, of the old Caledonian breed, are caught in the rising waters and swept off in the flood.

Pathways there are none, save the hunter's or the shep-

[1] Tacit., *Vit. Agric.*, cap. 10.

herd's track, which may be seen winding capriciously over hill or across heathy strath, and losing itself in the far-off hazy edge of moorland. No bridge gives passage to the wayfarer over the stream. When the snows melt, or the autumnal rains descend, and the waters are swollen, the traveller swims the flood or wades the ford, and goes on his way over black bog or trackless moor. The roads which are one day to afford the means of communication betwixt the territory of tribe and tribe, and link hamlet to hamlet, await the coming of a future age with its necessities and arts. They are not needed in this, for the hunter disdains their use, and the trader has not yet found his way to a land where there is neither taste to appreciate nor money to purchase his wares.

The seas around the coast are even more solitary than the land. Seldom or never is the white gleam of sail seen upon them. They are vexed with frequent tempests, which, descending upon them from the north, raise their waters in mountainous masses, and hurl them against the shore as if they would drown the land; and even when the tempest has spent its fury and the billows again subside, it is not to sparkle gaily in the light like the seas of southern climes, but to lie sullen and dark, as if they still harboured their angry mood, and but waited an opportunity of renewing the war against the great rocks that guard the coast. In the long line of its rockbound shore, no beacon light shines out to guide the mariner, and no harbour opens amid the waves to give shelter to his vessel, which, driven by the winds, reels onward to inevitable shipwreck. To these very real and formidable dangers, the imagination of the mariner added others, which were only the more alarming that they were vague and unknown. Rumour spoke of the region as overhung by perpetual darkness, and abounding in unknown perils and monsters of dreadful shape; and when the navigator found himself drawing nigh this haunted shore, he put his helm about and bore away to other and safer coasts. "If we trust the description of Procopius, Scotland was the real infernal region of the ancients, to which the souls of the dead passed in Charon's boat from the opposite shore of Germany; and where, of course, Ulysses must have gone to converse with them." [1]

"From earth a night
There of dim clouds ascends, and doubtful light."

Such was the Scotland which presented itself to the eyes of its first invaders, Agricola and Tacitus. What an intense earth-greed must have possessed the Roman when he coveted this poor country!

[1] Pinkerton, *Enquiry into the History of Scotland*, vol. ii. 50.

CHAPTER XIV.

THE CALEDONIANS AS PAINTED BY HERODIAN.

We advance to a yet darker feature of our country in its first beginnings. The inhabitant was as untamed as his rugged land. Those who occupied the southern half of our island, where, as the fruits of the earlier Roman invasion, a considerable cultivation of the soil was already to be seen, were known by the name of Britons. Those who inhabited the northern division, the men who roamed over the bleak moors and dark hills we have described, were called Caledonians or Picts.[1] The Scots—the contingent thrown in to attemper the general population, and give to it its predominant quality, if not its numerical strength—had not yet arrived in a country which was to bear their name in after ages. The Greek historian Herodian, who has given to our early ancestors a place in his sketches of the campaigns of Severus, may have unduly deepened the shades of his picture. He never was in Britain, and could relate only what others told him of the country and the people. But his descriptions may safely be taken as the portraiture of the Caledonian current at Rome in the age of the Emperor Severus. Herodian paints the men of Caledonia as going naked, only encircling their necks and bellies with iron rings, as others array themselves in ornaments of gold.

Their country, he tells us, abounded in swamps, and the

[1] "That the Caledonians and Piks were one and the same people is now universally allowed."—Pinkerton, i., 105.

vapours exhaled from these miry places by the heat filled the air with a continual murkiness. The natives traversed their bogs, wading up to the neck in mud, wholly regardless of the discomfort and defilement of person to which they subjected themselves. They had no raiment to soil, and a plunge into the first stream would cleanse their persons. Battle was to them a delight, and the greater the carnage the higher their satisfaction. Helmet and habergeon were unknown to them; protection for their persons they sought none, save a narrow shield of wicker-work covered with cow-hide. They carried no weapon into the fight but a javelin or lance, and a sword girded on their naked loins.[1] Their bravery, their contempt of danger, and their recklessness of life, made them no despicable antagonists, even to the legions of Rome. Their flight was sometimes more fatal to the enemy than their attack. The barbarian, burdened only with his few simple accoutrements, skimmed the surface of the quaking bog with agility and safety, and was soon out of reach of his pursuers, while the Roman soldier, weighed down by his heavy armour, sank in the morass and was held fast, till his comrades came to extricate him, or the foe he was chasing returned to slaughter him. Herodian can hardly conceal his chagrin that these untrained and unclothed warriors should have adopted a mode of fighting so alien to all the established usages of war, and which placed their opponents in so many points at a disadvantage. It was hardly to be expected that the Caledonians would consult the convenience of their haughty invaders or give them-

[1] "The primitive Celtic dress," says Pinkerton, "was only a skin thrown over the shoulder, and a piece of cloth tied round the middle. Gildas mentions the last as the dress of the Scots or Irish in his time."—Vol. ii. p. 144.

Herodian says, "Tantum scuto angusto lanceaque contenti, præterea gladio nudis corporibus dependente." Lib. iii. 268.

selves the least concern whether their mode of defence agreed with or crossed the usages of Rome.¹

Their appearance, as Herodian has depicted it, must have been uncouth in the extreme. Hardly have we courage to look calmly at the apparition which his pen has conjured up. We are fain to persuade ourselves that the historian has given the rein to his imagination, and produced a picture such as would grace his pages rather than one that would find its likeness on the moors of Caledonia. And yet there must have been some foundation for the statement, otherwise it would not have been so publicly made by writers of name, and in an age when it was so easy to test its truth. The Caledonians were in the habit, so Herodian assures us, of tatooing their bodies, after the fashion of the New Zealanders and the American Indians of our own day.² What we would have accounted a disfigurement they reckoned an embellishment. It cost them no little pains, and some suffering to boot, to effect this ingenious metamorphosis of their persons. By means of a hot iron the Caledonian imprinted upon his limbs the figures of such animals as he was most familiar with, or as he chose to make the symbols or interpreters of his predominating dispositions, much as the

¹ *Herodiani Historia Cum Angeli Politiani interpretatione latina*, Vindocini, 1663, lib. iii. p. 266-268. Neque enim vestis usum cognoverunt, sed ventrem atque cervicem ferro incingunt: ornamentum id esse, ac divitiarum argumentum existimantes, perinde ut aurum cæteri barbari.

² The statement of Herodian that the Caledonians painted their bodies, acquires confirmation from the well known passage in *Claudian*:—

"Ille leves Mauros, nec falso nomine Pictos,
    Edomuit."
        "He the fleet Moor subdued; and painted Pict
            Not falsely named."

And again—
                "Ferroque notatas,
    Perlegit exanimes Picto moriente figuras."

        "They on the bodies of the dying Picts
            Saw the rude figures, iron-graved."

knight of our own day blazons on his shield the figures which are most suggestive of the virtues or qualities he is emulous of being thought to possess. The parts of the body touched by the hot iron were rubbed over with the juice of the plant called woad, and this brought out in blue the figures which the iron had imprinted upon the person. We can imagine the barbarian, after completing this strange adornment, surveying himself with no little pride, and thinking how formidable he should look in the eyes of his enemy, blazing all over with the shapes of monstrous and terrible animals. Before going into battle he was careful, we are told, to deepen the colour of these wild figures in order to heighten the terrors of his appearance.[1]

Besides this curious emblazoning, worn on the person, and not after the more convenient fashion of modern times, on the shield, one other circumstance helped to make their aspect savage and terrible. This was their manner of disposing of their hair. Their locks, dark and matted, hung down, shading their faces and clustering on their shoulders. This arrangement served in some sort as a vizor. It may have stood them in some stead on occasion, but it would tend to hide the fire of their eye, and so diminish the terror of their countenance, unless, indeed, when the wind blew aside their locks, or the action of battle momentarily parted them, and then their faces, burning in fury, would gleam out upon the foe.[2]

Strange looking personages, indeed, must these forefathers of ours have been, if their first historians have not done them

[1] *Herodiani Historia*, lib. iii. 267. Quin ipsa notant corpora pictura varia et omnifariam formis animalium quocirca ne induuntur quidem, videlicet picturam corporis ne adoperiant. Sunt autem belliciosissima gens atque audissima cædis.

[2] It does not appear that the name *Pict* was an ancient one, or long continued. It probably came from the Romans. Finding the Caledonian warriors figured over with these strange devices, they would naturally speak of them as *picti*, or painted men.

injustice. Blue men, figured all over from head to heel with the representations of horses, bullocks, wolves, and foxes; traversing their wilds with foot almost as swift as that of the roe and deer which they chased; stalking by the shore of their lakes and their seas in the pride of barbarian independence, disdaining to plow or weave, to dig or plant, their loins begirt with skin of wolf, their long hair streaming in the wind, their dark features brightening with keen delight when the chase was to begin, or kindling with the fire of a yet fiercer joy when battle was to be joined. Were these uncouth progenitors to look up from their resting-places on lonely moor or underneath gray cairn, it is hard to say which would be the more astonished—we or they? We to see the men who went before us, they to behold the men who have come after them: we to behold the Scotland of the first century, they to see—striking contrast—the Scotland of the nineteenth!

CHAPTER XV.

CALEDONIAN HOUSES—LAKE DWELLINGS.

Let us at this stage bestow a rapid glance on the dwellings of the inhabitants of Scotland during the first centuries of our era. The retrospect on which we now enter will bring under the eye a very different state of things from that existing at this day, and will exhibit as great a contrast between the new periods of our country's history in this particular, as that seen in the details which have just passed under our review.

The Scotland of the nineteenth century is perhaps the most perfect country on the globe. We do not say that it is the grandest: it is the most complete. It combines within its narrow limits every variety of landscape—river, lake, ocean, frith, arable plain, the flourishing wood, the dark hill. It has thronged cities, lonely moors where browse the antlered herd, crags where the eagle builds her nest, and summits so lofty that, in certain seasons, the white gleam of the snow is seen upon them all the summer through. Gathered here into narrow space are all the natural beauties which the traveller must elsewhere seek for over vast areas. This is not a judgment springing from a too fond love of country, and an eye unfamiliar with the scenery of other, and what are sometimes called fairer lands. It is a conclusion which has been deliberately come to after a comparison, by personal observation, of Scotland with nearly all the countries of Europe, with, too, the more famous of the lands of Asia, and with some of those of Africa. Without being unjust to these countries, we are entitled to affirm that the landscapes of Scotland have a quiet grace, a picturesque beauty, and a delightful gradation of scenery, from the homely up to the romantic and the grand, not to be met with within the same limits in European or Asiatic countries. But these endowments and attractions are the gift of nature, and the only share man has had in them is that he has helped to develop them by a careful and skilful cultivation of the soil. Not so those other attractions to which we now turn. These are more purely the production of man, and so form a more definite measure of the advance of the inhabitants.

It is the Scotland of the first century to which we return —that which was startled by the news of Agricola's invasion. What a difference betwixt the edifices of the land from which Agricola had come and those of the country in which he was now arrived. The former was then in its glory. The echoes of the footsteps of the great Cæsar, and the eloquent accents of Cicero yet lingered amid its temples and statues. The golden house of Nero crowned the Palatine. The Pantheon, with its roof of burnished bronze, had not yet lost its pristine grandeur. The little temple of Vesta, the matchless grace of which twenty centuries have not been able wholly to efface, rose like a white blossom in marble on the banks of the Tiber. The titanic pile of the Colosseum was slowly rising, storey on storey, to its completion. Many a senatorial villa and classic temple gleamed out along the Apennines; and scattered over the plains at their feet were towns and villages without number. Scarcely was there crag or fountain in all that fair land which the art of Greece, working in the marble of Italy, had not adorned with statue or shrine, or crowned with other architectural glory. Such was the land which the Roman general had left. How different that into which he had come!

At the period of which we speak there was not a stone edifice in all Scotland. None are known to have then existed, for there are no architectural remains which date so far back as before the age of Agricola. The first masonry the Caledonians saw most probably was the line of Roman wall which stretched across betwixt the Forth and the Clyde. Whether they took their first lesson in stone-building from it we do not know. There were already, and had been before Cæsar's time, stone structures in their country; but these were reared in connection with their religion, and were of the same rude and simple kind with the memorial pillars and stone altars which the natives of those lands whence they had come, and whose rites they had brought with them, set up for worship; for history shows that the first labours of man in the department of stone-building is in connection with religion. He finds for his own dwelling a tent, or a cave, or a chamber in the earth, but he erects his altar above ground, and performs his rites in the face of the sun. Such rude temples there were already in Scotland, of which we have already spoken. But though the Caledonians, by some marvellous and as yet unexplained contrivance, demanding skill as well as strength, were able to set up immense blocks as altars of sacrifice, their art did not teach them to construct dwellings for themselves.

Of what sort, then, were the habitations of the early Caledonians? They must needs have shelter from the elements, and they must needs have a place of retreat in which to sleep at night. Their abodes, in sooth, were not greatly superior to those of the animals which they pursued on their mountains. They dug holes in the ground, and in times of war, or during the cold of winter, they burrowed in these subterranean dwellings, as did the Germans of the same age. In times of peace, or in the fine weather of summer, they left their cave in the earth, and lived above ground in rude habitations constructed of wattles and mud, and thatched with reeds or straw, of which we have spoken in a former chapter. From these humble beginnings rose the Scottish cities of the present day. While the capitals of Asia and of other lands have been slowly descending from splendour to ruin, and are now little better than mounds of rubbish, the cities of Scotland, in the same interval, have been rising from the wigwam on the moor, with the cold mist creeping round it, to the queenly metropolis that nestles at the foot of its great rock, which rises crowned with its grey castle, "a poem in stone," looking down on the silvery bosom of the Forth, and the rich plains of the Lothians.

Besides the habitations we have described, the underground cave and the structure of wattles with its roof of thatch, there was another class of dwellings which were common in Scotland. They mark, it is probable, a second stage in the humble architecture of early Scotland, seeing their construction displays a little more ingenuity and mechanical art than the rude structures that preceded them. These are known as lacustrine or lake dwellings, being found on the shores of lakes. This peculiar class of habitations is common to Scotland, with other countries of northern Europe, more especially Germany, Italy, and Switzerland. They are the memorials, we are disposed to think, of unsettled times. The swampy ground on which they stood, and the cold air of the lake that overhung them, must have made them unhealthy as places of human habitation, and we can hardly see what could tempt the natives to select such sites, unless the presence of danger, which would make the facilities of defence and escape the first consideration in the choice of a place of abode. In the case of sudden attack, the occupants could cut the passage that connected them with the shore, and insulate their dwelling; and if this did not secure their safety, they could plunge into the waters of the lake, or escape in their canoes.

Abundant materials for the construction of these dwellings were ready to hand. Their builders, shouldering their stone hatchet, or their bronze axe, repaired to the nearest wood, and cut down the trees fittest for their purpose. Dragging the trunks to the lake, they drove in rows of piles, partly on the shore, and partly in the water, and laying the timbers crosswise on the top of the piles, they formed a floor a few feet above the surface of the lake. Over this first flooring they laid a second, consisting of a layer of stones, or a paving of flags. This permitted a fire —a welcome arrangement in so damp and comfortless a dwelling—to be kindled, and a little necessary cooking to be done. When we dig down through the soil and turf which have accumulated above these abodes of an ancient time and an ancient people, and lay bare their remains, we find the signs of their former human occupancy clearly traceable in the ashes and charred wood which lie in heaps in the middle of their floors. Mixed with these long extinguished embers are the bones of the horse, the ox, the sheep, the deer, and other animals, the flesh of which served the inhabitants for food. Hand querns are also found, which testify to a little cultivation of the soil, and the use of farinaceous food at their meals.

Among other fragments of these banquets of two thousand years ago, are a few culinary utensils. Some of these are of clay, others of stone. Plenty, rather than elegance, doubtless reigned at these entertainments, yet the presence of these simple vessels shows that a little care had begun to be taken in the preparation of the viands, and that the meals eaten at these tables were not confined to one dish only. Nor was the adornment of the person altogether overlooked. We trace, even in these rude abodes, the presence and pride of female beauty in the little trinkets, such as beads of flint and bronze, which turn up at this day in these ancient heaps of debris. Some of these articles are of Roman workmanship, showing that lake dwellings continued in use down to a comparatively late period. It only remains to be mentioned, that in the floor of these lacustrine abodes, which stood overlapping the margin of the lake, it was not uncommon to cut a small opening, something like a trap door, through which the fish, as they swam underneath, could be speared and caught, and so a not unwelcome addition made to the dainties of the table.

There was yet another class of lake dwellings of a superior order known to the Scotland of those days. These distinctly point to times of danger, and show that the desire of safety was a predominant feeling in the selection of these extraordinary retreats. The lake dwellings of which we are now to speak, stood not on the bank, but in the lake itself, at some considerable distance from shore, having the water round and round, broad and deep, and serving as a moat for their defence. The inmates had access to the land by a long narrow pathway of planks, resting on stakes. This pathway or bridge could be cut on the approach of danger, much as the drawbridge of a castle is lifted in the face of an enemy. When the Caledonians would construct a lacustrine abode of this sort, they selected a low island, or sandbank, covered by the lake to no great depth, and proceeded to set up their structure in the following wise. They first enclosed the site with a row of strong stakes. Outside this paling they constructed a breastwork of timber, consisting of great oak beams, laid horizontally, and having upright stakes mortised into them. Great rounded trunks of trees, piled upon the others, and kept in position by the upright stakes, rose like stone rampart round castle, and completed the fortifications of these lake citadels, which must have been of no contemptible strength.

Within the area enclosed by this wooden rampart was laid first a flooring of logs. Over this were put beams of oak, and to give a yet more solid footing to those who lived aboard these places, half castle, half ship, and adapt the floor to their every purpose, there came last of all a pavement of flat stones. On this upper covering was placed the hearth. The walls that rose on these foundations have long since disappeared, but there can be no doubt that they were composed of the same materials, and built up with the same care, which was bestowed on the substructions. The oak forest, as we have said, was the quarry to which the builders of those days had recourse. To fell a tree was an easy matter compared with excavating a block. Had their knowledge of art, or the tools with which they worked enabled them, they would doubtless have reared their lake dwellings of stone. There are such lacustrine fabrics. The same emergency has compelled men to the adoption, in historic times, of the same expedient to which these rude people in far-off ages had recourse. Instead of a Scotch or a Swiss lake, let us take the shallows of the Adriatic. Venice is a superb example of a lacustrine dwelling. The terror of the advancing Goths drove the population of the north of Italy to seek a refuge in the mud flats at the head of the Adriatic Sea. There they built them a city. Its founders, however, chose, not the oak, but the marble with which to construct their lacustrine palaces, and though Venice still keeps its head above the mud of the Adriatic, it is as really a lacustrine creation as any of the buried lake dwellings of Scotland.

The most perfect specimen of a lake dwelling, or crannog, which as yet has come to light in our country, is that of Lochlea, near Tarbolton, Ayrshire. It was excavated in 1879. About forty years before this time the surface of the loch having been lowered by drainage, the site of the crannog became visible in summer time as a small island about seventy-five yards from the southern shore. On a second drainage taking place, the piles of which the crannog was constructed showed their heads in a circle of about twenty-five yards in diameter. Running round them there was found, on excavating, a breastwork of stakes and oak beams, in the manner we have already described, as usual in such structures. Within was a flooring of rough planks resting on transverse beams of oak. These were covered atop, near the centre, with a pavement of flat stones, which had been used as a hearth. The goodly dimensions of the fire-place is suggestive of abundance of good cheer, and of numerous retainers or guests. The castle was no hermitage. If such luxuries as grew beyond seas were not to be seen in it, it was amply stored, doubtless, with such fare as was supplied from the lake in which it stood, and the pastures and woods that lined the shore.

This central apartment—the kitchen and dining-room in one, for the meal was probably eaten in the same chamber in which it was cooked—was farther enclosed by a circle of upright piles, and these by an outer circle connected with the former by transverse beams, forming a strong breastwork all round the central pavement. Mixed with the ashes on the hearth were found the bones of the usual animals, together with instruments of deer-horn, querns, wooden dishes, spindle whorls, and numerous iron implements and weapons, such as spear-heads, knives, dirks, a wood-cutter's saw, a mortise-chisel, and similar articles. A long row of stakes, running landwards, showed that a gangway existed by which the inmates could hold communication with the shore. This gangway could be cut with scarce more labour, and in nearly as brief a space, as it takes to lift a drawbridge, and when thus severed, the castle was completely insulated. We have been contemplating the remains of structures older, probably, than the foundations of Rome.

Most touching it is to read these simple records of a world which has so utterly passed away—not a world that existed in some far-off region, but one that flourished on the very soil on which we are daily treading, and under the same sky beneath which our modern life is carried on. Our country is a book written all over with antique tales, of loves and hates, of banquets and battles, which were acted and ended before those of which Homer sang were begun. Not a league can we journey, not an acre can we turn up, but we light on another and yet another fragment of this hoary, weather-worn, yet veritable chronicle of the olden land and the olden men.

Beneath the dark surface of Lochar moss lie embedded the skiffs in which the aborigines were wont to traverse its waters—oak-trunks scooped out into canoes by means of fire and a stone hatchet.[1] On the banks of the Clyde the tiny ships of these "ancient mariners" have been dug up in great numbers. A stranded canoe was found beneath old St Enoch's, Glasgow. Another was dug up at the cross. Others have been exhumed in other quarters of the city, still farther from the present bed of the river. This ancient craft—how different from the iron-clads to be seen at this day on the Clyde!—are of various sizes, from six feet in length by two in width to eighteen feet by six. In

[1] Wilson, *Prehistoric Scotland*, pp. 30-40. Edin. 1851.

those days the waters of the Clyde, instead of flowing between the stone quays, which now confine them, spread out into a noble estuary, from five to ten feet in depth, covering the site of the city, and when the west winds prevailed, lashing with their waves the base of the hill on which now stands the cathedral. It looks a wild dream, and yet it is an indubitably attested fact that fleets of canoes once careered where the streets and churches and business marts of Glasgow are now spread forth, and no inconsiderable part of the commerce of the empire is transacted in our day.

The same magical changes have been wrought along the banks of our other estuaries and rivers. The ocean overflowed the carse lands of Stirling and Falkirk, in an age long past, and the whale gambolled where now the ploughman is seen tracing his furrow in the rich soil. In the same district the yellow corn waves every autumn over buried canoes and the skeletons of sea monsters with harpoons of deerhorn beside them. In the face of the cliff that bounds the carse on the north, at an elevation to which the tide never rises in our day, is still visible the iron ring to which the fisherman made fast his boat at eve. A broad ocean-frith, bounded by straight lines, struck far up into the country where now the Forth picturesquely winds through hamlets and orchards and corn-fields. The valley of the Tay has undergone similar changes, the result of the upheaval of the land, and the consequent lowering of the sea-level around our shores, and of the retreat of the ocean from our estuaries. Hills that once rose steeply from the waters of our friths, have now a belt of delightful plain at their feet, with homesteads and church steeples rising above their woods. The domain of the finny tribes, still sufficiently ample, has been somewhat curtailed thereby, but the acquisition is a valuable one to the inhabitants of the land. The portions thus gifted to

Scotland by old ocean are among the best corn-producing and fruit-bearing soils which she possesses. It is farther to be noted that the gift was a late one. The early Caledonian, if we may judge from the signs we have indicated, did not possess these lands. They came after his day, a little while before the advent of civilised man, for he only could profitably use them. It follows that we have a larger and also a richer Scotland than our ancestors knew. For in addition to the moors and mountains, which, though comparatively barren, the Caledonian, nevertheless, dearly loved and battled for with a stout heart and a stalwart arm, as the patriotic struggle we are now to relate will clearly show, we at this day possess many thousands of acres of carse lands, which not only contribute largely to fill our barns, but delight the eye, seeing they form our softest and sweetest landscapes.

CHAPTER XVI.

ROMAN PERIOD OF BRITAIN—ENGLAND INVADED BY CÆSAR, AND SCOTLAND BY AGRICOLA.

SUCH as we have described it had Scotland been from immemorial time. How impossible at that hour to have formed a true augury of its future! To a visitor from the polished and storied East, what a dismal picture would both the men and the country have presented! A land savage and untameable beyond all the lands of earth! Its air thick with tempest: its surface a bleak expanse of bog and heath and dark forest: a wild sea rolling in upon its harbourless shore: and its inhabitants of aspect even more repulsive than their country: their bodies tatooed all over: their loins begirt with the hide of wolf: their matted locks darkening their faces: brandishing the javelin with dexterity, but disdaining all knowledge of the plough or spade, and scorning acquaintance with any useful art. Here, would the visitor have exclaimed, is a land doomed to irretrievable barbarism! Here is a race whose lot it is to be hewers of wood and drawers of water to the rest of the nations! How astonished would such visitor have been if told that a day would come when this barbarous land would be one of the lights of the world—a fountain of purer knowledge than ever emanated from Greece, and a seat of wider power than Rome wielded, even when she called herself, and was called by others, the mistress of the world. But not as summer cloud settles on mountain top does glory descend on a nation. It must agonize before it is crowned. A severe discipline, prolonged through centuries, must Scotland undergo, before it can be worthy of so great a destiny.

Not for some time did its preparation for its great future begin. Defended by a stormy strait, and not less by the vague rumours that invested the lonely isle with something of mystery and horror, the first settlers in Britain were long left in undisturbed possession of their country. No one thought it worth his while to invade their quiet, or rob them of their wild independence. The warriors who were overrunning the world, intent on higher conquests, disdained to turn aside to a little country where there were no wealthy cities to spoil, no richly cultivated fields to rob, and where there was just as little fame as wealth to reward the arms of the conqueror. The Mede, the Persian, the Macedonian had successively passed it over. Not so the fourth great conquering power that arose in the earth. Impelled by that insatiable thirst of dominion which was implanted by Providence for its own high ends, the Roman eagle saw and alighted upon our shores. Henceforward our country belongs to history.

Julius Cæsar had frequent occasion to be in Gaul. When residing in Paris, he had heard tell, doubtless, of a wild country in the North Sea that lay only some two hours' sail from the coast of France. It was visited by few, save the adventurous merchants of Gaul, and traders from the Levant, who exchanged with the natives the products of the East for the tin of the Cornish mines. It is even possible, when war or negotiation called him to the coast, that Julius may have seen, in a favourable state of the atmosphere, the chalk cliffs of that island gleaming white across the narrow channel that parted it from the Continent. For Roman to see a spot of earth of which Rome was not mistress, was to have the tormenting thirst of conquest and occupation straightway awakened in him. This island, which rose before him in the blue sea, Cæsar resolved to add to the list of countries which had already received the yoke of Rome. Fitting out a fleet of eighty vessels, he crossed the Channel, and arrived before Dover. This was in the year 55 B.C.

Rumours of impending invasion had preceded the fleet across the strait. And now the rumour had become a reality. There were the dreaded galleys of invincible Rome lining their coast. Straightway a forest of barbarian spears bristled along the cliffs that overhung the shore, and thousands of dark faces scowled defiance down upon the invaders. Did they know that the Power to which they offered battle was the same which had conquered the earth? We can fancy a little disdain kindling in the eye of Cæsar when he saw the poor barbarians rushing headlong upon the bosses of Rome's buckler. Be this as it may, the great warrior showed unusual hesitation in launching his legions upon the barbarous shore to which he had led them. Though little accustomed to pause in the face of danger, Cæsar judged it prudent, in sight of the cliffs and the spears that topped them, to seek a more approachable part of the coast as a point of disembarkation. He gave orders to his fleet to move up channel.

But the fleet limbs of the Britons carried them along the shore faster than the ships could sail eastward. When the galleys halted off the flats at Deal, Cæsar saw, to his dismay, that the cloud which had lowered over the cliffs of Dover had shifted, and now hung ominously over that part of the coast where his fleet was moored. A vast and variously armed host, consisting of war chariots, cavalry and foot soldiers, stood prepared to resist the landing of the invader. To seize this barbarous shore, Cæsar saw, would prove a harder task than he had reckoned upon. His soldiers, clad in heavy armour, would have to struggle with the fierce and fearless natives in the sea, and would fight at great disadvantage. While he delayed to give the word to land, the standard-bearer of the tenth legion, by a bold action, decided the fortune of the day. Leaping into the water, he called on the men to follow their eagle. Instantly a torrent of warriors, twelve thousand in number, poured down the sides of their vessels, their armour gleaming in the westering sun of an early September day. The Britons, burning with fury, rushed into the tide to oppose their advance. A desperate grapple ensued betwixt the two. The waves were dyed with blood. Many a Briton and Roman went down together in the sea, locked in deadly embrace. But the heavy mass and stubborn valour of the Roman legionaries bore back the undisciplined hordes of the British, and before the sun had gone down, the invaders had made good their footing on shore. Britain was now linked to Rome.

Slowly the Roman eagle made its way into the interior of the country. That power which had trodden down the nations like the mire in the streets, encountered a fiercer resistance in our island than it had experienced in some countries, the inhabitants of which, more perfectly trained to arms, might have been expected to have met the aggressor with a stouter opposition. Cæsar had invaded Britain, but it could not be said that he had conquered it, much less that he occupied it. It mattered little to win victories in a country where the conqueror was master of the ground only on which the battle had been fought, and which he might, the next day, have to recover by force of arms. Only to the Thames

were the Romans able to hew their way into the land. The
corn which was now ripe in the fields, and the bullocks that
fed in the meadows, supplied the legions with food. They
cut broad pathways through the forests to facilitate their
advance. To guard against surprise, they cleared out the
wood-built villages and towns that nestled in the forest
glades or on the open plain. The palisades of timber that
enclosed them went down at the stroke of the Roman axe.
The brand and the sword did the rest. It was a horrible
business. An hour or so, and a smoking heap of ashes,
soaked with blood, alone remained to show where the Briton
had dwelt, and where his young barbarians had played. In
the words of Tacitus, "they made a solitude and called it
peace." After a year of this inglorious warfare, Cæsar grew
tired of it, and turned his face towards his own land. Great
changes were impending at Rome. The republic was about
to pass into the empire; the arms of the legions were needed
at home, and the Romans were to taste something of the
slavery which they had inflicted on others. On a day in
September, before the equinoctial storms had set in, Cæsar
embarked his soldiers, and set sail across the Channel. It
was ten o'clock at night, and the darkness soon hid from his
eye that shore to which he had made his first approach just
a year before, and which he was now leaving never more
to return. "The deified Julius," says Tacitus, "though he
scared the natives by a successful engagement, and took
possession of the shore, can be considered merely to have
discovered, but not appropriated, the island for posterity."[1]

After this, Britain had rest from Roman invasion for the
space of ninety-eight years. But if the mailed legionary was
not seen in the land all that while, the Italian merchant
found his way hither and settled in its cities, Cæsar having

[1] Tacitus, *Vita Agricolæ*, c. 13.

shown the country to him. Now began to be seen on our soil the early blossoms of commerce, and the first buddings of art. This was a little compensation for the year's calamities which the country had endured from the Roman sword. The reigns of Augustus, of Tiberius, and of Caligula followed, and passed in peace. But our country's discipline was not yet at an end—it was only at its commencement. In the time of the emperor Claudius an effort was made on a greater scale than before to subjugate the country. In A.D. 43, Aulus Plutius was sent to Britain at the head of an army of 50,000 men. He entered the country unopposed. He fought numerous battles, and in the end carried the Roman arms and the Roman yoke from the Straits of Dover to the Tweed. The campaign, which had for its issue the subjugation of England, threw, at the same time, a gleam of glory upon the nation.

When we look back we can discern, through the obscurity of the many centuries which have since elapsed, the colossal figure of the British leader and patriot, Caractacus. This hero, barbarian though he was, nobly stood up against the master of the world for the independence of his native land. He was worsted in the patriotic struggle, but he manifested in defeat, as in the conflict that preceded it, a magnanimity of soul which contrasted grandly with the essential littleness of the man who had vanquished him. By the strength of the legions, Caractacus was finally driven into the mountains of Wales. Being captured, he was carried in chains to Rome, and exhibited to the servile mob of the capital, along with his wife and daughters, in a triumphal procession. He strode onward along the *Via Sacra*, wearing his chains as Cæsar might have worn his purple. When the procession was over, the captive prince was conducted to the palace on the Palatine, and presented to the emperor. Caractacus is said to have given vent to his wonder, as well he might, that one who was so sumptuously housed, and whom so many fair and mighty realms called master, should have envied him his hut in his far-off native wilds. The dignity with which he bore himself in the imperial presence won the respect of Claudius, and he ordered his chains to be struck off. Did the emperor know, when he gazed on the British chief, that he stood face to face with the representative of that empire which in future days was to succeed his own, and by the beneficence, not less than the vastness of its sway, far eclipse it?

As yet, not a legionary had crossed the Tweed: not an acre of soil did Rome possess in Scotland. Another half century was to pass away before the march of the Roman arms should reach the northern country. The year A.D. 80 was to open a new era to Caledonia. That remote and mountainous land was now to make acquaintance with a power, which, ere it touched our soil, had carried invasion and conquest into almost all quarters of the habitable globe. Scotland was among the last of the countries which was destined to submit her neck to the yoke of that haughty mistress whose own arm, palsied by political and moral corruption, was about to let fall the sceptre of the world.

The general who carried the Roman sword into Scotland, Julius Agricola, was one of the ablest and also one of the most clement which Rome had sent forth on the conquest of Britain. He combined the qualities of the statesman with those of the soldier, and retained by wisdom what he won by valour. Tacitus paints him as a model of military virtue. He was trained to the knowledge of affairs by service in various grades and on many fields. He never shirked hardship or danger. He welcomed labour as joyfully as other men do rest. He displayed great intrepidity in performing the services assigned him, and equal modesty in speaking of them. Thus he escaped jealousy and attained renown. He shunned pageantry and scorned pleasures, and used his high post, not for his own aggrandisement, but the greater profit of the state. Vigilant, he knew all that went on, and while he rewarded merit, he punished only the graver faults. If at any time he dealt the enemy a heavy blow, he followed it up with offers of peace: thus he was at once severe and conciliatory.[1] Such was the man who now came to subjugate Scotland to the Roman obedience. But when we reflect that this portrait was drawn by the pen of his son-in-law, we may be disposed perhaps to make allowance for a little unconscious exaggeration on the part of the historian. But after all deductions, Agricola stood far above the average Roman of his day.

By this time England was included within the pale of Rome. But this did not satisfy the imperial government. The southern province was not secure so long as the more warlike north remained unconquered: the tempest would ever be gathering on the great mountains and rushing down with destructive fury on the lowlands. Every successive Roman governor who entered Britain had it as his special task and his highest ambition, to conduct the legions to the extreme northern verge of Caledonia, wherever that might be, and affix to his name the much coveted designation of Britannicus. Agricola, of course, came cherishing the same hope which had inspired all his predecessors. Unless he accomplished this conquest he accomplished nothing. He was at the head of a powerful and well-disciplined host; he was versed in the command of armies; he was to meet half-armed barbarians, whose jealousies and rivalships made them even more open to attack than their wretched military

[1] Tacitus, *Vit. Agric.*, c. 4, 5, 8.

equipments. It was no unreasonable expectation, therefore, that when he went back to Rome it would be to tell that now at last the limit of the empire on the north was the polar wave. His quarrel lacked but one element of success: it had no foundation in justice.

Before turning his face towards Scotland, he took every precaution lest revolt should spring up behind him. He conciliated the southern Britons by equalising and lightening the heavy taxes which his predecessors had imposed upon them. He strove to draw their activities away from arms, and divert them into channels of industry. He embellished their country with temples and towns. He educated the sons of the chieftains in the accomplishments and arts of Italy, and the British youth now began to use the Roman tongue, and to wear the Roman toga. In these soft indulgences they forgot the hardy exercises of the field. There is a strong undertone of contempt in the words of Tacitus when he describes these changes. "Baths, piazzas, and sumptuous feasts," he says, "were called by the ignorant people 'civilisation.' They were in reality the elements of slavery."[1]

Having made all safe in his rear, Agricola began his march towards the North. His route lay along the eastern side of the island. We gather from his historian that he signalised the beginning of his march with a stroke of arms. A border tribe, the Ordovices, who had been troublesome to his legions, he punished with extermination. The terror of the blow would travel faster than his standards, and help to open their way. Even before crossing the Tweed he had a presage of the unfamiliar land to which he was advancing in the mountain ridges and deep narrow gullies of what is now known as Northumberland. And even after he had crossed the Tweed, he did not all at once come in contact

[1] Tacitus, *Vit. Agric.*, c. 20, 21.

with the true Caledonian fierceness. He had to fight with the country rather than with the natives. And no better ally could the natives have had. Their country, while it offered shelter to themselves, threw manifold difficulties in the way of the invader. The hills, the rocky glens, the woods, and the morasses were so many ambushes where the Caledonian might lurk, and at any hour of the day or night, spring upon the Romans, entangled in the bog, or caught in the defile. And having delivered their assault, they could evade pursuit and defy attack, by a speedy retreat to the fastnesses known only to themselves. The Roman general saw that the task he had undertaken was one that would test to the uttermost the endurance and bravery of his troops, and exercise all his own wariness and skill. But he dared not turn back before barbarians. He must keep his face turned toward that unknown north, where the Roman eagle had never yet been seen, and to which, therefore, Agricola the more longed to point its flight. Those who submitted experienced a ready clemency: those who opposed had to endure a terrible chastisement. The red prints which the conqueror left behind him, and the terrible rumour that travelled in front of him, opened his way into the land, and without fighting a single battle he reached the summit of the Lammermoors, whence he looked down on the plains of the Lothians and the waters of the Firth of Forth.

Here was convenient halting place. Nature herself, by drawing a strongly marked line across the country, appeared to say that here Agricola should stop. Two great arms of the sea, the one issuing from the eastern and the other from the western ocean, ran far into the land, cutting the island well nigh in two, and forming, as it were, a southern and a northern Scotland. By joining the two seas by a line of fortresses, Agricola would be able to protect the country behind him, now subject to his arms, and guard against surprise or irruption from the yet unconquered territory in front. Accordingly he constructed, as we have already said, a chain of forts, running from east to west, beginning at Borrowstonness on the Forth, and ending at Bowling Bay, near Dumbarton, on the Clyde. Agricola put garrisons in these forts. They were the first tracing out of that rampart which was erected subsequently on the same tract, and which came to be known as the Wall of Antonine.

The great hills which from this point might be seen towering up in the northern sky, warned Agricola that should he attempt to extend the limits of the empire in that direction, he would encounter far more tremendous obstacles than those over which he had had to fight his way to reach the point where he now stood. And the Caledonians, when they reflected on the strength of the power whose soldiers scowled defiance upon them from their forts, might have remained content with the freedom of their mountains, and their exemption from a yoke now borne by their southern neighbours. But considerations of prudence did not weigh with either side. The Caledonians grew impatient to recover what of their soil they had lost, and the Romans began to covet what of the country they did not yet possess. Prowling hordes stole down from the highlands of Stirlingshire and Perthshire to espy the weak points in the Roman entrenchment, and take advantage of them. The soldiers in the forts were kept continually upon the alert. Their eye must never be off those hills in the distance, which any moment might send forth from their glens a torrent of warriors, to force their line with sudden and headlong rush, and carry slaughter and devastation into the country beyond it. The three years that followed the construction of the rampart were full of surprises, of skirmishes, and battles,

which often left the ground on which they were fought,
as thickly covered with the bodies of Roman dead as with
the corpses of the slaughtered Caledonians.

The third year of his stay enabled Agricola to enlarge his
acquaintance with the country and its tribes. Transporting
his army across the Forth he traversed Fife to the banks of
the Tay. The expedition left its inglorious traces in huts
burned, harvests ravaged to feed the legions, and spots
red with the marks of recent skirmish. Tacitus says that
"the tribes were devastated." He does not say that they
were conquered. In truth, Agricola himself confessed that
the expedition was abortive, when next summer—the fourth
—he proceeded to construct his famous line of forts, between
the Forth and the Clyde, by which, as the historian remarks,
he "removed the enemy, as it were, into another island."

In the fifth summer, Agricola turned his arms against the
tribes of the Argyleshire hills, or scattered along the Ayrshire coast. What provocation they had given, or what advantage he could reap from slaughtering them, it is hard to
say. It enabled him, however, to report at Rome that he
was master of the lonely rocks and gloomy mountains of the
western sea-board. The real motive of his western raid,
Tacitus hints, was the hope of crossing the sea to Ireland.
That island was large. Its soil and climate were excellent.
It had numerous harbours, the resort of merchants. It
would be an easy conquest; a single legion, Agricola reckoned,
would suffice to subdue it. It lay between Britain and
Spain, for the geography of the age was not exact, and its
occupation would help to consolidate the empire; and, adds
Tacitus, with sarcastic bitterness, "remove the spectacle of
liberty from the sight of the Britons."[1]

Meanwhile the eye of Briton did not need to look so

[1] Tacitus, *Vit. Agric.*, c. 24.

far as across the Irish Channel for the odious spectacle of liberty. That hateful sight was close at hand. The imperial Eagle, having ventured on a short flight to the banks of the Tay, had again retired within the lines of the Forth, leaving the great hills of northern Caledonia, with the free and fierce tribes that inhabited them, untouched by the Roman yoke. Ireland must stand over till the legions had finished with Britain. Agricola again took up the thread of his Caledonian expedition, interrupted for a season by his western episode. He advanced warily, step by step, like one who gropes his way in a difficult country and amid foes of unknown numbers and force. The roads were enfiladed; every wood was suspected as a possible lurking place; an army of half-naked warriors might any moment start up on the hill-side, or be vomited forth from the ravine. There came rumours of uprisings from the Grampians. A conquest which appeared so easy when viewed from the distance of Rome, was seen to be full of hazards and difficulties when looked at on the spot.

Agricola called the fleet to his aid, issuing orders that it should operate along with his land forces, and be ready at any moment to render assistance to the legions. He made his galleys sail up the firths, in the hope that a sight so unusual might strike terror into the barbarians, and fill their imaginations with the idea that his ships could sail over mountains—to use Cromwell's phrase, borrowed from Cornelius Nepos—as well as over seas. He explored the harbours on the coast, but was careful to enjoin the fleet never to move so far off as to lose sight of the land army. The ships faithfully obeyed the orders of their general, keeping so close in that the marines, as Tacitus informs us, often came ashore to visit their comrades in the camp, and while all three, infantry, cavalry, and marines, caroused together, they would entertain one another with tales of the valiant deeds they had done and the wonderful adventures which had befallen them in this strange land: "now the 'wilds of the mountain and forest,' now the 'hardships of the storm and the billows,' here the 'land and the enemy,' there the 'subject ocean,' were compared with the exaggeration natural to soldiers."[1] So passed the sixth summer of the Roman stay in Caledonia.

Season followed season, and the conquest of northern Britain was not yet accomplished. It is evident that the Roman commander feared to strike a decisive blow. His historian does not admit this in so many words, but the real state of matters is plain from his statement, that "the native tribes assailed the forts, and spread terror by acting on the offensive: and the timid, with the appearance of being prudent persons, advised a retreat behind the Bodotria (Forth), and to evacuate the country rather than be expelled." The outlook at that moment was decidedly gloomy for the invaders. Nor did an incident which occurred just then help to brighten it. A cohort of Usipii, levied in Germany, was brought over to assist the legions. Not liking the country or the service, it would seem, they broke into mutiny, massacred the centurion and Roman soldiers which had been incorporated with them in order to their being drilled, and again embarked in their galleys and put to sea. A tragic fate was in store for them on the ocean. Without pilot or chart, they were driven hither and thither at the mercy of the waves. When their provisions failed, they assuaged the pangs of hunger by feeding on the flesh of those of their comrades whom the inexorable lot adjudged to that revolting use. The survivors, after passing through these horrors, were captured by the Frisians and sold as slaves.

[1] Tacitus, *Vit. Agric.*, c. 25.

The same summer, the seventh if we rightly gather, would have brought with it another and even greater disaster to the Roman arms, if a timely discovery had not warded off the blow. The ninth legion lay encamped within two miles of Loch Leven, and the Caledonians, in whose eyes the prestige of the Romans was waning, resolved to test their invincibility by forcing upon them the wager of battle. They planned a night attack on their entrenchment. When the evening fell, veiling the waters of the loch, and the summit of the neighbouring Lomond, there was neither sight nor sound of enemy. But when the darkness had fully set in, the Caledonians mustered, and stole in silence upon the sleeping camp. Striking down the sentinel, they forced the gateway, poured in in a torrent, and threw themselves with fearful suddenness and violence upon the soldiers. The darkness of night hid the fierce struggle betwixt Caledonian and Roman. In the consternation that reigned a terrible slaughter was being enacted in the camp. Not a Roman would have seen the dawn, had not Agricola, informed of what was going on by his scouts, sent his light troops at their utmost speed, to save his legion before it should be exterminated. He himself followed with the legionaries. The shouts of the troops, now arrived at the entrance of the entrenchments, and the gleam of the standards in the early light, made the Caledonians aware that succours had been sent the Romans, and that they were now being assailed in the rear. So far from feeling panic, they turned and confronted the newly arrived troops, and the gateway became the scene of a terrific struggle. The exit was beginning to be blocked up with the bodies of the slain. But the Caledonians, bravely continuing the fight, forced their way out with no great loss, through living and dead, and made their escape to their bogs and fastnesses.

The Romans, who had narrowly escaped what would have been a calamity and disgrace, claimed this affair as a victory. The Caledonians, on their part, gathered heart and hope from the incident. It showed them that the Roman was not the charmed invincible warrior their fears had painted him, and that it was possible even yet to cast the invader out of their country, or if he should refuse to quit it, to make it his burial-place, and preserve for their sons the freedom which their fathers had transmitted to themselves. The wisdom and method with which they proceeded to make arrangements for continuing their defence were not a little remarkable. They sent messengers through all their mountains with invitations to the clans to meet and confer touching the position of affairs. We gather from the historian of the campaign that the summons met a universal and willing response. The tribes assembled, probably by their delegates, though their place of meeting is not known. The question debated was, of course, submission or war? If they should resolve on submission the way was easy: easy at its beginning, the bitterness would come in the end. But if they should resolve to continue the struggle, they must wage it with united arms. If they should stand apart, tribe from tribe, their great enemy would devour them piece-meal. Their only chance of victory, and with victory escape from slavery, lay in their union. This policy, at once so obvious and so imperative, was adopted. The Caledonians agreed to merge the interest of chief and clan in the mightier interest of country. They buried their feuds, and clans that never met before save to shed each other's blood, now met to embrace and march in united phalanx against the foe. They had learned that they must first conquer themselves would they hope to conquer the Romans. The outcome of all was the formation of a grand confederacy, to which the priests added the sanctions of religion by the offering of public sacrifices. With a not unsympathetic pen does Tacitus record briefly these touching arrangements on the part of this remnant of the nations to withstand a power which had overrun the world.

War being resolved upon, they vigorously set about the adoption of measures for its successful prosecution. We trace in these the superintendence of a mind not unacquainted with military tactics. Some of the Caledonians had gone south to assist the Britons when the Romans invaded them, fearing, as John Major has quaintly put it, that "if the Romans should dine with the Britons, they would sup with the Scots and Picts."[1] In their English campaigns they had acquired a knowledge of strategy which stood them in good service now. They removed their wives and little ones, and doubtless also their old men, to places of security. They enrolled and armed the youth. They repaired their mountain barriers. They arranged the number of spears which each tribe should place on the field when the day of their great final stand should arrive.[2]

Their mountains were alive throughout with the din of preparations. Every glen rung with the stroke of the craftsman's hammer. The iron war-chariots were being got ready, swords scoured and sharpened, arrows pointed, and flint heads chipped by the thousand. In short, and to express it in a familiar modern phrase, "the heather was on fire," and if Agricola will not come to the "Grampians," the "Grampians" will go to Agricola.

---

[1] Timebant enim omnes ne si Britonibus Romani pranderent, cum Scotis et Pictis cœnarent.— *Historia Majoris Britanniæ, per Joannem Majorem*, cap. 12, 3d ed., Edin., 1740.

[2] Tacitus, *Vit. Agric.*, c. 27-29.

CHAPTER XVII.

THE BATTLE OF MONS GRAMPIUS.

AGRICOLA was aware that a storm was gathering on the north hills. Intelligence had been communicated to him that embassies were passing betwixt tribe and tribe, that chieftains formerly at feud were now knit together in bonds of amity, that thirty thousand armed men were now available, and still recruits were pouring into the native camp, that a combination of the states had been formed, blessed by the priests, and that the Caledonians, their fierce and warlike enthusiasm roused to the highest pitch, were prepared to stake all on a supreme effort for freedom.

This cloud in the north, which was growing bigger every hour, made the Roman commander not a little uneasy. He had now been seven years in Britain, but the Roman arms had been unable to advance beyond the line of the Forth. For five years they had remained stationary. The legions had passed the summer in skirmishes, reaping the inglorious trophies of villages burned, and their inhabitants slaughtered. The tempests of the northern sky had furnished them with an excuse for resting in camp during winter, and refreshing themselves after the toils of the summer campaign. Agricola saw that he could no longer make the war an affair of skirmishes. He must attempt operations on a larger scale. He must strike a blow for the subjugation of the whole of Caledonia, otherwise he should find himself overpowered by numbers and be driven out of the country.[1]

Accordingly, forming his army into three divisions, and commanding his fleet to cruise on the coast, and strike terror by devastating the parts within its reach, he began his march to the north. He traversed the territory lying betwixt the Forth and the Tay, without, so far as appears, seeing the enemy or meeting opposition. As the legions climbed Moncreiff Hill—for it lay upon their route—they had their first view of the valley of the Tay. As they beheld the strath running far to the north, with the Tay issuing from the bosom of the distant Grampians, much as the Tiber appears to do from the Sabines to one looking from the Capitol at Rome, the soldiers burst out in the exclamation, so often attributed to them since, "*Ecce Tiberim!*" For the valley of the Tay, in its general arrangements of city, river, and mountains, is the valley of the Tiber over again—but without its sky. There is this one other point of difference betwixt the two. The Tay rolls along in a crystal clearness, which the Tiber, as it issues from Etrurian fountain, and sweeps onward through the Clitumnus vale with "yellow wave," might well envy.

Beyond the Tay, stretching almost from side to side of Scotland, is the "Great Strath," bounded on the south by the Sidlaws—soft as Apennine—and walled in on the north by the lofty Grampians. Across this plain lay the march of the legions. The Romans might a second time have exclaimed, "*Ecce Campaniam*," for the region they were now traversing, the modern Strathmore, in the vastness of its open bosom, and the magnificence of its mountain boundary, may not unworthily be compared with the great champaign around the eternal city—another Campania, but without its

[1] Tacitus, *Vit. Agric.*, c. 20.

"Rome," and also without that rich garniture of Patrician villa and olive-grove which clothed the Italian plain in the days of the Romans. Somewhere on the northern boundary of this great Strath, where the level ground merges with the hills, at a place which Tacitus designates "Mons Grampius," the Caledonians had assembled their forces, and there waited for Agricola in the resolution of offering him battle. The historian does not identify the locality where this first great Scottish battle was fought, beyond placing it at the foot of the Grampian chain. It has been the subject of many conjectures since. The long line of country, extending from the Tay to the shores of the German Ocean, has been anxiously but fruitlessly searched, if haply a spot could be found that fulfils all the conditions of the famous "Mons." Some have found this battlefield, as they believed, at Ardoch, on the north slope of the Ochils, near Dunblane. Their reason for fixing on a spot so far from the Grampian chain is that at Ardoch there occurs the most perfect example of a Roman camp that is to be seen in all Scotland: an excellent reason for concluding that the Romans were here, but no proof that here they engaged the Caledonians. Besides, the stay of a night, or even of a few nights, would hardly have resulted in the construction of entrenchments, which, after eighteen centuries, would be found so complete and beautiful as are the Roman remains at Ardoch.

Others have found the site of this famous battle on the plain betwixt Meigle and Dunkeld, near the foot of the mountains. Others place the *Mons Grampius* of the historian far to the eastward at Fettercairn above Laurencekirk. There the Grampians swell up into lofty rolling masses, and by a long descent merge into the plain. The supporters of this view rest it mainly on the statement of the historian, that the battle was fought in the sight of the ships. This, however, is rather the inference of historians than the statement of Tacitus, who only says that the fleet kept pace with the advance of the army. The ships could not have been in sight at either of the first two mentioned places, unless, indeed, the fleet had sailed up the Tay. But if the action took place toward the eastern extremity of the Grampian chain, the German Sea would be on the right flank of the Roman army, and ships moored off the shore would be quite in sight. Agricola had given orders for the fleet to sail along the coast northwards, keeping equal pace with the progress of his troops on land, to give, if need were, mutual succour. After the battle the army fell back, as we shall see, on its line of fortresses, but the ships held on their way to the north, and entering the Pentland Firth, sailed westward into the Atlantic. The discovery that followed belongs to peace rather than to war.

"By Agricola's order," says Tacitus, "the Roman fleet sailed round the northern point, and made the first certain discovery that Britain was an island. The cluster of isles called the Orcades, till then wholly unknown, was in this expedition added to the Roman empire. Thule, which had lain concealed in the gloom of winter and a depth of eternal snows, was also seen by our navigators."[1]

Every hour the tide of war was rolling nearer to the foot of the great mountains. From the tops of their frontier hills the Caledonians looked down on the great strath at

[1] Tacitus here expressly affirms that this was the first discovery of the Orcades, or Orkney Islands. There is some reason, however, to think that he was mistaken. Eutropius and Orosius say that Claudius not only subdued a number of British princes, but that he discovered the Orcades. An inscribed tablet from the palace of Barberini, Rome, seems to confirm this, when it speaks of Claudius as the discoverer of several barbarous nations. The probability is that the Orkneys were first discovered in the time and manner that Eutropius and Orosius say, but that islands so remote and insignificant, were lost sight of, and all knowledge of their discovery lost by Agricola's day.

their feet, and watched the progress of the armed host across it. Goodlier sight, yet one more terrible, had never before greeted their eyes. They had seen their clans go forth to battle, armed with the simple weapons which their limited knowledge of art had taught them to fabricate. But here was war in all the panoply and pomp with which Rome, in the noon of her power, was accustomed to carry it on. Here were her cohorts, marshalled under their ensigns and eagles, clad in panoply of mail, the gleam of their brazen shields lighting up the moors through which their track lay with an unusual but terrible splendour. To the Caledonians how inscrutable the motive which had brought these men from a country whose plains poured out corn and whose hills were purple with the grape, to the very ends of the earth, to a land of nakedness and hunger, where no glory was to be won by conquest, and no profit was to be reaped from possession! But whatever the motives or hopes of the invaders, to the Caledonian, his brown moors and naked hills were dear, and he was prepared to defend them to the last drop of his blood. The signal is given from the hill-top that the enemy is near. It flashes quickly along the whole Grampian chain, from where Ben More lifts its giant head in the west, to where the range sinks into the German Sea on the east.

The summons finds the warrior tribes not unprepared. From the shore of dark lake, from the recesses of deep glen, from moor and wood, the sons of the mountain hurry forth to meet and measure swords with the invaders of their native land. Gathering in marshalled ranks on the plain, their great hills towering behind them, they stand face to face with the legions of Rome. The chief takes his place at the head of his tribe. For lacking control, and left to itself, the wild valour of the mountains, like the tempests that gather and burst on their summits, would have dashed itself against the mail-clad phalanxes, and been annihilated. The supreme command of the confederate Caledonian tribes was assumed by a leader whom history has handed down to us by the name of Galgacus. The pen of Tacitus has ascribed to him the glory of valour and the virtue of patriotism. A stout and patriotic heart he must in very deed have possessed, to stand up at the head of his half-naked warriors against the conquerors of the world, and do battle for the dark mountains and heathery straths in his rear, and which were all that was now left him of his once free native land. This first of Scottish heroes—the pioneer of the Wallace and the Bruce of an after-age—appears for a moment, and passes almost entirely out of view. We hear little of him after the battle in which he lost victory but not honour.

The Caledonian army was thirty thousand strong. So does Tacitus say, repeating, probably, the rough guess of his father-in-law Agricola. The Romans were twenty-six thousand; and their number would be known to a man. Numerically the two hosts were not very unequally matched; but in point of discipline, and especially of equipments, the overwhelming superiority lay with the Romans; and when one thought of the vast disparity between the two armies in this respect, it was not difficult to forecast the nature of the tidings which would fly fast and far through glen and strath at the close of the day. Meanwhile, the muster for battle goes on with spirit. The Caledonians will go back to their hills as victors, or they will die on the moor on which they stand.

There is an open space betwixt the two armies, and the Caledonians take advantage of it, before battle is joined, to show off their war chariots in presence of the Romans. It is an early and eastern mode of fighting, which one hardly expects to find practised in Agricola's day, at the foot of the Grampians. Yet so it was. The Caledonians fight after the same fashion as the heroes before Troy. They fight as did the five kings of Syria when they crossed Mount Hermon in their war chariots, and assembled by the waters of Merom, to do battle with Joshua. The country is rough: probably there are no roads: but the nature of the surface has been taken into account in the construction of these cars. The wheel is a disk of metal, it is fixed on a revolving axle-tree, and the seat is placed between the two wheels. The machine, skilfully handled, could be driven with great rapidity over uneven ground, with but small risk of being upset. The chariots flashed to and fro in the open ground in presence of the armies, the chief acting as charioteer, and the combatants seated in the car. To see their sharp, naked scythes projecting from the axle and glittering in the sun, one could imagine with a shudder the red furrow they would plough in the packed ranks of battle, driven swiftly over the field. But in actual fight these war chariots lost much of their terrors. A thrust of the sword or of the spear brought the steeds, to which they were yoked, to the ground, and the chariot with its apparatus of slaughter lay stranded on the battlefield. The Roman soldiers, it is probable, contemplated this exhibition with more of curiosity than of dismay. They had encountered these engines of destruction in eastern campaigns, and knew that they were not altogether so formidable as they looked.

It was the recognised duty of the historian in those days not to permit battle to be joined till first the leaders on both sides had, in fitting phrase, harangued their troops. Tacitus gives us the speeches delivered on this occasion by Agricola to the legions, and by Galgacus to the Caledonians. He does not state in what language the latter spake, or who reported and interpreted his words to him, but nothing could be finer or more fitting than the speech of the barbarian leader to his soldiers. In terse, yet burning words, Galgacus denounces the ambition of Rome, and paints the miserable condition of the nations enslaved to her yoke: a condition, he adds, which they, the noblest of all the Britons, had never beheld, much less undergone.[1] "There is now no nation beyond us," continues the Caledonian leader, "nothing save the billows and the rocks, and the Romans, still more savage, whose tyranny you will in vain appease by submission and concession. The devastators of the earth, when the land has failed to suffice their universal ravages, they explore even the ocean. If an enemy be wealthy, they are covetous ; if he be poor, they become ambitious. Neither East nor West has contented them. Alone, of all men, they covet with equal rapacity the rich and the needy. Plunder, murder, and robbery, under false pretences they call 'empire,' and when they make a wilderness, they call it 'peace.'"[2]

Tacitus himself might have pronounced this oration in the Forum. He could not in terser phrase or in more burning words have denounced the crimes of an empire which, built up in blood, was spreading effeminacy and serfdom over the earth. And had he ventured on so scathing a denunciation, the nations, east and west, would have clanked their chains in sympathetic response. But not a syllable of all this durst any one at that hour have uttered at Rome. If spoken but in a whisper, its echoes would speedily have reached the ear of the gloomy Domitian in the Palatine, and before the sound of the last words had died away, the head of the speaker would have rolled on the floor of the Mamer-

---

[1] "Nobilissimi totius Britanniæ."
[2] Tacitus, *Vit. Agric.*, c. 30-32.

tine. Tacitus, therefore, puts the speech into the mouth of Galgacus, and thunders it forth to the world from the foot of the Grampians.

Agricola also addressed his soldiers. His speech was that of a general who contends for conquest alone. It is more remarkable for the topics which are left out than for those which the speaker introduces and dwells upon. It was hardly possible for the Roman soldier to feel the sentiment of patriotism. He fought not for country but for the world—for his empire embraced the world—and this object was far too vast and vague to awaken or sustain patriotism: and Agricola made no appeal to a feeling which he knew did not exist in his soldiers. The uppermost idea in the mind of a Roman, and the phrase that came readiest to his lips, was the greatness and glory of Rome. It was this that formed the key-note of Agricola's address to his army. He flatters their pride, by glancing back on the toils of their past marches, so patiently borne, and the glory of their many victories, so bravely won. He next turns to the battle about to be joined, and holds out the hope of victory by a consideration not very complimentary, one should think, to their courage, even that the bravest of the Caledonians were now in the grave, slain by the Roman sword, and that there remained only the feeble and the timid; one great day more, and the perils of the campaign would be ended, and the limits of the empire would be completed by the inclusion of the territory on the north of the hills at the foot of which they stood, and which was now almost the only portion of the habitable globe over which Rome did not sway her sceptre. The speech, Tacitus adds, fired the soldiers, and they flew at once to arms.[1]

The two armies were now drawn up in order of battle.

[1] Tacit., *Vit. Agric.*, c. 33, 34.

Agricola formed his soldiers into two lines. The first consisted of auxiliary infantry, with three thousand horse disposed as wings. The second line was formed of the Roman legionaries, the flower of his army; for it was a maxim of the Romans in their wars to expose their foreign troops to the brunt of battle, and while lavish of the blood of the mercenary, to be sparing of that of the Roman soldier. It was a proud boast when a general could say that he had won a battle without the loss of so much as one native life. The main body of the Caledonian army was drawn up on the plain in front of the Romans. The reserves were stationed on the heights behind, rising row on row, and overlooking the scene of action. They were to watch the progress of the battle, and, at the critical moment, rush down and decide the fortune of the day.

At its commencement the battle was waged from a distance. The Caledonians let fly showers of flint arrow-heads, and the Romans replied by a discharge of their missiles, which, however, were less effective than the "dense volleys" of the enemy. Galled by the shower of flints, the Romans were losing in the fight. When Agricola perceived that his men were giving way, he ordered three cohorts of Batavians and two of Tungrians to close with the foe and bring the encounter to the sword. The Caledonians met them, shouting their war-cry, but the change in the battle placed them at great disadvantage. They carried long swords, the downward stroke of which did terrible execution, but at close quarters the length of the weapon made it unserviceable. It got entangled and could not be easily raised to deal a second stroke, and having no point it was useless to thrust with. His little round shield, moreover, left great part of the body of the Caledonian exposed to the weapon of his adversary. What made the conditions of the fight more unfavourable for the Caledonian, was that the armour of the Roman legionary was admirably adapted for a hand to hand encounter. He always carried into battle a short, sharp sword; he covered his person with a large oblong shield, and when the Caledonian approached him with his long sword, the Roman received the weapon in its murderous descent on the rim of his brazen buckler, and before his adversary had time to repeat the blow, he had despatched him with his sharp dagger-like sword. From the moment that the fight became a close one, the chances were against the native army: for what availed the brawny hand of the Caledonian when the weapon that filled it was so ill adapted to its work. That was no equal combat in which half-armed and half-naked men contended with mailed legionaries, whose daily work was battle, and who fought with what we should now style "weapons of precision."

The fight was fierce and sanguinary, and went on hour after hour. The Batavians, dashing the knobs of their bucklers in the faces of the Caledonians, and stabbing them with their short swords, forced them back over the dead-encumbered plain towards the hills. Other cohorts, catching the fury of the Batavians, rushed to that part of the field, and throwing themselves on the ranks of the hill men, and striking with sword and buckler, increased the butchery. Pressing forward in their eagerness for victory, they bore to the earth, and left in their rear, numbers who had received no hurt from the sword. To increase the confusion, the chariots became entangled with the masses of fighting infantry, and the affrighted horses, left without charioteers, careered wildly over the field, their terrible scythes mowing down friend and foe along their blood-marked track.[1]

The reserves posted on the heights had been quiet obser-

[1] Tac., *Vit. Agric.*, c. 36.

vers of the fight so far. But now they rushed down with intent to outflank the Romans and assail them on the rear. If they had been able to execute their manœuvre, they might even yet have retrieved the fortunes of the day. But Agricola had foreseen and provided against this contingency. Four battalions of cavalry, kept in reserve till this moment, met them as they advanced, and put them to rout. And now the Roman general had recourse to the same stratagem which the Caledonians had attempted against himself. He ordered the wings of the van to push forward past the flanks of the Caledonian host, and fall upon its rear, thus enclosing it before and behind with walls of steel. "And now," says the historian of the battle, " a strange and awful scene presented itself on the open plain. They pursued, they stabbed, they made prisoners, and ever as a new relay of captives was brought in, the former batch was put to the sword. Here a company of armed men would be seen in flight, there unarmed natives, not knowing what they did, would charge the foe and rush upon death. Weapons and bodies and mangled limbs lay everywhere, and the ground ran blood."[1]

The day was lost. Overpowered and broken, the Caledonians now began to leave the field, where they had so stoutly resisted, but where further resistance was vain. The soaked plain behind them, steaming with fresh, warm gore, and dotted with ghastly heaps of stiffened corpses, of bodies still palpitating with life, of dissevered limbs, broken swords, shivered lances, and the multifarious wreck of battle, showing where the fiercest struggles had taken place, was an awful monument of the bravery of the men who had dared to battle with Rome for country and liberty. "Barbarians!" So did the Romans call the men whose corpses lay strewed upon the red moor. It might be so, yet their haughty foe

[1] Tac., *Vit. Agric.*, c. 37.

could not withhold from them the tribute of heroism and the higher praise of patriotism.

There are few now who will have much difficulty in deciding which of the two, the barbarian of the Grampians, or the imperial slayer from the banks of the Tiber, was the nobler being. Those who could make such a stand for their fathers' graves and their children's homes, showed that they had elements in them which needed only to be disciplined and developed to take the place in the world now occupied by those who were trampling them down as if they were the vilest and most worthless of the nations. Had Agricola encountered on the south of the Tweed anything like the obstinate valour that met him on this moor, neither he nor his soldiers would ever have got within sight of those mountains, at the base of which they offered this smoking holocaust to Rome.

The flight of the Caledonians was now general. They could flee but in one direction, to their great hills even, the woods and glens of which offered them escape from the sword of their cruel foe. The Romans followed them, but they were severely punished for their temerity; for the fugitives would turn suddenly at times on detached parties of their pursuers, and cut them off. Night fell, and the darkness put an end to the carnage on both sides, the Romans desisting from the pursuit, and the survivors of the Caledonian host making their way without further molestation to their mountain fastnesses. Tacitus says that they left ten thousand dead on the field and in the flight, and that the loss of the Romans was three hundred and forty men.[1] The difference of numbers is startling, even making allowance for the great inferiority of weapons on the part of the Caledonians, and we have great difficulty in believing that the numbers have not been dimin-

[1] Tac., *Vit. Agric.*, c. 37.

ished on the side of the victors. In a hand-to-hand encounter, lasting for many hours, it could hardly be that the loss was so unequal. The Caledonian dead would, of course, not be counted, but only roughly guessed at; but if half the number the historian says lay on the field, what a trophy, ghastly yet noble, of the resolution and devotion of the natives, and, alas! what a sumptuous banquet for the wolves of the woods and the eagles of the hills!

Agricola and his men passed the night on the battlefield. The general was not able to assure himself that the victory was his, or that the battle might not have to be renewed on the morrow. With ten thousand of the enemy dead around him, and his own army comparatively intact, one would have thought that he would have felt more at his ease. But the terror of the Caledonians was still upon him. But if the general was anxious, his soldiers were not so. Tacitus tells us that the camp was a scene of jubilation. The victory had brought the soldiers store of booty, and as regards the horrors around them, they were accustomed to such sights, and had learned to regard them with indifference. Nevertheless, despite the elation of the camp, the historian hints that the hours of the night were made doleful with "the mingled lamentations of men and women," who stole back to the field to search for and carry off their dead or wounded relatives. With the first gleam of dawn on the summit of the Grampians, these mourners desisted from their melancholy task, and vanished. When day fully broke, "it disclosed," says the historian, "more broadly the features of the victory: the silence of desolation all round, the lonely hills, the smoking ruins in the distance, and no human being visible to the scouts."[1]

The silence that brooded round Agricola's camp, so em-

[1] Tac., *Vit. Agric.*, c. 38.

phatically marked by the historian, was deep, doubtless, and it would be felt to be all the deeper by contrast with the shouts, the clash of arms, and the shrieks of terror or of pain with which it had rung the day before. Now that terrible noise had subsided into a yet more terrible stillness. The dead were at rest. The wounded! had they, too, ceased to moan? And the wolves, that already scented the corpses, were they, too, creeping stealthily down from the hills, and gathering in silence round the feast the Roman sword had prepared for them? But what of the shielings on moor and edge of loch, or by mountain torrent, from which these stalwart forms had come, that now lay still and stark on this field of death? Was there silence, too, in these dwellings? Alas! loud and bitter must have been the wail of mother and wife in the glens and straths of the great mountains, when, instead of the loved ones for whose return they waited, there came tidings of the great slaughter. But that cry of agony and woe was too far off to be heard by Agricola, and too far off to startle the ear of the wearer of the purple at Rome.

This was the first of the historic battles of Scotland, and it is interesting to reflect that it has been described to us by the pen of the prince of Roman historians.[1] Of the many fields stricken on Scottish soil during the eighteen centuries that have since elapsed, few have been so bloody as this

---

[1] We had almost said the first of war correspondents—a class which has sprung up in our own day, and which, at great risk and toil, have made us so familiar with what goes on on battlefields, and whose minute, graphic, and often brilliant descriptions, achieved in circumstances of great difficulty, are not unworthy of their great pioneer. We may also be permitted to express our surprise that Scottish historians should have passed over this great battle so lightly, or have so little perceived the influence it had on Scotland for centuries after, so that now, for the first time, have the full details of it been laid before the English reader.

one. But this blood was not shed in vain : it bore fruit in the centuries that followed. The ruthless slaughter of that day burned into the soul of the Caledonians a sense of wrong, and a hatred of the Roman name, which made it impossible it should ever be repeated by Roman sword. Its remembrance nerved them to resistance, and not unsuccessful resistance, in the campaigns of Severus. A mightier host—it was more than double the number of Agricola's —did that emperor lead against them. He had come, too, after great preparations, and with the firm determination to subdue them. But the dark day at the foot of the Grampians was still fresh in their memory, and nothing daunted by the mailed legions, and the terrible threats of Severus, who offered them the bitter alternative of submission to the Roman yoke, or extermination by the Roman sword, they concerted their plans, and patient as well as fierce, wise as well as brave, they perseveringly carried them out, and in the end completely baffled the invader. The land he had come to subdue became the grave of his army.

And farther, the triumph of Agricola—won after this bloody fashion—taught a great and much needed lesson to the Caledonians, and started them upon a new career. When the Roman fleet appeared on their coast, and the Roman army marched into their country, they were fermenting and consuming in the miserable and inglorious quarrels of tribe. The apparition of this terrible Power woke them up to a sense of their madness and danger. They saw that the cause of country was greater than the cause of tribe. They hushed the din of their wretched rivalries and petty feuds, and reserved their blood for worthier contests and nobler aims. The sight of the legions did not appal them; it but sobered and united them; it evoked the instinctive fierceness and valour of the race, and they rose up, no longer an assemblage of clans, but a nation, and, uniting their hearts and their arms, they stood for their country against an enemy of tremendous strength, and of pitiless as boundless ambition. It was in this field, at the foot of the Grampians, that the cause of Scotland's independence received its first baptism.

Since that day the great struggle has never wholly gone to sleep. Its career has been checkered. It has seen not a few dark years, and even some dark centuries; nevertheless it has lived, and gone onward, though not always at a uniform rate of progress. After the Roman there have arisen other opponents with which it has had to do battle. It has had, too, to transfer its combats to other arenas besides that of the stricken field, and wage its war with other weapons than the sword. It has been called to fight in Parliaments, to wrestle in the cabinets of kings, to contend in synods and assemblies, and to suffer glorious death on the scaffold and at the stake. But in all varieties of fortune, in the sunshine of success or in the darkness of temporary defeat, it has never parted with the hope of victory, and has ever demeaned itself as befits a cause which is that of eternal righteousness, and which has wider interests bound up with it than those that exclusively appertain to the little country in which it has been waged. Looking back from the advanced stage which the long conflict has now reached, we can see that the "first *straik* of the fight" was given on that purple moor at the foot of the Grampians—purple, not with the bloom of its heather, but with the blood of its children, poured out in torrents by the Roman sword.

Agricola did not venture on following the Caledonians into their mountains. He had had sufficient experience of their fighting qualities on the plain, and he could not tell how it might fare with his soldiers should he pursue into the fastness of the Grampians, tribes so fierce and warlike, and which, though defeated, were not crushed. He led back his army by slow marches within the chain of fortresses which stretched betwixt the Forth and the Clyde.

This was now the eighth year that Agricola had been in Britain, and yet how little progress had he made in the work of subjugating Scotland! Instead of advancing boldly into the land, he lingers summer after summer on its border, under the shelter of his forts. Nothing could be a stronger proof of the stout resistance which his legions encountered, and the fear with which the fierce and warlike tribes of the country had inspired him. He had undertaken a task evidently which he had not strength to accomplish. For a moment, and only for a moment, had the Roman eagle soared as far northward as to the foot of the Grampians, to leave there the print of its talons in blood, and again turn southwards, and seek security within the line of its forts.

CHAPTER XVIII.

EXPEDITION OF SEVERUS, AND WITHDRAWAL OF ROMANS FROM BRITAIN.

To follow the tide of the imperial conquests in Britain in its every flow and ebb is no part of our plan. A mightier power than the Roman entered our country about this time, the early conquests of which we wish we could clearly trace and minutely chronicle; but its footsteps are in silence, and meanwhile we must give our attention to a power whose battles are with "confused noise," and its victories with "garments rolled in blood." It is the fortune of the Roman arms in Britain now to advance, and now to recede. The frontier of the empire is never for more than a few years on end stationary and fixed. It is a moving line. Now it runs between the Tyne and the Solway, coinciding pretty nearly with what is now the "Border," and including the England of our day, Northumberland excepted, a county which, from the ruggedness and picturesqueness of its surface, seems rather to claim affinity with the northern land. And anon, the line that bounds the empire is pushed onward to the Firth of Forth, and is made to embrace the southern shires of the modern Scotland. We have seen the attempt of Agricola to carry it even farther to the north, but that attempt was foiled by men whose valour was the better half of their armour. Here, then, is the extreme northern verge of the Roman world, and here we can imagine the sentinel going his rounds, his attention divided betwixt the prowling native hordes outside the wall and the play of light and shade on the green Ochils in the distance, a happier man than Domitian, who, though master of an empire which touched the Nile and the Euphrates on the south, and the shores of the Forth on the north, dared not stir across the threshold of his palace for fear of the dagger.

Soon after his battle, Agricola was called to Rome to receive from his dark and jealous master the double gift of thanks and a cup of poison. His line of forts was converted into a continuous fortification, probably about A.D. 139. It formed a triple rampart, consisting of earthen or turf wall, of broad ditch, and military road, thirty-six miles in length. The wall ran along in the middle, and was twenty feet high. It had the ditch on its outward or north side, forty feet wide and twenty deep. The causeway, or military road, was on the inward side. At every two miles throughout its whole extent rose a tower by which intelligence could be signalled from end to end with a speed not greatly below that of the modern telegraph. Antoninus Pius being emperor, the work bore his name, though constructed by his lieutenant, Lollius Urbicus. After eighteen centuries, traces of Antoninus's wall still remain in the form of grassy mounds; and the traveller by rail betwixt the cities of Edinburgh and Glasgow has the satisfaction of thinking that he is being carried along on the almost identical line that formed the northern boundary of the greatest of ancient empires, over the forgotten site of Roman camps and towns, and the resting-place of many a now nameless warrior.

Within less than thirty years from the battle of Mons Grampius, we find the north Britons again gathering in force, descending like a cloud on Agricola's line of forts, driving the Romans before them, and recovering the territory which the invader had wrested from its original occupants to subject it to Rome. Again the boundary of the empire has receded to the Solway. Here an arrangement of sea and land, not unsimilar to that which farther north had attracted the military eye of Agricola, offered itself to the leader of this renewed invasion, and of this a similar advantage was taken. The Emperor Hadrian, about A.D. 120, built a wall between the Tyne and the Solway, seventy miles in length, again joining the eastern and western seas. Hadrian's wall was vastly stronger than Agricola's fortifications; it was of solid masonry, laid down in courses of great and carefully hewn blocks of freestone, strengthened with square massy towers at short distances, in which garrisons were lodged, and defended on the side towards Scotland by a broad ditch, while within, on the English side, ran successive parallel rows of earthen ramparts. Onward it went, straight as an arrow, turning aside for no inequality of ground, climbing the brow of the loftiest eminence, and again, by steep and rapid descent, seeking the valley. It was a prodigious undertaking; lofty and broad, like battlements of city — indeed, of superfluous strength — and finished almost like wall of palace. Its magnificent remains impress with wonder the beholder at this day, suggesting, as they do, the many millions that must have been lavished upon it, the hundreds of thousands of men employed in rearing it, and the engineering skill that superintended the whole. How much must Rome have respected, not to say feared, the valour of those barbarians against whom she erected this mighty bulwark! and how much must she have prized those provinces which she was careful to defend at a cost so immense, and with labour so prodigious!

But Rome could not abide within this limit. The fortification of Hadrian was not to be a final boundary; it was only a temporary halting place, a convenient base whence Rome might conquer northwards. And soon that insatiable hunger of sea and land, which animated the mistress of the world, began again to stir within her. Antoninus Pius had now assumed the purple. Not content with the now well-cultivated meadow-lands of England, he began to covet the country of moorland and mountain that stretched away to the north from Hadrian's wall. By dint of fighting, he again advanced the Roman dominion to the old line of Agricola, and once more the sentinels of Rome took up their position on the shores of the Forth and the Clyde, and their eagles were again within the shadow of the great mountains. Antonine strengthened the new frontier by converting, in the manner we have already said, Agricola's line of forts into a regular fortification, and at the same time he attempted to carry out, by means of military forts and camps, a semi-occupancy of the country on the north as far as to the foot of the Grampians.

But the near approach of the Romans to these hills awakened anew the tempest which had only slumbered. Patriotism may burn as strongly in the breast of the barbarian as in that of the civilised man, though it may not be able to express itself so finely; and one must grant that the love of liberty and of country, mingled with and ennobled that thirst for vengeance which animated the fierce and warlike tribes which now rushed down from their mountains to raise the cry of battle against a power which, mistress though she was of the fairest kingdoms on the globe, had sought them out at the end of the earth to put her yoke upon their neck.

The legionaries retired before the storm that rolled down upon them from the hills. They fell back to Antonine's wall at the Forth. The barbarian host followed them thither, their numbers increasing doubtless as they advanced. Even the fortification the legionaries found untenable against the fierceness of northern assault, and they had to retreat to the stronger and more southern wall of Hadrian. Again the limits of the empire are rolled back to the Solway.

It was now the year A.D. 204. The reigning emperor, Severus, incensed by these repeated affronts to the power of Rome offered by barbarians, resolved on striking a blow which should quell, once for all, the insurrections of these northern tribes, and annex all Britain for ever to the empire. In order to this, he raised an army, which he led in person, so intent was he on the accomplishment of his design. An old man—he was now sixty—racked with gout, and unable to keep the saddle, he made himself be carried in a litter at the head of his soldiers.[1] He entered Scotland with an army of from fifty to a hundred thousand men. The Caledonians did not venture battle. This mailed and disciplined host which followed Severus was odds too great to be met in the open field. They remembered the slaughter which Agricola had inflicted upon them with half that number of soldiers a century ago, and they profited by the lesson. They sought to deprecate the wrath of the gouty old emperor by meeting him at Hadrian's wall with offers of peace. Their terms were scornfully rejected. They must first taste the vengeance of Rome, and know of what a crime they had been guilty when they rose in insurrection against her. Severus gave orders to have the roads cleared, the bridges repaired, and every obstruction removed out of the way of his troops. Thus began their march northwards.

[1] Herodian says—Senex, et morbo articulari laborans: tanta autem animi virtute quanta nemo (unquam) vel juvenum. Igitur iter ingressus lectica plurimum vehebatur, nulloque cessabat loco.—*Herod. Hist.*, lib. iii. p. 265.

Around them, day after day, as they advanced into the land, were silent moors and gloomy forests, but inhabitants there were none that were visible. The Romans eagerly courted battle, the Caledonians as eagerly avoided it. But the legions soon began to feel that the enemy, though invisible, was never far away. The Caledonians, concealed in their numerous ambushes, which the woody and marshy country afforded them, and secure in their mountain fastnesses, left their powerful invader to wage unprofitable war with the pathless forests, the naked rocks, and the fierce tempests of the great mountains. If the natives ventured from their lurking-places, it was only to fall on his flank and rear, and after cutting off his detached parties, to vanish once more in the friendly mist or in the dark wood.

They contrived to make their very herds bear their part in this great national struggle. The food magazines of the Romans were getting low. The Caledonians made them welcome to replenish their exhausted stores from bare moor or haunt of wild boar in wood or thicket, if they were able; but they had taken care that no supplies should they glean from field or barnyard. They had not sowed that the Roman might eat. Ziphiline, in his abridgment of Dion Cassius, tells us that at times they would leave a few head of cattle, as if by oversight, in the way of the legions. It was a tempting bait to hungry soldiers. They would rush upon the beeves, but as they were making merry over their prize, and in the act of bearing it off, a band of ambushed Caledonians would start up, fall upon the spoilers, and handle them so severely, that it was rare that even one escaped to carry tidings of the trap into which they had fallen. The snare was sure to be set for their comrades on the morrow. The misery the Romans endured was extreme. Worn out with their march through bogs and woods, they sank on the earth, begging their fellows to kill them that they might not die by the hands of the Caledonians.

Continuing his march in this fashion, triumphant over woods, moors, rocks, and hills, everything, in short, but the natives, Severus traversed the chain of the Grampians, descended on Strathspey, and at last reached the shores of the Moray Firth. His army encountered, in their route, hardships tenfold greater than would have been those of the most fiercely contested battle. They had to hew their way with the axe through dense forests, they had to bridge rivers, and with spade and pick extemporise roads over wild mountains. In these exhausting toils, to which were added the frost and snows of winter, fifty thousand men, it is said, perished. Even here, on this northern shore, Severus had not reached the extremity of this wild land. He could descry, rising on his startled sight, still further to the north, the precipices that line the coast of Caithness, and the great mountains that rise in the interior of Sutherlandshire. And as regarded the natives, whom he sought to conquer, he had driven them into hiding, but he had not compelled them to submission. The emperor waited here on the southern shore of the Cromarty Firth, uncertain whether to retreat or to go forward, and his stay was so prolonged that it gave him opportunity to mark the long light of the days in summer, and the equally long darkness of the winter nights.

At length Severus, breaking up his encampment, set out on his return journey. The Caledonians, feeling that each day's march brought them a new enlargement and liberty, were careful to put no obstruction in the path of the retreating host. The emperor halted at York, and there he received tidings that startled and enraged him. The whole north was in insurrection behind them. How would this inglorious campaign tell at Rome? An army wasted, but no conquest achieved! No train of captives, and no waggons laden with rich spoil had he to lead along the Via Sacra, and evoke the plaudits of the populace when he should re-enter the capital! Only the wolves of Badenoch fed with Roman flesh! It had been foretold that Rome he should never more see; and it required no gift of prophecy to presage that a sickly and gouty old man like Severus would never return from a campaign prosecuted amid the mists and snows of Caledonia. The master of the world had failed to make himself master of Scotland. The emperor died at York in A.D. 211, as he was planning a terrible revenge upon tribes whose crime was that they had dared, "at the extremities of the earth and of liberty,"—to make use of the words which Tacitus puts into the mouth of Galgacus—to assert their independence at the cost of the glory of Rome.

From the hour that Severus breathed his last, the Roman dominion in Britain steadily declined. The evil days had come upon Rome herself. Torn by faction, and weakened by profligacy at her centre, attacked on her extremities by the natives of Germany and Scythia, she had to gather in her armies, in order to repel that ever-increasing host of assailants whose vengeance she had provoked by her oppression, and whose cupidity she had awakened by her riches. After an occupancy of well-nigh five centuries, the Romans, in A.D. 414, quitted our shores, never more to return.

It was passing strange that the mistress of the world should so intently covet our remote and rugged isle. Her sceptre was swayed over the fairest realms and the richest kingdoms of earth. Egypt was hers; she stored her granaries and fed her populace with the harvests of the Delta and the corn of the Nile. The wealthy cities of Asia Minor, replenished with the various elegances and luxuries of art and commerce, were hers. Hers were the dates and spices of Arabia; the coral and the pearls of the Indian seas; the ebony of Ethiopia; the gold, the silver, the iron, and the tin of Spain; the fruits and wines of France; the timber and hides of Germany: in short, everything which tree or field, river or ocean, yielded between the Euphrates and the Atlantic, for hers was the ample and fertile territory which in former days owned the sway of the ancient Babylon. More precious treasures by far than any which the soil produces, or the handicraft of man creates, did she possess. Greece had laboured, and Rome had entered into her labours. What was the wealth of the mine or of the mart compared with the intellectual treasures—the thinking of the greatest sages of the heathen world—which had descended to her as a peerless heritage! And yet, as if it had been nothing to possess a world, so long as she lacked the little Scotland, she strove for centuries to seize and hold that diminutive territory. For this end she freely lavished her blood and treasure. She sent great armies to subjugate it, and these, as we have seen, were at times led by the emperor in person; and when insurrection threatened to deprive her of her conquests in this remote quarter, yet greater armies did she send to make sure her hold upon them. Such attractions had our heath-clad, storm-swept, and sea-engirdled country in the eyes of her who was "Lady of Kingdoms." This is out of the common course, and cannot be explained on the ordinary principles of ambition. The hand of Providence is here. Our island had been chosen to act a great part in the future; it was to become a fountain of loftier and purer influences than any that ever emanated from the Roman capitol, or the Greek acropolis; and it pleased Providence to employ the sword to begin our education for our high destiny.

We behold the Romans quitting our shores. What benefits do they leave behind them? The Roman occupancy, it is to be taken into account, lasted nearly five hundred years; that is, about as long as since the battle of Bannockburn to the present hour. Such was the duration of the Roman period in southern Britain. Its length in Scotland was somewhat shorter, being only about three centuries and a half, and its area only a comparatively narrow strip of the country. In either case there was sufficient time to allow of great changes. And great changes did take place. The face of the country was changed; the manners and dwellings of the people were changed; arts and literature, cities and city life were introduced, especially into that part of Britain which forms the modern England. In what is now Scotland, the action of the Romans was less continuous, their frontier oscillating between the Forth and the Solway, and the impression they made on Northern Britain was less marked. The men of the hills did not so readily respond to the strong touch of the Roman hand as did their neighbours, who occupied the soft meadows and breathed the milder air of the south.

To secure their hold on the country the conquerors found it necessary to cut down woods, drain marshes, and construct roads and bridges. Their roads were great undertakings; they were the links that knit the most distant provinces to the capital. Starting from the golden milestone of Augustus, in the capitol, they traversed the empire in all directions: this running off towards sun-rise, that stretching away towards the western sea; this turning towards the torrid south, and that towards the frozen north. These roads were solidly made, as befitted an empire that deemed itself eternal. Their bed was filled in with successive layers of gravel and stones, and they were finished atop with large hewn blocks of tufa, so smooth that the luxurious Roman found no inconvenience in driving along upon them in a carriage without springs. The tempests, the earthquakes, and the wars of two thousand years have not entirely obliterated them. Vestiges of the Roman roads, in a wonderful state of preservation, are to be seen at this day, not in Italy only, but in almost all countries that once formed part of the empire of Rome.

The great road that ran northwards to Britain terminated at Boulogne. Resuming, on the English side of the Channel, on the shore of Kent, it held a straight course to London. From London it ran northwards like a white ribbon stretched across the green land, rising and falling as it passed on from mountain-top to mountain-top. Trodden by the myriad feet of centuries, and ploughed by the torrents of two thousand winters, it can yet be traced, with numerous breaks, on the face of the country, and is known as "Watling Street." This great road was continued into Scotland. Crossing the valley of the Tyne near Hexham, it ran on by Jedburgh, skirted the Eildon Hills, traversed the Pentlands, and taking a westward slant to Cramond, held on its course to Camelon, on the Roman wall. This was not the only line of communication which the Romans maintained in Scotland. A second road started from near Carlisle, and running on by Langton, it was prolonged to the western extremity of Antonine's wall, near Old Kilpatrick, Dumbartonshire. Nor were Camelon and Old Kilpatrick the terminating points of the Roman roads in Scotland. The invaders had frequent occasion to act on the north of the Forth and of the Tay, and needed highways for the passage of their armies. The strath of the Earn, and the valley of Strathmore were traversed by Roman roads, which ran on till they touched the Grampians. This great chain seemed a natural boundary, setting limits to the engineering operations as well as to the military conquests of the Roman power; the solitary instance of Severus excepted. What a contrast between the dreary and silent wilds amid which these roads drew to an end, and the pomp and luxury, the trophies of conquest and the symbols of empire which crowded the Forum, where they took their rise! We can imagine the Caledonian, as he crosses them in the chase, pausing for a moment to call up the contrast, which, after all, he could but dimly realise.

The Romans, moreover, encouraged husbandry. England was greatly greener and fairer in the last centuries of their occupancy than when Cæsar first touched its shore. Its naturally rich soil responded to the hand of the Roman farmer in abundant harvests. Its corn now began to be carried across the Channel and sold in the markets of France. Scotland, it is probable, with a less fertile soil, did not mark an equal agricultural advance. Nevertheless, with so practical a people as the Romans in it for more than three centuries, it could not be but that rows of fruit-trees now cheered the spring with their rich blossoms, and broad corn-fields gladdened the eye in autumn with the gold of their ripened grain, where aforetime had been brown moor or dark wood. The sixth legion continued to be stationed at York for three hundred years, and the soil around that ancient city is, to this day, the better for their residence. Roman remains, too, are often dug up in it—altars, images, pottery, and even fragments of Roman furniture.

The trade and commerce of Britain did not owe their beginning to the Romans, but doubtless they received a great impulse from them. The tin of Cornwall drew the Phœnicians first of all to our shores, and these early merchants gave us our first lessons in commerce. In exchange for the ore of our mines, the Phœnicians bartered the fruits of the East, and doubtless also the curious and costly articles wrought on its looms, and in the workshops of Asia. They paid for what they carried away, at times in coin, but more commonly in rich robes, in cutlery, and in weapons for war. The war chariots in which Cæsar found the natives of Britain taking the field are just as likely to have been brought across the sea, in the large Phœnician vessels, as to have been manufactured in the country. The spirit of trade thus awakened at the south-western extremity of our island would soon spread along the shore, extend inland, and finally centre in the capital, which bore the same name it does at this day. The Romans called it Augusta, but viewing the new name as but the livery of the conqueror, it dropped it and resumed the old British appellation of London. Tacitus[1] makes mention of London, describing it as a city renowned for the multitude of its merchants, and the extent of its commerce. But though they did not originate, the Romans greatly stimulated the commercial and trading operations of the early Britons. The arts they introduced, and the greater wealth that followed: the richer harvests, the consequence of an improved industry, the more numerous exports the Briton now carried to the foreign market, and, above all, the roads with which the conquerors opened up the country, administered stimulants to trade, and furnished facilities for its prosecution, which till then had been unknown in Britain.

The Romans were great builders as well as great road makers. The wall of Hadrian remains, even in its ruins, an imperishable monument of what they could plan and execute in this way. Besides the great works undertaken for military purposes, they were the founders of towns and the builders of villas. This holds true mainly of England. Beyond the Forth the barbarian remained master of his

[1] Londinum copia negotiatorum et commeatum maxime celebre.—Tacit. *Ann.,* xiv. 33.

moors, and repelled with scorn the touch of that imperious hand which sought to refine, but which sought also to enslave. Yet the Caledonian was not able wholly to keep out the subtle and permeating spirit of progress which Rome brought with her. It is calculated that there were forty-six military stations and twenty-eight large cities between Inverness and London.[1] In most cases towns grew up around the military stations, just as in the middle ages burghs sprung into existence beside the baron's castle; the inhabitants being naturally desirous of planting their dwellings where they had most chance of protection. These towns were most numerous along the line of the two walls. In the belt of country traced out between the Tyne and the Solway by Hadrian's rampart, there would seem to have been about a score of towns, great and small. These, judging from their remains, contained theatres, temples, and baths, such as the Romans were wont to frequent in their own country in quest of relaxation and amusement. On the line of the northern wall a considerable Roman population existed. There was a large Roman town at Camelon, in the neighbourhood of Falkirk, and another at Castlecary, where was also a Roman station, right through the centre of which now runs the railway.

In the south of England, Roman villas and towns were frequent. Several of the latter have been disentombed of late years. One of the latest to be laid bare was the Roman town at Wycomb, six miles east of Cheltenham, at the Coltswold hills, near the sources of the Thames. On the soil being removed, an almost entire town disclosed itself, the seat of an activity and life long extinct. The line of streets and the arrangement of the town were plainly visible. The foundations showed where private dwellings or where pub-

[1] Cosmo Innes, *Scotland in the Middle Ages*, p. 42, Edin. 1860.

lic edifices had stood. There was all that could minister to the luxury and the amusement of the citizen: baths, amphitheatres for his entertainment, temples for his devotion, and a tomb to receive him when dead. The tesselated pavement remained in many places; much buried money, including coins of all the emperors, was dug up on the site. Emblem of the men who used it, this treasure, prized dearly once, and kept bright and shining, passing rapidly from hand to hand, had long since been abandoned to rust, and trodden under foot, and has ceased to have part or lot in the business of the world.

The numerous remains of Roman villas which have been discovered in England we take as a certain indication that the Italian gentleman of that age, in many instances, chose south Britain as a place of residence in preference to his native land. Nor is it surprising that he should do so, for England, even the England of that day, had some attractions which Italy could not boast. Few countries in the world can compete, in point of soft and beautiful scenery, with the tract lying between Worcester and Bristol. There swellings more graceful, woods more umbrageous, and richer pastures than are to be found in Italy, regale the eye. The air temperate, the fields green all the summer through, no severe alternations of heat and cold as in Italy, the milk and butter delicious, the "roast" such as England only can show, the spring-time how pleasant! the air loaded with the odours that exhaled from the blossoms of the numerous fruit trees; even the dog-days tolerable; autumn, with its clear, crisp air, wooing one a-field; the dwelling embellished with the elegances of Italian art, and the library table covered with the productions of the Italian muse; it is difficult to discover why the self-expatriated Roman should not find life just as enjoyable in England as at home, and, if he loved quiet, perhaps a little more enjoyable. In the meadows of the Trent and the Avon, he was far removed from the turmoil and intrigue with which faction was now filling Italy. York, and the country around it, seem to have had not a few charms for the Romans. It was a favourite resort of theirs, and even to this day there is a Roman air, an imperial halo, as it were, round that old city. There Constantine, the first Christian emperor, was born, and there Constantius Chlorus lived and died.

It only remains to specify, as the final benefit bestowed by our invaders, the introduction of the law and literature of Rome. For the wild justice of the native chiefs there was now substituted the regulated and equitable procedure of the Roman code. In the calm, passionless judge who occupied the tribunal, and who saw the *cause* but not the *parties* before him, the Briton was able to see the difference, in some degree, between law as a principle, and law as a mere force. The Roman tribunal became the open door through which he obtained a glimpse into an ethical world which had hitherto been veiled to him. His belief in the right, and his resolve to practise it, would be strengthened. This was a greater, because a deeper, and more lasting benefit than any direct and immediate advantages, though these were great, which flowed from a righteous administration. Some of the towns were privileged with municipal government, and thus was gradually created a sense of corporate rights. Not a few of the youth of Britain began to study the literature and to speak the polished tongue of Rome. They were henceforth conscious, doubtless, of a subtle but powerful influence revolutionising their whole intellectual being, and imparting a capacity for pleasures of a more refined and exquisite nature than any they had tasted heretofore.

Thus it came to pass that when the five centuries of their occupancy came to an end, and the Romans bade a final adieu to our country, they left behind them, in their roads, in their tribunals, in their municipal corporations, in their marts and channels of commerce, domestic and foreign, and in the mental discipline of their literature, not only the entire framework of civilisation, as it then existed in the empire itself,—a civilisation which, as we shall see, was afterwards wholly swept away,—but what was far better, a young but pure Christianity which was destined to form the basis of the ultimate and enduring civilisation of Britain. When that civilisation which Rome imparted had, like a too early blossom, or an untimely birth, perished and been forgotten, that which the Gospel gave lived and flourished in the expanding power and growing prosperity of the country.

CHAPTER XIX.

CHRISTIANITY ENTERS BRITAIN.

We pause in this rapid narration of events to take note of the entrance of two mighty forces into Britain. These two powers were to find in our country the main theatre of their development, as well as a centre of propagation and a basis of action upon the nations of the world. So intimate is the alliance betwixt them, and so reciprocal the help they tender to each other, that they may be regarded as not twain, but one. These two forces are Religion and Liberty. Their rise, and their steady, onward progress, till at last they culminate in the creation of a State which exhibits to the world the model of a more perfect liberty than it has seen anywhere else, is one of the most delightful studies to which history can address herself, and one of the most ennobling spectacles on which one's attention can be fixed. To recount the kings that fleet past us, as if they were so many shadows, and of whom some, it may be, are simply the creations of the chronicler's pen; to describe in stately rhetoric the feuds that convulsed barbarous ages, and paint the battles in which the men of those times delighted to shed one another's blood, were a task which would bring with it much labour to the writer, and but small profit to the reader. History has a much higher function. It is, or ought to be, occupied mainly with the *life* of a nation. And by the life of a nation is meant that predominating intellectual and moral quality which gives it corporate identity and substantive being, and in virtue of which it performs its allotted share of the world's work, and tenders its special contribution towards the accomplishment of the grand plan of Him who has assigned to each of the nations its time, and its place, and its mission.

Two thousand years ago, Scotland was a land of painted men. Why is it not a land of painted men still? Why is it at this day a land of civilised men? What has taken the darkness from the face of the savage, quenched the demon-fire in his eye, and kindled there the light of intelligence and kindliness? "Twenty centuries," some will say, deeming it a sufficient explanation of the amazing transformation Scotland has undergone, "twenty centuries have passed since the day when Pict and Scot roamed their moors as savages; and it is impossible that these many ages should pass over them and leave them unchanged." This is an explanation that deceives us with a show of meaning which it does not contain. The same twenty centuries have passed over the Zulus of Africa, and at the end of them they are precisely where they were at the beginning. Not a footbreadth have they advanced. The first explanation only calls for a second. Why have the twenty centuries, which have proved themselves such powerful civilising agencies in Scotland, shown themselves so devoid of all civilising power in Africa? More than time and opportunity is needed for progress. The principle and the capacity of progress must first be implanted. It may be said that Scotland, surrounded with the civilisations of Europe, could hardly fail receiving an impulse from without, and becoming inoculated with the principles that were stirring in its neighbourhood; whereas Zululand lay remote and isolated. There was nothing to give it a start. This might be accepted as the solution so far, were it the fact that the civilisation of Scotland is simply a copy of the civilisation of its neighbours. But it is not so. It is a civilisation which is peculiar to Scotland, and is unique among the civilisations of the world. It has sprung up on its own soil; it is of a higher type, and has given to the people among whom it has taken root and developed a strongly-marked and sharply-defined individuality of national life—a richer and broader life, ever ready to expand and overflow, yet ever ready to call back its current within the embankments of right and law.

We trace progress in the stone age, we trace progress in the bronze age, especially do we trace progress in the iron age; but the civilisation of these epochs is not the civilisation of the Scotland of to-day. Nor would the civilisation of those eras ever have risen into the same type with the Scottish civilisation of our own era, however much it might have improved the Scots as cultivators, or as artizans, or as soldiers. It would have left them barbarians at the core, liable to be dominated at times by the beast within them; and to break out into those awful excesses which ever and anon deform the fair and tranquil surface of Oriental civilisations, and of some civilisations nearer home. The civilisation of Scotland is not æsthetics, it is not art, it is not science, it is not even law; it is diviner than these. It is conscience.

How came it? An influence descended on our wild country when no man was aware. It came unheard amid the din caused by the conflict of Roman with Briton. It found for itself a home in the hearts of the people, and from this deep seat it began to work outwards. It changed first of all, not the land, but the men who inhabited it; not their faces, but their hearts; extinguishing with quiet but omnipotent touch, the passions that raged there, and planting in their room feelings altogether new. From this day forward there was a new race in the country. There had been breathed into its sons a new moral life, and all who partook of that new life became one, being knit together by a stronger bond than the "one blood," even the "one heart." The tribes and the races which had hitherto parted Scotland amongst them, now began to be fused into one nation. Of these "stones of the wilderness," to use the metaphor of the Great Teacher, this power raised up "children to Abraham." Or, in plain language, out of Picts and Scots it formed, in process of time, jurists and legislators, philosophers and orators, champions of liberty and martyrs for the truth.

This new life created two great necessities. The first necessity was liberty. The man who was inspired by this new life must be free; for the life must needs act according to the laws of its nature, otherwise it must cease to exist. The second necessity was law—freedom under rule. The new life being moral, brought with it a moral sense, in other words, conscience. But conscience does not more imperatively demand that it be free from human control than it demands to be free to obey divine authority. These two necessities—contradictory in appearance, but entirely harmonious in their working—conferred on the individual to whom this new life came the capacity for freedom, by combining therewith the capacity for obedience. That capacity passed over with the individual into the state. The nation felt the same need of liberty as the individuals composing it, and it felt equally with them the obligation to use this liberty within those great landmarks which the new life which had originated the necessity for it had reared around it. The first and fundamental virtue of a nation is obedience. Obedience is essential not simply to the welfare, but to the existence of society. But the one faculty capable of rendering obedience is conscience. Where there is no conscience there can be no obedience. Society may be held down or held together by force, but that is not obedience. But conscience being the strongest power in man, and by consequence the strongest power in society, can be governed only by the strongest or highest authority—that is, by the Divine; but in order to render obedience to the Divine authority it must be emancipated from the undue interference of human authority. Hence it is that the two things, order and liberty, are bound up together. They who cannot obey cannot be free. And thus it is that the moral sense or conscience of a nation must, in every instance, be the measure of its liberty. The one can be neither more nor less than the other. Not *less*, because less would constitute an invasion upon the domain which conscience claims as its own. And not *more*, because more would be equally a trespass upon the domain where law reigns: a breaking through the limits which the moral sense has set to the exercise of liberty.

It is because these too necessities—the necessity for order and the necessity for freedom—have been so fully developed and so evenly balanced in Scotland, that this country has attained so perfect and symmetrical a liberty, deeply founded in a sense of law, buttressed by intelligence, and crowning itself with noble achievement. Therefore, of all historical studies, that of Scotland is the most instructive. It is eminently so at this hour when the nations are in a state of transition, and are looking out for models. Where in all history is there a finer example or better school? We are here taken down to where the first springs of national liberty have their rise. We are here shown that the creation of a moral sense is the deepest foundation-stone of States, if they aspire to become great. Arms, arts, science, law, liberty, in their order, but first CONSCIENCE.

Let us follow the entrance of the new life into our country

so far as the dim and fragmentary traces it has left in history enable us to do so.

From what we know of the state of the world at the beginning of our era, we conclude that Christianity would, in no long time, reach the boundary of the Roman Empire, and even the barbarous tribes beyond it. The deep slumber of the Pagan world had been broken. There was a universal expectation among the nations that a great personage was to appear, who was to give a new touch to humanity, and recall it from the tomb to which it seemed hastening. There were facilities for intercourse and the rapid communication of thought such as no former age had enjoyed. Armies were coming and going to the ends of the earth. Many of the subordinate officers in the Roman legions were converts to the Gospel, and soldiers of Jesus not less than of Cæsar. The merchants of the wealthy cities of Asia Minor were diligently seeking out new channels for their commerce. The flourishing trade carried on betwixt the Levant and Britain had found new routes over the Alps in addition to the ancient road by the Pillars of Hercules. The wealthy traders of Ephesus, Corinth, Antioch, and other cities, the seats of flourishing churches, as well as of skilful craftsmen, often visited Rome, and at times extended their journey to Gaul, and crossing the Channel to Britain, went on to London, a city even then well known to merchants. Among these visitors were, doubtless, some earnest and zealous Christians who were intent on higher objects than gain, and who would gladly avail themselves of the opportunity now put in their power of communicating the "great tidings" to those with whom they came in contact. Trade and war opened the way of the Gospel into many countries. It followed the victories of Trajan beyond the Danube into Eastern Europe. "At this epoch" (close of second century), says Philip

Smith, "there is good reason to believe that the faith of Christ had been received in every province of the Roman Empire, from the Tigris to the Rhine, and even in Britain, and from the Danube and the Euxine to Ethiopia and the Lybian desert; that it had spread over a considerable portion of the Parthean Empire, and the remoter regions of the East; and that it had been carried beyond the Roman frontiers to the barbarous tribes of Europe."[1]

It follows that some considerable time before the Roman eagle had taken its final departure from Britain, the dove, with the olive branch of the Gospel, had lighted upon our shores. The first footsteps of Christianity are recorded in the book of "Acts," and following the track of its first missionaries, as there recorded, we are led over the various countries of Asia Minor, across the Egean, and onward to the two great capitals of Europe—Athens and Rome. But there the history leaves us. We cannot gather from the inspired record that apostolic feet ever touched our remote shores. If we would follow Christianity to Britain, we must seek other guides. Secular historians, engrossed with other matters, have found no time to chronicle the progress of a kingdom, the nature of which they did not understand, and the future greatness of which they could not foresee. Their allusions to Christianity are only incidental, often depreciatory, and at times bitterly hostile. Even Tacitus has no other name to give it than "a pernicious superstition." Still their brief and uncomplimentary references enable us to infer that the Gospel entered our country at an early period; but in what year, or who was its first missionary, or who, of all the Britons, was the first to embrace it and to be baptized in the name of Christ, we have no information. One would like to

[1] *The History of the Christian Church*, by Philip Smith, B.A., p. 78. Lond. 1884.

trace the links of that chain which led to a result at the moment apparently so trivial, but in its consequences so unspeakably important and grand, as the conversion of our poor country. Who would have thought of enrolling the despised and barbarous Britain, in the brilliant procession of cities and kingdoms then crowding to the feet of the "Crucified"—Athens, Alexandria, Rome, Carthage? Who would have presumed to add the name of our little country to that of these four great trophies of the Cross, much less foreseen that one day it would be accounted the greatest trophy of the five? The Gospel will receive lustre from the philosophy of the Greek; it will derive prestige and help from the arms of the Roman; but what can the painted Briton do for it? But the Gospel came not to borrow aid, but to give it. The philosophy of Greece, no more than the barbarism of Scotland, could help the Gospel till first the Gospel had helped it. But this was a truth not then understood; and so Britain entered the pale of Christian states with hardly a line from any historian of the period to notify the fact or tell posterity when it occurred.

But though we know not who was the first of the nation of the Britons to forsake the altars of the Druid and to pray in the name of Jesus, our imagination can picture the scene. We see the skin-clothed man withdrawing from his tribe, forgetting the excitements of the chase and of the battle, and seating himself at the feet of the missionary. Entranced by the story of the Cross, he drinks in the words so new and strange, and he asks to be told them again and again. He listens till the ruggedness of his nature is melted, and the tears are seen coursing down his cheeks. What a power to subdue is shown to lie in that simple story! The barbarian hears it, and he is a barbarian no longer. He rises up from the feet of the missionary, another heart within him, and a new world around him. He has been raised all at once into a higher sphere than that of mere civilisation. He straightway becomes a member of a holy society, and from that moment his name stands enrolled in a citizenship more illustrious than that of Athens or of Rome. No wisdom known to Greece, no power wielded by Rome, could have so changed the man and lifted him up to where he looks down not only upon his former barbarism, to which he can never more return, but even upon the lettered and polished civilisations of the world, which till now had looked down upon him.

But though we know neither the day nor the hour when the Gospel entered Britain, there is a vast amount of proof for the supposition that it entered early. There is a great concurrence of testimony—scattered allusions in the classic writers, and numerous direct statements in the Christian fathers—all going to show that in the course of a few decades after the crucifixion, the "great tidings" had reached the extremities of the Roman world, and had passed beyond them. The nations had become, in a sense, of one language, and the world, in a sense, but one country, by the network of roads constructed for the passage of the legions, and which opened easy intercourse and communication from Damascus to Cadiz, and from the Tigris to the Tweed. Along these highways sped the heralds of Christianity, conquering in years nations it had taken Rome centuries to subdue.

The first indication we have that the Christian day had broken in Britain is of a touching kind. It comes from the prison of Paul, and is contained in the last lines his pen ever traced. Writing to Timothy, the aged apostle, now waiting martyrdom, sends from Rome the salutations of Pudens and Claudia[1] to his former companion and fellow-labourer. Who are these two whose names Paul inscribes

[1] 2 Tim. iv. 21.

in his letter and lays down his pen for ever ? Pudens is the son of a Roman senator, and Claudia is his wife. But of what country was the lady ? It cannot be affirmed as an established fact, but there is strong grounds for believing that she was a Briton, and the daughter of a British king. The proofs that strongly lead to this conclusion are as follows. *First*, Martial has left us two epigrams, written at Rome at a date coinciding with Paul's last imprisonment, in the first of which he celebrates the marriage of a Roman of rank, named Pudens, with a foreign lady named Claudia. In the latter epigram, he tells us that this Claudia was a Briton. So far the information of Martial. Next comes Tacitus, who mentions that certain territories in the south of Britain were ceded to King Cogidunus as a reward for his stedfast allegiance to Rome.[1] This occurred while Tiberius Claudius was emperor. But *third*, in 1723 a marble was dug up at Chichester, with an inscription in which mention is made of a British king, who bore the title of Tiberius Claudius Cogidubnus. In the same inscription occurs the name of Pudens. According to a usage prevalent among the Romans, the daughter of this king would be named Claudia. Here we have a remarkable concatenation. It is made up of very diverse parts, and these parts come from very opposite quarters, yet they all perfectly fit in together, and form a consistent body of proof. First, we have the Pudens and Claudia of Paul's letter; next, we have the Pudens and Claudia of Martial's first epigram. Then comes his second, telling us that Claudia was a Briton. Next we have the casual statement of the Roman historian, that in the reign of Claudius there was a king in south Britain named Cogidunus, a favourite with the emperor. And last of all comes the marble slab exhumed in England in the eighteenth

[1] *Vita Agricolæ*, c. 14.

century, with the names of Tiberius Claudius Cogidubnus and Pudens upon it; the link between King Claudius and Pudens being, most probably, the marriage which Martial celebrates betwixt Pudens and a British lady of the name of Claudia, the very name which the daughter of King Cogidubnus must have borne. These facts shut us up to the conclusion either that there were two couples named Pudens and Claudia living at Rome at the date of Paul's last imprisonment, and that both couples moved in the circle of the Roman aristocracy, or that the Pudens and Claudia of Paul's Epistle to Timothy and the Pudens and Claudia of Martial's epigrams were the same persons. The last alternative appears to us by much the more probable. How interesting to think that we should have at least one British name on the page of the New Testament, and that of a lady who has won the praise of the noblest constancy in Christian friendship. When others forsook the apostle, scared away by the shadow of that doom which was now gathering over him, this daughter of Britain stood his friend to the last, and was neither ashamed of the chain of Paul nor terrified by the wrath of Nero.[1] The incident gave happy augury of what Britain would become when the day now breaking in its sky should have fully opened upon it.

The next notice which we meet with of British Christianity is on the page of Tacitus. It is of a like kind with the preceding, and strengthens it. The historian tells us that Pomponia Graecina, a noble lady, the wife of Aulus Plutius, who returned from Britain to receive a triumph at Rome, was accused of having embraced a "foreign superstition." This reference can hardly be to anything else than to Christianity. For this is the word which Tacitus usually

[1] J. Williams, M.A., *Claudia and Pudens*, Lond. 1848; Conybeare and Howson, *Life and Writings of St Paul*, p. 780.

employs to denote the Christian religion. No other religion would then have formed matter of accusation against any one. Every other religion was at that time tolerated at Rome, and the deities of all nations were admitted into the Pantheon, side by side with the gods of the empire. There was but one faith which it was a crime to profess, and but one worship which was stigmatised as superstition, and that was Christianity. This, in all probability, was the "foreign superstition" of which this noble lady was accused: she had brought it with her from Britain, and if our inference be correct, the Gospel had reached our shores before A.D. 56, while Paul and others of the apostles were still alive.

There is historic evidence in existence amounting to a presumption that the Apostle Paul made a journey to Britain and there preached the Gospel. It is true that recent ecclesiastical historians have dismissed this idea as one hardly deserving consideration; but the evidence that satisfied Usher and Stillingfleet is not to be lightly set aside. In the course of his long life and his incessant journeyings, Paul doubtless crossed seas and visited countries which have received no mention in the brief narrative of his missionary travels in the "Acts." We trace briefly the chain of testimony, leaving to the reader his own conclusions. The supposition that Britain was one of the unnamed countries to which the apostle's labours extended, takes its rise in Paul's own declared intention to visit Spain.[1] Next comes the testimony of Paul's fellow-labourer, Clemens Romanus. He, of all men, best knew the extent of the apostle's travels. Clement says that Paul, in preaching the Gospel, went to the "utmost bounds of the West."[2] This, replies Dr Hales, is a rhetorical expression. But those who regard Paul as the

[1] Rom. xv. 24.   [2] Epi., το τερμα της δυσεως.

pioneer of the Gospel in Britain contend that "the utmost bounds of the West" is the usual designation of Britain among the early Christian fathers, and that the "West" was a general term comprehending Spain, Gaul, and Britain. Theodoret, for example, speaks of the inhabitants of Spain, Gaul, and Britain as dwelling in the *utmost bounds of the West*. Nicephorus, speaking of the progress of the Gospel, says that it "has reached the western ocean, and the British islands have been evangelised." Other passages are adduced by Stillingfleet to show how common it is to include Britain in the "utmost bounds of the West," and that the phrase is not rhetorical but descriptive.[1]

In the second century (A.D. 179), Irenæus speaks of Christianity as having been spread to the utmost bounds of the earth by the apostles and their disciples, and particularly specifies the churches planted in Spain and among the Celtic nations. By the Keltæ, Irenæus had in his eye, most probably, the people of Gaul and Britain.[2] In the end of the second and beginning of the third century (A.D. 193-220), Tertullian commemorates Spain and the places in Britain inaccessible to the Roman arms among the countries conquered by the Gospel.[3] In the fourth century (A.D. 270-340), Eusebius says that some of the apostles "passed over the ocean to the British Isles." And Jerome, in the same century (A.D. 329-420), says that the apostle who did so was Paul, who, after his imprisonment, went to Spain, and thence passing over the ocean, preached the Gospel in the *western parts*.[4] Those who believe that by "western parts" Jerome meant Britain, found upon the passage in his epistle to Marcella in which he speaks of "the Britains, who live

---

[1] *Origines Britan*, p. 38.   [2] *Irenæus*, lib. i. cap. 2 and 3.
[3] Tert., *Adversus Judæos*, cap. 7.
[4] *De Script. Eccles.*, and in *Amos*, cap. 5.

apart from our world, if they go on pilgrimage, will leave the western parts and seek Jerusalem." [1]

In the fifth century (423-460), Theodoret bears his testimony to the fact that Paul, after his release from his first imprisonment at Rome, carried out his long meditated purpose of visiting Spain, and thence carried the light of the Gospel to other nations.[2] He states also that Paul brought salvation *to the islands that lie in the ocean.*[3] By "the islands that lie in the ocean," Chrysostom understands Theodoret to mean the British islands, and so, too, does Cave in his "Life of St Paul." The ocean was put in contradistinction to the Mediterranean, the sea of the ancients. It is now generally admitted that Paul spent two years (64-66) *in Spain* betwixt his two imprisonments at Rome.[4] From Cape Finisterre to the coast of South Wales is no great extent of sea. The apostle was used to longer voyages; and there would be no difficulty in obtaining a passage in one of the many trading vessels employed in that navigation.

The reader may not be prepared to concur with Usher and Stillingfleet in thinking that these testimonies are conclusive as to Paul's personal ministry in Britain. He may still hold it a doubtful point. But he will admit, we think, that these testimonies establish the fact that it was Paul who planted Christianity in Spain, and that, of all the members of the apostolic college, it was this apostle, eminently, who laid the foundations of the Western Church. There are messages which may be enhanced by the dignity of the messenger. But the Gospel is not capable of being so magnified. It matters not whether it was an apostle or a

---

[1] *Epist. ad Marcellam,* p. 128.   [2] In 2nd Ep. ad Tim. iv. 17.
[3] Tom. i.   In Psalm cxvi.
[4] Conybeare and Howson, *Life and Epistles of St Paul,* p. 746, Lond., 1870.

deaconess, like Phœbe, who first carried it to our island. We must be permitted to say, moreover, that it is not British writers, but early fathers of the Eastern and Western Church who have claimed as the first preacher of Christianity in our country, one of apostolic rank.[1]

The rapidity with which the Gospel spread in the first age is what we have had no second experience of. In all history there is no other example of a revolution so great accomplished in so short a time. The nearest approach to it is the Reformation in the sixteenth century, which, in the course of fifty years, spread over Europe, and had enrolled the half of its nations beneath its standard. But even that movement was slow and laborious compared with the rapid onward march of Christianity at the beginning of our era. No figure can express the celerity of its triumphant advance through the cities, provinces, and nations of an empire which was the world, but the figure under which its Divine Founder had foretold its conquests, even the lightning which suddenly darts forth from the cloud, and in one moment fills east and west with its blaze. For no sooner had the apostles and the disciples begun to proclaim the Gospel, till lo! the earth, in a manner, was lightened with its glory. Let us listen to Tertullian. The language may be that of the rhetorician, but the statements are those of open, undeniable truth and fact, otherwise the orator, instead of compelling the conviction and acknowledgment of those whom he addressed, and serving the cause for which he made his appeal, would have drawn upon himself the contempt and laughter of his hearers, and lowered, instead of raising, Christianity in the eyes of men. "We are but of yesterday," he says, "yet we fill all

---

[1] For a full and learned discussion of this point see *Tracts on the Origin and Independence of the Ancient British Church*, by the Bishop of St David's, Lond., 1815.

places of your dominions, your cities, islands, castles, corporations, councils, armies, tribes, the palace, senate, and courts of judicature; we have left to the heathen only their temples. We are able and ready to fight, but we yield ourselves to be killed for our religion. Had we a mind to revenge ourselves, we are numerous enough to take up arms, having adherents not in this or that province, but in all quarters of the world. Nay, should we agree to quit our homes, what a loss would our exodus be to the empire! The world would be amazed to see the solitude we should leave behind us. You would then have more enemies than friends, for now almost all your friends and best citizens are Christians. It would be more than a sufficient revenge to us that your city, if we were gone, would be an empty possession of unclean spirits. Therefore Christianity is not to be reckoned a pest to your cities, but a benefit; nor ought we to be accounted enemies to mankind, but only adversaries of human errors." These were eloquent and weighty words, nor can we doubt that they were true, seeing they were no harangue spoken to a popular and sympathising assembly, but a formal and earnest appeal in behalf of his brethren to the Roman governors.[1] But if such was the power of Christianity at the centre, we may imagine the rapidity and force with which the waves of its influence were then propagating themselves all throughout the empire, and amongst the barbarous tribes in the regions beyond, and Britain amongst the rest.

This early dawn of the Christian day in our country is borne testimony to by numerous historians. Eusebius says that "the faith of Christ began to be preached in the Roman part of Britain even in the apostles' times."[1] Gildas, the oldest of British historians, places this in the reign of Nero.

[1] Apology, chap. xxxvii. p. 46; and to Scapula, Deputy of Africa, chap. xxvi. p. 92.
[2] Euseb., *Præparat. Evangel.* lib. iii. c. 7.

Doubtless the disciples of the Gospel were then few in number, and in humble station. We can look for no organised church at that early stage. Those who had received the faith, fed upon it in secret, hardly daring to avow it, it may be, amid the troubles of the times, and the ignorance and barbarism of their country, but when the wall of Antonine was built, and the government of the Romans was extended to the Forth, and a comparatively settled order of things was established, there followed, Bede informs us, a corresponding extension of the Gospel, which had another period of revival and growth about a century later, under Marcus Aurelius.[1] In these comparatively tranquil days the disciples would begin to show themselves openly; they would draw to one another; the Christian legionary and the native convert would blend their voices in the same psalm, would kneel together in the same prayer, and thus small communities or churches would spring up in Britain by the same gradual and natural process by which the campagna around Rome was at that very time being covered with societies of believing men. Those of their number whom they deemed the fittest for the post they would appoint to preside in their worship, and when it happened that the little flock was visited by an ordained pastor, he would confirm their choice of instructor, and give the object of it more formal admission into office.

The wall of Antonine, which, as the reader knows, extended betwixt the firths of Forth and Clyde, set limits to the empire, but it could not bound the progress of the Gospel. In A.D. 196 we find that the day has fairly risen on Scotland. It is Tertullian who so unmistakably announces that the last watch of the long night was past, and that the morning had come. In that year this father published his treatise

---

[1] Bede, *Hist. Eccles.*, lib. i. c. 4.

against the Jews, and in it, while arguing with them that Jesus is the Messiah on the ground that in Him had been fulfilled what the psalm foretold, even, that "the uttermost ends of the earth would be given him for his possession," he adduces it as an undeniable fact that "those parts of Britain which Cæsar could not conquer have been subdued to Christ."[1] So, then, we behold the Christian missionary passing the sentinel on the Roman wall, the limit where the legions were compelled to halt, going on his way and penetrating the moors and mountains beyond, and spreading the triumphs of the Cross among the Caledonians of the north. Origen says of his time (A.D. 212), "the land of Britain has received the religion of Christ." These averments have the greater weight from the circumstance that they occur not in rhetorical but in controversial works, where every fact was sure to be sifted, and if in the least doubtful, was certain to be challenged. We know of no contradiction that ever was given to any of these statements.

A century after (A.D. 302) came the persecution under Dioclesian, which pushed Christianity outwards beyond its former limits. Of all the terrible tempests that burst upon the early church, this was the most frightful. It raged with a violence which threatened for a while to leave not one disciple of the Gospel alive, nor a single vestige of Christianity upon the face of the earth. Hundreds of thousands of confessors perished by every kind of cruel death; the flourishing churches of Asia and Africa were laid in ruins. The destructive sweep of that tempest was felt in Britain. The previous nine persecutions had not touched our shore, but this, the tenth and greatest, smote it with terrible force. "By this persecution," says Gildas, "the churches were thrown down, and all the books of the Holy Scriptures that

[1] *Contra Judæos*, cap. vii.

could be found were burned in the streets, and the chosen priests of the flock of our Lord, with the innocent sheep, murdered: so as in some parts of the province no footsteps of the Christian religion did appear."[1]

Of the Christians, some sought refuge in caves and woods; but many fled beyond the wall of Antonine, where they found among the Picts the safety denied them within the empire. Their presence gave additional strength to the Christianity of these northern regions. The storm passed; with Constantine came a period of peace, the sanctuaries which had been destroyed were rebuilt; from the blood of the martyrs sprang a numerous army of confessors, and the consequence was that in Britain, as in lands where the blow had fallen with more crushing force, and the ruin was more complete, the Christian Church rose stronger than ever, and filled limits wider than before. We may accept as the tokens of its prosperity the historic fact, that three of its chief pastors were present in the council of Arles, A.D. 314. This council was summoned by Constantine, and the three British pastors who took their seats in it, were Eborens, from the city of York; Restitutus, from the city of London; and Adelfius, from the city of Caerleon. The last was accompanied by a deacon. The Chronicle that records the fact gives the delegates the name of bishop, but is silent regarding the extent of their dioceses, the powers of their jurisdiction, and the mode in which they were deputed to the council. A church just emerging from a terrible persecution was not likely to concern itself about rich sees and lofty titles for its ministers. Words change their meaning, and titles expressive of high office and great magnificence in one age, may, in another, especially in a thinly-peopled and semi-barbarous country as England then was, designate only the

[1] Gillies, *Hist. Col.*, bk. i. chap. 1.

humblest rank, and the most limited powers. The three British bishops of the Arles Council were, in all probability, the simple shepherds of single flocks, each in his own city. It is observable that they brought with them a deacon but no presbyter; an omission for which it is not easy to account, save on the supposition that they themselves were presbyters, and that in the British Church of those days the same simple classification obtained as in the Philippian Church, where the only distinction among the clergy was that of " the bishops and deacons." We trace the continued existence of the British Church, and her recognition by the sister churches of the empire, in the presence of three British bishops in the subsequent Council of Sardica (A.D. 347). But we fail to trace any increase of influence and wealth on the part of the British pastors, for the three "bishops" who served in the Council of Sardica were so poor that they were indebted for their maintenance, during the period of their attendance, to the public exchequer, and had to endure the gibes of their southern brethren, who had already begun to ape the state of grandees of the empire.

Certain writers of the legendary school have affirmed that Britain sat in darkness till Rome, compassionating our doleful plight, was pleased to send the light to us, and that it was the monk Augustine, the missionary of Pope Gregory, who, in A.D. 596, first kindled the lamp of the Gospel in our island. The inference, of course, is that we are bound in all coming time to follow the guidance of her who was the first to lead us into the right road. The facts we have stated show how little foundation there is for that fond boast. Four hundred years before Augustine set foot on our soil, there had been Christians and a Christian Church in Britain. The fact is attested by a chain of evidence so conclusive as to leave not a shadow of doubt upon the point.

When those fathers, whose testimony we have quoted, wrote, the condition of the remote Britain was well known: the legions were continually going and returning; the ships of the Levant were constantly voyaging to and fro, and had the land been still Pagan, and the altar of the Druid still standing in it, the first legionary, or the first ship that returned from Britain, would have proclaimed the fact, that in that land, said to have its Christian sanctuaries and its Christian congregations, there was as yet neither church nor disciple; and what would the consequence have been? Undoubtedly, the opponents of Christianity, so watchful and malignant, would speedily have silenced its apologists by convicting them of the crime of propping up their cause by falsehoods. The Christian fathers maintained openly in their writings that the light of the Gospel had travelled as far as to Britain, and that from the mountains of the farthest north had come back echoes of the song sung at midnight in the vale of Bethlehem, and not one of the many vigilant and bitter enemies of Christianity dared to contradict them. Founding on the silence of foe, as well as on the testimony of friend, we conclude that there were disciples of the Gospel in Britain certainly by the middle of the second century, and probably before the end of the first.

It remains to be asked by what route did the first "light-bearer" arrive on our shore? Starting from Italy, did he cross the Alps, and traverse France? Or setting out from the Levant, did he sail through the Pillars of Hercules, and coast along by Spain? By whatever road the herald travelled, or in whatever guise, whether that of the soldier, or of the merchant, or of the missionary, thrice blessed the feet that first carried thither the "good news!" There were three channels, apart from direct missionary agency, by which the Gospel may have entered our land. It may have come to us in the ships employed in the commerce carried on betwixt Britain and Phœnicia. Or the legions who came to conquer our country for Cæsar may have brought thither tidings of one who was greater than Cæsar —a Saviour as well as a King. Or Britain may have been evangelised by its own sons. Its natives were beginning to be drafted off to serve in Italy and Greece, and on their return to their native land, what so natural as that they should inform their countrymen of what they had heard or seen of new and strange abroad. It is not necessary that we should suppose that by one only of these channels did the waters of life enter our country. It is much more probable that they flowed into our land by all three. Let us look at them again.

Had we taken our stand on St Michael's Mount, off the coast of Cornwall, any time during the first and second centuries of our era, we should have seen, approaching from the south, long lines of ships steering in the direction of the English shore. In these bottoms the tin of the Cornish mines was transported to the Levant. The crews that manned these vessels were from the trading towns of Phœnicia, and the seaports of Egypt and Greece, the very regions where the Gospel was then being preached, and where congregations were being formed. Aboard these ships were, doubtless, disciples of the Gospel, and it is not conceivable that they would visit this dark land and traffic with its natives without seeking to dispel their ignorance by speaking to them of the life and death and resurrection of Jesus of Nazareth. Thus would they convey to our shore a richer treasure than any they carried away from it. What greatly strengthens this view is the fact that our early Christianity bore unmistakably the stamp of the East. The great church festival of those days was Easter, and the manner in which this observance was kept was the main point of distinction between the Eastern and the Western churches. The Church of Asia Minor observed Easter according to a mode of reckoning which made the festival fall on the fourteenth day of the month, whatever the day of the week. The Church of Italy, on the other hand, observed Easter by a mode of reckoning which made the feast always fall on a Sabbath, whatever day of the month that might chance to be. The Christians of Britain, following another custom than that of Italy, always observed Easter on the fourteenth day of the month. On this great testing question they were ruled by the authority of the Eastern Church, and in this they plainly showed that their first christianisation came not from the city of the Cæsars, but from that land which was the cradle of the Gospel and the scene of the ministry of the apostles.

Among the historical authorities who have traced British Christianity not to a Latin but an Eastern source, we can rank the great name of Neander. After setting aside the legend of King Lucius, this historian goes on to say, "The peculiarity of the later British Church is evidence against its origin from Rome; for in many ritual matters it departed from the usage of the Roman Church, and agreed much more nearly with the churches of Asia Minor. It withstood for a long time the authority of the Romish papacy. This circumstance would seem to indicate that the Britons had received their Christianity either immediately, or through Gaul, from Asia Minor—a thing quite possible and easy, by means of the commercial intercourse. The later Anglo-Saxons, who opposed the spirit of ecclesiastical independence among the Britons, and endeavoured to establish the Church supremacy of Rome, were uniformly inclined to trace back the church establishments to a Roman origin, from which effort many false legends might have arisen." [1]

[1] Neander, *General Church History*, vol. i. p. 117.

But there is no inconsistency in supposing that, along with the traders and mariners on board the Phœnician ships, who, doubtless, were our first teachers, the Roman legionaries bore a part, though a subordinate part, in dispelling the darkness which had so long brooded over our land. Troops were continually arriving from Italy during these centuries, and among them, doubtless, were some, probably many converts of Christianity, for by this time there were numerous disciples of the Saviour in the armies of Rome. These, we may believe, would show an equal zeal to subdue the country to Christ which their fellow-soldiers displayed in conquering it for Cæsar, and they would talk of that of which their own heart was full with the poor natives with whom it chanced to them to mingle in the camp or in the city, and with whom, it may be, they sat in converse at eventide on the wall which bounded the empire of Cæsar, though not that of the Saviour.

And, as we have hinted, there was a third channel through which the message of life may have extended to our country. When the Briton or the Caledonian returned, at the end of his military service, from Italy, or from the more distant fields of Asia Minor, nothing more wonderful had he to carry back than the story of the "crucified." Of all the wonders he had to recount, and which he had witnessed abroad—Rome, then in its prime—the temples of Greece, as yet untouched by decay—the monuments of Egypt, not yet bowed down with age—all sank into insignificance compared with that of the Cross—the Tree on Calvary, on which the God-man had accomplished the world's redemption. We see the worn and scarred veteran rehearsing the amazing tidings to the circle of eager and entranced listeners gathered round him, till their hearts begin to burn, and they become, in their turn, preachers of the good news to others, their countrymen. Thus would the Gospel spread. By its own divine energy it opened barbarous hearts, unlocked the fastnesses of our country, penetrating where the eagles of Rome had feared to enter, replaced the stone circle of the Druid with holier sanctuaries, and his obscene rites with sweeter sacrifices, and, in process of time, the foreign mariner, voyaging on our coast, instead of the horrid war-whoop of tribe battling with tribe, which had aforetime stunned his ear, was now regaled by the "melody of joy and praise" which, borne on the evening breeze, came wafted towards him over the waters. Justly did the fathers of the primitive church regard the conversion of Britain as a signal fulfilment of ancient prophecy, and one of the most convincing proofs of the Gospel's power; for after the painted savages of Caledonia, what barbarism could not the Gospel tame? what darkness could it not illuminate? Although little could these fathers foresee that the day now breaking on the mountains of this poor land would gather brightness from age to age, till at last other and far distant skies would be filled with its refluent light.

CHAPTER XX.

THE CRADLE OF THE SCOTS.

The drama in Scotland opens before the arrival of the main actors in it. The Scots had not yet appeared in the country, nor was there at this time a Scotland in existence—that is, a country passing under that name. But it does not therefore follow that the recital we have given is aside from the main story, or that the events we have detailed refer to a race wholly distinct from that which forms the Scottish nation of the present hour. On the contrary, the men with whom the Romans maintained so arduous a warfare, and whose country the masters of the world were able only partially to subdue, contributed their blood and bravery to form that heroic race which, in a subsequent age, fought under the standards of Bruce, and which, in a still later age, rallied to the nobler battle for freedom which was led by Knox. In order to the formation of that race, there must be the accession of new elements, and there must also be the engrafting of finer qualities, but all this is seen to take place upon the aboriginal stock. There is no rooting out of the old trunk, no planting of a new tree. The old root—the top rising continually higher, and the branches spreading ever wider around—which had hold of the ground when Agricola crossed the Tweed with his legions, and which refused to be torn up, even by the iron of Rome, remained fixed in the soil, and still stands rooted in it.

But what was destined to form the main constituent in the nationality now in process of formation had not yet arrived, and for the coming of the Scots, preparation had to be made both in the country they were to occupy, and on the race with which they were to be mingled, and which they were to impregnate with their higher qualities. We have seen what manner of country Caledonia was when history first raises the curtain and permits us a sight of it; and we have seen, too, what manner of men they were who inhabited it. Country and inhabitant alike present themselves before us in all the rudeness and savageness of nature. The former is scarred and broken, upheaved in sterile mountains, or laid down in swampy plains by the long continued action of volcanic fires, and the storms of countless winters, the only agents which as yet have moulded it; and the latter is deformed by the play of ignoble passions and familiarity with rude and violent pursuits; and yet in both, are latent capabilities far beyond what the keenest observer might have guessed to be present, and which wait only the hour of development. Dreary as is the aspect of the country —a far extending vista of marsh and woodland, shut in by a wall of rocky mountain, and the sun able only at times to struggle through its thick air; yet its frame-work is such, that the hand of culture and skill may contrive to create in it landscapes more picturesque, and to fashion it as a whole into a more perfect and complete country than perhaps is to be met with in any other corner of Europe. And as regards the natives who know only as yet to paint their bodies, to brandish the spear, to hunt the boar, and to shout their war-whoop as they join battle with the foe, they furnish a hardy and vigorous stock which, when its native robustness shall have been tempered by an engrafting of the nobler qualities of knowledge and patriotism, may one day yield fruits which will delight the world.

It is necessary here to cast a glance back on that great movement of the early nations, which resulted in the second peopling of the earth. This will enable us to guess at the relation of the Scots to the other branches of mankind, and assign them their true place in the genealogical tree of the world. We have followed, in the early chapters of our history, the great wave of population, which, rising in the mountains of Armenia, and flowing northward betwixt the Euxine and the Caspian, rolled down the slopes of the Caucasus, and finally touched the shores of Britain. We know only the beginning and the end of this great march, but that enables us with certainty to infer much of what lay between. When history returns to the scene, reinforced by the light of archeology and etymology, we can discern that this great people, though divided into numerous septs, are sprung of the same stock, the Gomeric—the same that set out ages before from the heights of Armenia.

This great Cimric family, which needed no inconsiderable part of the northern hemisphere to accommodate its prolific swarms, was again divided into two great septs or clans. We drop out of view the numerous smaller tribes, each occupying its own little territory, and each bearing its special name, of which these two great divisions of the Cimric race were composed. The mention of them would but confuse our aim, which is to present a general outline of the ethnical arrangement of Europe, say from one thousand to five hundred years B.C., in order to reach the native region of the Scots, and fix the particular branch of the great ancestral tree on which they grew. The one Cimric family are divided into the northern and southern. The northern, who inhabit from the shores of the German Ocean to the confines of Asia, and beyond, are known by the general name of Scythians.¹ The southern, who dwell in Belgium and France, and overflow —for their lands were fertile—into the mountains of Switzerland and the north of Spain, were the Gauls. Both peoples, as Tacitus informs us, spoke the same language, though differing slightly in dialect, and that language was the Gallic or Celtic.

In process of time the memory of their common parentage was lost, and the tribes or nations of later formation, the Scythians and the Gauls, began to weigh heavily upon the earlier Cimric races, by whom the various countries of Europe—empty till their arrival—had been peopled. The Scythic or Gallic masses began to shift about, and gravitate to larger or more fertile territories, and the result of this pressure was to become mixed with their neighbours, and in some instances to displace them, and occupy in their room. It was thus that Britain, whose population till now was the early Cimric, received into it three new varieties, the Gaul, the Pict, and the Scot. There exists abundant evidence to show that all the inhabitants of Britain, from this early period onward, were all sprung from the same stock, though they arrived in our island by different routes, and are known by different names. There is a remarkable agreement on this point among the writers of highest antiquity and of greatest weight. And their testimony is corroborated by the evidence arising from substantial identity of language and similarity of religious rites. The ancient BRETONS, who were most probably the early Cimric settlers, for the Cimri are found in Britain a thousand years before Christ; and the PICTS, the same people

---

[1] "The ancients," says Strabo, "commonly called the northern people *Scythes.*"—Strabo, lib. xi.

with the Caledonians; the BELGÆ, or Gauls, in the south of England; and the SCOTS, in the west Highlands, were but four several branches from the same root, and that root Gallic or Celtic.[1]

The three quarters whence came the three importations by which the aboriginal population of Britain was partly mixed and partly displaced, were Germany, Gaul, and Spain. When Cæsar invaded Britain, he tells us that he found the inhabitants of the south of England, Belgic, that is, the Galli. He concluded, and concluded rightly, from the strong similarity betwixt the population of the south of England and the great nation of the Gauls on the hither shores of what are now known as France, Belgium, and Holland, and their substantial identity in speech, in manners, in their style of building, and in their mode of fighting, that the former were a colony from across the Channel, which the hope of plunder had drawn into Britain, and the rich pastures and milder climate of their new country retained in it. Tacitus, writing a century later, agrees in this opinion. And Bede, in the eighth century of our era, adds his testimony, when speaking of the same people; he says, "They were Celts, and came from Armorica," that is, Britany.

Cæsar, moreover, made inquiry touching the sort of people that occupied the interior of the island, but could learn nothing of them. There were no written records, no traditions, and no monuments to throw light on their origin. He could tell neither the time when they arrived in Britain, nor the country whence they came, and in these circumstances

---

[1] Such is the conclusion at which Buchanan arrives, after an exhaustive examination of all existing Greek and Latin authorities, together with the early English chroniclers, and though Pinkerton demurs somewhat to Buchanan's conclusion, it has not been seriously disturbed, much less overthrown, and may now be said to be all but universally acquiesced in

he had recourse to the Greek idea, even that they were aborigines, that is, men sprung from the soil on which they lived.

We now turn our eyes in another quarter. Our main interest centres in that multitudinous horde which have found a dwelling beneath the northern Bear, and who go under the general name of Scythians. "The original principle of motion," observes Gibbon, "was concealed in the remote countries of the north." It is not difficult to discover the latent cause to which the historian refers, and which has given birth to the numerous emigrations, at times destructive, and at times beneficent, which the north has sent forth. It converted the vast tract of land in Europe vaguely described as Scythia, extending from the Euxine to the shores of the Rhine, into a fountain-head of nations.[1] The snow-storms and icy winds of that region made it the nursing-ground of hardy constitutions, and of adventurous and valourous spirits. Jornandes calls it the "workshop of nations."[2] Its inhabitants were strong of arm and keen of eye; they were bold riders and dexterous bowmen. Their occupation was shepherds, but to the patient labourers of the fold they added the active exercises of the chase. They maintained their vigour, and perfected their courage and skill, by daily combats with the angry wild boar, or the not less ferocious tiger, ever ready to spring upon them from the thicket. And thus, though no two modes of life appear to lie farther apart than the pastoral and the military, all experience has demonstrated that the hardihood and patience learned in the one is an admirable training for the endurance and daring required in the other, and that nothing is easier than to

[1] Tacitus and Pomponius Mela call this vast tract *Germany*, and make it include all the northern nations of Europe to the Arctic Ocean. Strabo, Diodorus, Pliny, and, after them, Bede, speak of it as *Scythia*.
[2] Jornandes, *De Rebus Giticis*, lib. i. cap. 4.

transform the shepherd into the warrior. The terrible phalanxes which, in the fourteenth and fifteenth centuries, did battle, at times as the allies, and at times as the enemies of Austria, were drawn from among the herdsmen of the Alps; and in our own day, in the British army, the regiments most distinguished for their heroism are those which have been recruited from the sheep-walks of Sutherlandshire. Scythia, a land of shepherds, became a school of war, and a camp of soldiers.

If we are to believe the Greek writers, this people were as distinguished for their strength of understanding as for their vigour of body. Dio bears his testimony to their intelligence. Thucydides says that the Scythians in point of valour and wisdom were the first of nations.[1] And Herodotus testifies that they were both learned and wise.[2] The names still survive of individuals among them eminent in law, in medicine, in philosophy, and in poetry. As regards their courage, let their enemies testify. When no Roman could be found to lead the armies of the empire in its last struggles for existence, two generals of this nation, Stilicho, a Vandal, and Belisarius, of Thrace, by their intrepidity and valour delayed for a short space, they could not prevent, the fall of Rome. In that age it was to Scythia, not to Italy, that men might turn in the hope of finding the virtues of temperance, of fortitude, of hospitality and humanity.

It is true, no doubt, that *Scythia* has come to be equivalent, in the vulgar apprehension, to *Barbaric*. But, as has been well observed, "their enemies have been their historians." There are some to whom virtue in a garment of Scythian fur will appear barbarism, and vice in the spangled robes of dissolute Italy, civilisation. The Scythians formed a main element in that Gothic inundation which, when the

[1] Thucyd., lib. ii. cap. 21.   [2] Herod., lib. iv. cap. 46.

"original principle of motion, which was concealed in the countries of the north," had attained its perfect development, and the cup of Rome was full, rolled down upon the effeminate empire and crushed it. And though we have no wish to diminish the terrors, the sufferings, and the agonies of that awful time, it may yet be doubted whether the sack and burning and slaughter which accompanied the overthrow of the empire by the Goths was nearly so great as the butcherings and blood-sheddings, the holocausts of cities, and tribes, and nations, by means of which Rome had, in a former age, effected the conquest of the world. It was partial displacement, not total extermination which the Goths inflicted. The victors mingled with the vanquished, and soon became one people with them. They did not destroy with blind barbaric rage; on the contrary, they spared much which they deemed tasteful in architecture, wise in legislation, and good in institutions. In that invasion, it is true, there were leaders of terrible name, for the mention of Attila and his Huns still thrills us, and it is also true that the progress of the northern arms was marked by some scenes which are to be ranked amongst the darkest in history; yet, as Pinkerton has observed, the preservation of "the language of Italy, France, and Spain, which is mere Latin corrupted by time, sufficiently shows that very few of the old inhabitants perished." "The Romans," he adds, "often shed more blood in one war than the Goths in conquering the Roman empire."[1]

In pursuing our argument, we have been carried past that point in our narrative where the Scots make their first appearance, not indeed as yet as a distinct nationality, for they still lie embedded in the great Scythic mass, and have

---

[1] Pinkerton, *Dissertation on the Origin and Progress of the Scythians, or Goths*, Preface, xi.

not been blocked out, and made to stand apart on the human stage. We must turn back some centuries. Prior to the general outbreak of the Scythic nations by which the Roman empire was overthrown, smaller emigrations had gone forth from this prolific source of young and hardy races. About five hundred years before Christ, according to ancient writers, the Scythians began to press upon the Cimbri, or Celts, and pushing them before them, compelled them to fall back into the western parts of Europe, which they had been the first to people. One of these adventurous bands, by a long and circuitous route, found its way to Scotland. Almost all ancient testimony points to Scythia as the original cradle of the Scottish race.

And first, as to the name *Scots*. Though, as Innes[1] observes, it is not met with till the third century, it can hardly be questioned that it is the same as *Scyths*. There is a resemblance betwixt Scythæ and *Scoti*, and only a difference in the pronunciation according to the different accent of the several peoples that spoke of them. Thus as *Gethi*, *Gethicus*, are the same as *Gothi*, *Gothicus*, so also from *Scythæ*, *Scythicus*, come *Scoti*, *Scoticus*. Gildas, in the sixth century,[2] and Nennius in the ninth, use the names *Scythæ* and *Scoti* for the same people.

King Alfred, in his translation of Bede, and other writers of that time, use *Scytisc* for *Scottish*, so that *Scyt* and *Scot* were synonymous. Several of the classic writers do the same thing, making use of Scythia and Scotia, and Scyth and Scot alternately. The Irish writers uniformly say that the Scots were Scythians, and Nennius tells us the same thing.[3] Ware confirms this origin of the nation when he shows that *Scythæ* and *Scoti* were but different names for

[1] Innes, vol. ii. 536, Lond. 1729.   [2] Gildas, cap. 15.
[3] Pinkerton, ii. 46.

the same people, and that both are called *Scutten* by the Germans.[1] The two names, Scythe and Scot, signify the same thing—an archer or bowman. The Welsh, as Camden observes, call both Scythians and Scots by the term Y-Scot. And from them the Romans, who now began to encounter them on the battle-field, called them *Scoti.*

We see the colony of shepherds and hunters setting out from their northern dwelling uncertain where their journey may end. They do not, like other emigrants, leave home and country behind them. Their tent is their home, and their camp is their country, and around them are their associates, their herds and flocks, and their whole possessions. Every few days' march places them under fairer skies, and in the midst of richer pastures. They seek, if haply they may find, a country which has not yet been taken possession of, and where they may have room to follow the same wandering and pastoral life they have led in the north. On their route lies Germany. In that age it is little better than a vast forest. They thread its woody mazes, they swim its rivers, and make an occasional short halt in its woody glades. Its sea-coast is cleared, but is already occupied by earlier emigrants. They must go onward, but neither in the regions beyond do they find permanent settlements. The lagunes of the Rhine have not yet been drained, nor have the dykes of Holland been built to restrain the waves of the North Sea which overflow where, in a future age, meadows with their kine, and fair cities with their thriving populations are to be seen.

The Scythic host go on still towards the south. They are now in the territory of the Belgæ. A vast champaign country; its surface, which is made up of woods, grazings, cultivated fields, and towns, stretches onwards to the Alps.

[1] Pinkerton, ii. 49.

The emigrants which we beheld leaving Scythia have been buried on the way, and the bands we now see wandering hither and thither amid the rivers, forests, and vinelands of Gaul are their sons of the second or third generation. The richer soil on which they now tread, invites them to become cultivators and strike permanent root, but the disposition to wander is still strong in them, and the Belgae are no ways enchanted with the prospect of having as neighbours these children of the north, who can play the warrior as well as the shepherd, and who may one day become their masters. They may pass through Gaul, but they cannot remain in it.

From this point two routes are open to them. They may traverse the Pyrenees and descend on Spain, or they may cross the sea and enter Ireland. Should they adopt the first, there is ample room for their swarms on that magnificent and fertile expanse, which stretches along at the foot of the Pyrenees, now known as the plains of Castile; or, if that tract is claimed by earlier comers, they can turn to the vast and goodly mountain-chain that runs along on its northern edge, pushing its bold, towering masses far into the Atlantic, now known as Cape Finisterre. There they may follow the pursuits which had occupied them in their primeval home. The valleys will afford pasturage for their flocks, and they can hunt the boar in their woods and rocks. Or, if they should direct their march on Ireland, they will find a thinly-peopled island ready to receive them, with a milder air than northern Gaul, and richer pastures, which the midsummer heats do not burn up.

The common tradition is, that they came round by Spain. Their stay in that country would seem not to have been long. The Iberia of that day was the battle-ground of the Carthagenians and the Romans, and the Scythic colony, or Scots, for we must begin to call them by the name, which they were afterwards to bear, quitted a land that was full of broils and misery, and crossed the sea to Ireland. Hardy and warlike, they fought their way from the south to the north of the island, and there, growing into a numerous people, they sent across a large colony, or, rather, successive colonies, to Scotland, which laid the foundations of the Scottish nation.

We have followed, as above, the course of those emigrants which, describing a compass by Gaul and Spain and Ireland, ultimately entered Scotland on the west. From them springs the line proper of the Scottish nation. But some considerable time before their arrival, a body of kindred people had entered Scotland on its eastern side. The great Scythic stream flowing southward would seem to have parted on its way, and the diverging current, taking a westward course, crossed from Jutland to our shores; or, it may be, this last was an independent migration, originating in the same prolific region, and set in motion by the same propelling principle as the migration of which we have spoken. Travelling by a shorter route, they anticipated the others, and appeared in Scotland, probably about three hundred years before Christ. Nennius says that the Picts came to Orkney nine hundred years after Eli, which would fix their arrival in our island at the period we have mentioned, and would make it contemporaneous, or nearly so, with the supposed entrance of the Belgæ into southern Britain.[1]

[1] Innes (*Crit. Essay*, vol. i. p. 47) makes the Picts a detachment of the Belgæ, and brings them from Gaul. There is nothing in this inconsistent with the view given in the text. They were not Cymric, but Celtic, and were, probably, the second grand immigration which reached our shores, coming either by way of Gaul, or across the German Ocean. The Picts are first mentioned by Eumenius in his panegyric on Constantius, A.D. 297, then by Ammianus Marcellinus in the fourth century. They appear, too, in the verse of Claudian. Dr Skene, in his "Four Ancient Books of

Tacitus, who is the first to mention them by the name of Caledonians, gives it as his opinion that they were of German origin.[1] And Bede says that they came from Scythia, the vague appellation, as we have said, of northern Europe. Though of Scythian origin, and therefore the kindred of the Scots, they do not make their appearance in history under that name, but as Picts or Caledonians. The former name they received most probably from their custom of painting or tattooing their bodies, after the manner of certain tribes inhabiting about the parts from which they had come.[2] Displacing the ancient Cymric inhabitants, or, what is more probable, mingling with them, they came to occupy the eastern half of Scotland.

They brought with them to our island the northern iron. Nursed amid the icy blasts of Scythia, the rains and frosts of Caledonia did not dismay them. They were wild, hardy, brave. Their swift foot and sure eye bore them in safety over the treacherous bog, and through the gloomy, trackless wood. They were addicted to the chase, as the relics of their feasts attest. They were terrible in battle. They met Agricola at the foot of their own Grampians, and conducted

Wales," says, "The inferences to be drawn from tradition clearly range the Picts as a people with the Gaelic division of the great Celtic race." In the sixth century the Picts of Buchan were of the same race as the Scots of Down.

[1] Tacit., *Vit. Agric.*, c. 11.
[2] The Geloni in Thrace, Virgil informs us, were accustomed so to adorn themselves. And Claudian, speaking of them (lib. i.), says. "Membraque qui ferro gaudit pinxisse, Geloniis."
"And the Geloni who delight
Their hardy limbs with iron to imprint."
The same poet mentions the Getæ in Thrace as ornamenting their bodies in a like fashion. Other Gothic tribes did the same. When the Romans built their wall across the island, it is probable that of the natives whom it parted in two, all on the south, under the sway of Rome, ceased to paint their bodies, while those on the north continued the practice, and so were specially denominated Picts.

themselves in such a manner as fully to satisfy his legions of their intrepidity and skill in war.

They rushed on the foe in their chariots. To their early predecessors, the Cymri, the war-car was unknown. We trace in this an advance in the arts. They joined battle with a shout: they grappled with the enemy at close quarters, and while covering themselves with their small, round shields, they strove to pull their antagonist from his horse or his car, with their long hooks, and despatch him with their swords. Their common dead they buried: their great men they honoured by burning, selecting the most odorous of their woods for his funeral pile. The ashes were put into an earthen urn, and the barrow thrown up was in proportion to the rank of the chief whose remains it covered.

Their dress was a skin thrown over their shoulders, and a cloth tied round their loins. The Roman writers, who saw them only in summer, speak of them as going naked. It is possible that even their scanty winter clothing they deemed an encumbrance in the warmer months, and went abroad in their bare skin, the rich fanciful picturings on which were to them as a garment;—a more modest attire, after all, than the transparent robes in which the Roman beauties of the period were beginning to array themselves. Their power of enduring hunger was great. They could subsist for days on the roots that were readiest to hand. But when they feasted, their voracity made amends for the rigour of their previous abstinence. They mustered in rows along the four sides of their great hall, their chief in the middle. The board groaned under whole carcases of roast boar, reindeer, horses, and oxen. To this substantial fare, freely partaken of, was added a pot of goodly dimensions, brimful of mead or beer, from which the guests drank as oft and as deeply as they pleased, using for this purpose cups made of horn.

Then came the song of the bards, celebrating the last fought battle, and bestowing fitting praise on the heroes who had fallen in it. It was loud, wild, passionate, and highly metaphorical, but the better adapted on that account to delight an audience no ways critical.

The tiger and other beasts of prey have their combats and their victories, but they never celebrate their wars in verse. Their conflicts never rise above the low groove of mere animal passion and brute rage. Not so man: not so even barbarian man. With his combats there always mingle in some degree mental and moral sentiments. It is these, when the strife is over, and the animal passions have subsided, that vent themselves in song. Hence war, with all its miseries, is, in rude ages, an educating and elevating process. The beasts fight for food or to gratify their rage, and never get beyond these sordid objects. The lion is not a more chivalrous combatant to-day than he was a thousand years ago. He but caters for his cubs, or he ravens for himself. Man fights, first, to display his prowess, next he combats for his clan, and finally he does battle for country and liberty, all the while the brute instinct in him is weakening, and the higher faculties are developing apace, and embracing in their aims still grander objects. Of the songs of love and war sung on these occasions, and they were many doubtless, not one remains. The very language of the Picts has perished. Only one word has come down to us, preserved by Bede, *Peanfahel*.[1] It is thought to mean "the

---

[1] So was it when Sir Walter wrote the "Antiquary." Since that time there has been discovered a considerable number of Pictish words. The phonetic changes in these exhibit Pictish as occupying an intermediate place betwixt Cymric and Gaelic. Dr Skene thinks that Cymric and Gaelic has each a high and low dialect, like high and low German, and that Pictish was a low Gaelic dialect.—Forbes' *Life of St Ninian; Historians of Scotland*, vol. v. p. 277; Skene's *Four Ancient Books of Wales*, p. 138.

head of the wall," that is, the eastern end of Antonine's wall, and to be identical in site with the modern town of Keneil. The universal language of Europe at that day was the Celtic in its various dialects, and it is probable that the speech of the Picts differed only slightly from that of the Scots, the Welsh, and the Gauls. It is hardly necessary to add that the religion of the Pict was Druidism, and that he repaired to the oak wood and the stone circle to worship.

CHAPTER XXI.

THE COMING OF THE SCOTS.

In the previous chapter we traced the progress of the Scots from Scythia, that "workshop of nations," to Ireland. There can be no doubt regarding their starting point; but there is some variety of opinion touching the route by which they travelled. They may have crossed from the Cymric Chersonesus, and passing betwixt the mainland of Scotland and the Orkneys, entered Ireland on the north. Or they may have taken the longer and more circuitous road by Gaul and Spain. There is a concurrence of early Irish tradition in favour of the latter route, and in deference to that tradition we have adopted it as that by which these Scythic emigrants travelled. But it is of more importance to enquire, at what time did the Scots arrive in Ireland?

Some have placed their advent so early as the tenth or twelfth century before Christ. This opinion has neither proof nor probability to support it. If the Scots were in Ireland ten centuries or even five centuries before the Christian era, how comes it that of the historians and geographers that speak of Ireland, not one mentions the name of the Scots till the third or fourth century? Ptolemy, the geographer, in the second century, enumerates some score of different races as inhabiting Ireland, but the Scot is not of the number. Cæsar, Diodorus Siculus, Strabo, Mela, Tacitus, Pliny, though they mention Ireland, know nothing of the Scots. The name by which the country was then known among the writers who speak of it, was *Hibernia, Ierne,* or *Britannia Minor;* and they had no name for its inhabitants save *Hyberni* and *Hyberionæ.* The first writer in whose pages the term *Scoti* appears is Ammianus Marcellinus in the end of the fourth century, and he speaks of them as a people who had been wanderers through diverse countries, and who even yet were hardly settled down in their new homes.[1] Having made their appearance, the Scots do not again pass out of view. On the contrary, they continue to make their presence in Ireland felt, as they do also in the country on the hither side of the Irish Channel; and hardly is there a writer of any eminence in the ages that follow who has not occasion to speak of them. Claudian, Jerome, Orosius, Gildas, all make mention of the Scots. This is wholly unaccountable on the supposition that this people had been resident in Ireland for twelve or thirteen centuries, but it perfectly accords with the theory that makes their arrival to fall at the beginning of the Christian era, or soon thereafter. As spoken of by their first historians, the Scots have about them the air of a new people. They are of hardier fibre than the soft and peace-loving aborigines among whom they have come to dwell, but with whom they do not mix. Ammianus hints that the disposition to roam was still strong in them, and already, before they have well established themselves in their new abodes, they are on the outlook for larger territories, and have their curraghs ready to pass over and explore the land, whose blue mountain-tops they can descry on the other side of the narrow sea.

The world was then on the eve of one of its greatest revolutions. The north was about to open its gates and send

---

[1] Amian. Marcel., lib. 27. *Scoti per diversa vagantes.*

forth its numerous hardy races to overflow and occupy the fertile lands of the south. The manhood of the Greeks and Romans was extinct. There was neither piety in their temples, nor virtue in their homes. The Senate was without patriotism, and the camp without courage. A universal dissolution of moral principle had set in, and society lay overwhelmed. Unless the world was to stand still or perish, new races must be brought upon the stage. The Frank was to be planted in Gaul, the Goth was to inherit Spain, the Vandal was to have possessions in Africa, and the Astrogoth and Lombard were to pitch their tents in Italy. Of all this offspring of the fruitful north, it is a historic fact that the Scot was the first born. He occupied the van in this great procession of nations which we see about to begin their march to the south: for he was the first to leave his northern home and set out in quest of a new country. He arrived too early on the scene to fare well in this new partition of Europe, for Rome was still strong, and kept the gates of her fairest provinces closed against the northern hordes. Had he come later, when the empire was more enfeebled, the Scot might have been able to choose his lot amid the corn-lands of Spain, or the vineyards of Italy, like the Goths, the Huns, and other swarms who followed him. As it was, he was constrained to turn northwards, and fix his abode under the humid skies of Ierne, and amid the heath-clad mountains of Caledonia. Nevertheless his was the better part. If the inheritance assigned him lay at the extremity of Europe, and looked rugged and barren, compared with the happier allotments of others, it brought with it a countervailing advantage, which was worth, ten times over, all possible attractions of soil and climate. It made him all the more able to maintain his liberty and his faith. A new and deeper slavery was preparing for the nations. The Scot, standing afar off, was the last to come under the yoke of the second Rome, and among the first to escape from it.

As we dimly descry him on his first appearance in Ireland, the Scot has about him a marked individuality. He is seen moving about, a man of iron among figures of clay. His arrival brings the country into historic light. He takes upon himself the burden of ruling the land, and he infuses something of his own spirit into the natives. The aborigines appear to have been a submissive and unwarlike people, who occupied themselves in tending their herds of cattle and swine amid their woods and bogs. Such at least would seem to have been the report brought of them to Agricola. The Roman general had been able to do little more than stand his ground before the Caledonians at the foot of the Grampians, with the Roman army in force, and yet he undertook, with a single legion and a few bodies of auxiliaries, to subdue and occupy Ireland.[1] Plainly Agricola recognised a vast difference betwixt the spirit of the men on this side of the Irish Channel and on that. And such do the aborigines of Ierne appear, as seen in the earliest Irish writings which we possess. We refer to the "Confessions of Patrick."[2] Being the autobiography of Patrick, and not the history of Ireland, it is only side-glimpses which it gives us of the inhabitants of the country; but these are full of interest, and amply bear out all that we have said regarding the character and relative position of the two races then inhabiting Ireland, the *Hiberni* and the *Scoti*. There is seen to be a marked

---

[1] Tacitus, *Vit. Agric.*, c. 24.

[2] *Confessio S. Patricii.* We shall have frequent occasion to refer to this work at a subsequent stage of our history. All that we deem it needful to say of it here is, that it was written by himself in the fifth century, and first published by Ware from very ancient MS., and its authenticity is acknowledged by all the learned.

distinction between the two. The Scots are the military class; they are the nobles. So does Patrick style them when he has occasion to speak of them in his "Confession," and also in his letter to the Irish chieftain, Coroticus. But his language is different when he has occasion to refer to the aboriginal inhabitants. The latter are spoken of as the commonalty, the sons of the soil,[1] a quiet, yielding, and inoffensive people, dwelling carelessly in their pleasant insular abode, plowing their fields, reaping their harvests, skilled in the rearing of cattle and swine, but inexperienced in the art of war, from the sight of which their situation happily removed them; yet destined, a few centuries later, to attain the fame of learning, and then Ireland would shine in a glory which would attract to its shore the youth of Europe, to drink in the wisdom of its schools.

Very different is that other people who now make their appearance, and whose career is destined to be so eventful. It is in Ireland that we first meet them. But Ierne is not their native soil. They have arrived in it, Ammianus Marcellinus tells us, after long wandering through many countries, and, doubtless, divers perils. They give kings to their adopted land. They send an armed expedition across the Channel, to aid the Picts in overrunning the Provincials, and driving back the Romans. They are constantly finding work for the legions which guard the frontiers of the now tottering empire. Now it is the Scots that conquer, and now it is the Romans, and the belt of country between the two walls becomes the scene of many a bloody fray. They go back again to Ireland, but soon they return in strength to Scotland, and settle down in it as if they felt that for better

---

[1] Patrick often uses *Scoti* and *Reguli* as equivalent terms. To the term *Scottus* he adds often the word *nobilis;* whereas he has no other appellative for the native Irish but *Hyberione*, or *Hyberni genæ*, the common people. Both Bolland and Tillemont take notice of this distinction.

for worse this must be the future land of the Scots. They still cherish their warlike spirit, and are on the outlook for a foe. The Roman has vanished from Britain, but the Saxon has come in. The Scots unite their arms with the Picts, and push back the new intruder. At length the two form one people. The northern rover now appears on their shore, but it is only to find a grave. The barrows on the northern and western coasts of our island, where sleep the Viking and his followers, "slain with the sword of the Scot," show that their prowess had not suffered decay. The Dane had conquered the Saxon, but he cannot prevail against the Scot. For ages the nation maintains its independence in a country which some would have deemed not worth possessing, and which more would have deemed not worth invading, but which nevertheless was the object of repeated attack on the part of its powerful neighbours, but with no other result than to renew from age to age, and to work into the soul of its people, the love of country, and the passion of liberty. In this summary of the Scottish people we have gone a few centuries forward, and must now retrace our steps.

CHAPTER XXII.

THE PLANTING OF THE SCOTTISH NATION.

The Scots make their first appearance on the stage of British history in the year A.D. 360. At this date they did not own an acre o land out of Ireland, and they had as yet planted no colony on the Caledonian side of the Channel. Ulster was still the headquarters of their race, and the sway over them was exercised by princes of the renowned line of the Hy Nial. But in the above year we see them crossing the sea, and for the first time, so far as is known to history, setting foot on the shore of their future home, not as colonists, but only in the character of strangers, or rather of military adventurers. On this side the Channel they promise themselves larger scope for the restless and warlike spirit that stirred so strongly within them. The Caledonians are still dwelling amid their old hills, but now they have come to be known by the name of Picts. The new name, however, has wrought in them no change of sentiment towards the Romans, or effaced the remembrance of the cruelties they suffered at their hands. The Picts, that is the Caledonians, still cherish the hatred which the terrible campaigns of Agricola and Severus burned into them, and the growing embarrassments of the empire present at this moment a tempting opportunity of vengeance, of which they are not slow to avail themselves. They welcome, perhaps they invite these hardy fighters, the Scots, to wit, from across the

Irish Channel. Store of booty, the excitement of battle, and, after the fight, pleasant allotments in the conquered land, were the inducements, doubtless, held forth by the Caledonians to the Scots of Ulster to join them in a raid upon the enfeebled and dispirited garrisons cantoned along the Roman wall. The whole earth was rising against Rome, the North and the East were in motion, why should they let the hour pass without calling their old enemy to a reckoning for their fathers' blood? It was the quarrel of Scot not less than of Pict, for should the tottering empire recover its strength, what could they expect but that Rome would come back upon them with her scheme of universal empire to be set up in the midst of an enslaved earth. The Scots must not promise themselves exemption in the Irish Sea, or think that there they were beyond the reach of this all-embracing tyranny. Rome would find them out in their isle, hitherto inviolate, and they should have to wear her chain with the rest of the nations.

Perhaps these considerations of policy were not needed. To the Scot, with his keen spirit and sharp sword, it may be that adventure and battle were inducement enough. But whatever the motive which drew them across the Irish Channel, here are the Scots fighting side by side with the Picts against their common foe, the Romans. The theatre on which we find the allied host slaughtering and burning is the wide district lying betwixt the two walls, that of Antonine on the Forth, and that of Hadrian on the Solway. The inhabitants of that intermediate territory had come to be a mixed race, made up of Briton and Roman, with perhaps a few strangers of Caledonian, that is, Pictish blood, who had stolen down from the region of the Grampians to settle in the pleasant vales of this more fertile and picturesque land. This mongrel population passed under the general name of Meatæ, and afterwards when the Scots came to mingle with them, and still farther diversify their blood, they were sometimes spoken of as Attacotti.[1] Lying between the Roman and Caledonian provinces of Britain, they were exposed to assaults on both sides. It was from the north that the present storm burst upon them. Besides the grudge which both Scot and Pict bore the men of this district as the subjects of the Roman power, the region offered special attractions to the marauder. It had for a long time—with frequent intervals of lapse, however—been in possession of the Romans, and was now redeemed from barrenness. But its blooming cultivation speedily withered beneath the feet of the invaders. We see the allied host of Pict and Scot bursting over the northern wall, never a strong defence, and now weaker than ever—driving away or slaying the natives, and planting themselves down in their fields and dwellings. The success of the spoilers drew them on into the good land beyond. There was neither spirit in the Britons, nor power in their Roman protectors to check the ravages of this wild host. Onward they swept, giving free licence to their swords and full scope to their rapaciousness, till they had reached a line south of London. Here this pitiful work was at length put a stop to for the time. Theodosius, esteemed the best general of his age, and the father of a line of emperors, was despatched against them from the Continent with an army, A.D. 369.[2] On arriving, he found that all that had been left to Rome in Britain was a narrow strip along its southern coast. Homesteads in ashes, fields pillaged, terror everywhere, showed who, for the time, were masters of the country, from the foot of the Grampians to almost the English Channel. Theodosius, on arriving, found Kent

---

[1] Attacotti bellicosa hominum natio.—*Ammian Marc.*, xxvii. 8.
[2] Ammian Marcel., lib. xxviii. c. 8.

swarming with the northern hordes, and had to fight his way to Augusta, "an old town," observes Ammianus Marcellinus, "formerly named London." Roman discipline prevailed over the wild fury of the invading tribes. The northern tempest was driven back to its native birthplace. The Roman dominion was re-established, and the limits of the empire were once more extended as far north as to the Forth. The territory lying between the two walls was erected into a Roman province, and named in honour of the reigning emperor Valentia. It was a short-lived principality, for the Romans retiring from Britain soon after, the name, which was the badge of subjection, fell into disuse when the legions departed. It is curious to mark that the Scots, when they first come before us, are seen battling with Rome. How often in after years were these two powers fated to come into conflict, though not precisely after the same fashion in which we here behold this little band of vagrant warriors measuring swords with the mistress of the world?

The weakness of the empire was too marked, and her British provinces were too tempting to permit the spirit of invasion long to sleep. In A.D. 384, just fifteen years after Theodosius had re-extended the Roman government in north Britain to the old line of Antonine, the Scots and Picts are again seen in arms; again they swarm over the northern wall, and again they rush down like an inundation, carrying slaughter and devastation throughout the ill-starred territory that intervenes betwixt the Roman power on the south, which is waxing feebler every year, and the continually growing mass of warlike barbarism which presses upon them on the north. The intervals that divided the episodes of invasion were becoming shorter, and every new raid was being attended with more calamity and bloodshed than the one that had preceded it. On this occasion, the region itself yielded a contingent to swell the army of plunderers. The Meatæ and Attacotti were becoming disaffected to the Romans; their invaders had sown the seeds of revolt amongst them; and they possibly judged that should they cast in their lot with the Picts and Scots, their condition would be less miserable than if they retained their allegiance to a power which had become unable to defend either their lives or their heritages. They had the alternative of plundering or of being plundered. They did not long hesitate. Seizing brand and torch, they threw themselves into the stream of marauders, and went on with them to slay and burn. The few veterans left on the wall of Hadrian looked down with dismay on this multifarious horde, surging at the foot of their feeble rampart. They might as well have thought of keeping out the sea when the tide is coming in, as of preventing their irruption into the province they had been appointed to guard. The hostile tribes scaled the wall and rushed down in a torrent, or flood rather, on the rich holms and corn-lands of England. The Romans again came to the help of the afflicted provincials, and driving back the invaders, gave them another short respite from rapine and slaughter.

Rome, which had so long fought for glory, was now fighting for existence, and the overburdened empire would have relieved itself by abandoning Britain, had it not been that it needed its revenue to replenish its exchequer, drained by the numerous armies it was compelled to maintain to quell the insurrections on its frontier. But now the Picts and Scots were gleaning more from Britain than its Roman masters, and the time evidently was near when the province would be left to defend itself. One effort more, however, did the expiring empire make on behalf of its wretched subjects. Again the barbarian host had gathered in aug-

mented numbers and fiercer audacity. Again they were
seen dashing over the Roman walls and spreading like an
inundation over the territory occupied by the provincial
Britons. The torment of the land was great, and its cry
for assistance was loud. This induced Stilicho, the vigorous
minister of the effeminate Honorius, in A.D. 400, to respond
with help. The country was once more cleared by the sword
of the legionaries, and the Picts and Scots being driven out,
the frontier of the empire, so often effaced and so often
traced out anew, was once more drawn along the ancient
line of Antonine's wall. It was superfluous labour. The
hour had almost come when the wall would be levelled,
never again to be rebuilt. In anticipation of their near
departure from Britain, the Romans repaired the breaches
in the rampart, and otherwise strengthened it, and having
performed this last friendly office to the Britons, they took
leave of them, committing the wall to their keeping, with
some friendly advice to the effect that as henceforth they
should have to rely upon themselves for protection against
their troublesome neighbours, it would be their wisdom to
cultivate a little hardihood and courage, and not lean on an
empire which, having now to fight for its seat and capital
in Italy, was in no condition to lavish either money or
soldiers on the defence of its distant provinces.

Meanwhile, heavier cares began to press upon Stilicho,
the minister who was heroically struggling to uphold a falling empire. Civil war within and barbarian insurrection
without, gave token to Rome that the horrors of her overthrow would be great as her territory had been wide, and
the darkness of her night deep, as the splendours of her noon
had been brilliant. The ancient terror had departed from
her name; her legions had lost their old discipline and
bravery; one man alone, energetic, upright, and patriotic,

strove to redeem from ineffable and universal contempt the venal, debauched, and cowardly crowd that inherited the names and bore the titles, but lacked the virtues of Rome's ancient patricians. In the distant and unknown regions of Scythia, storm after storm was gathering and rolling up against the empire. The legions on Hadrian's wall, in the far north, were recalled in this hour of extremity. The garrisons of the Rhine were withdrawn; and the Gothic hordes, swarming across that river, rushed through the passes of the Julian Alps to assail her which had so often sent her legions through the same passes on a like errand. Italy, which now disclosed her fruitful face to their greedy eyes, did but the more enflame the courage of these terrible warriors. The youthful and luxurious Honorius fled in terror from his palace of Milan, at the approach of Alaric. The victory of Stilicho on the bloody field of Pollentia (A.D. 403), only delayed for a short while the catastrophe of the empire. It was one man against nations. No skill, no bravery could suffice against odds so tremendous. The north continued to send forth through its open gates horde after horde. Rome fell: and with her fall darkness descended upon the world. The volume of Holy Writ alone can supply us with adequate imagery to depict the confusions and horrors of that awful time: "The sun became black as sackcloth of hair," "the stars of heaven fell unto the earth," "and the day shone not."

On the extinction of the Roman dominion in Britain it is not surprising that our country should fall back into the darkness in which it had been sunk before the arrival of Julius Cæsar. Dissevered from the Western world, mixing itself in no way with the affairs of the struggling nations around it, it passes out of sight. For a full century it is lost. Did Britain, retired within her four seas, enjoy security and quiet, while the nations of the Continent were enduring the throes of a revolution unexampled before or since in the history of the world? Among the last indications of its condition, just before the curtain drops upon it, is the despairing cry of the aboriginal Britons to the Romans for help against the barbarians. The document to which we refer is the well-known letter of the Britons to Ætius, the Roman governor in Gaul, which has been preserved by Bede. Never was more pathetic supplication addressed to ruler. "To Ætius," say they, "thrice consul, the groans of the Britons. The barbarians drive us to the sea—the sea throws us back on the swords of the barbarians. We have, alas! no choice left us but the wretched one of being drowned or butchered." This lamentable cry leaves us in no doubt what the country's fate was during this unhistoric century. It was a century full of wretchedness and horror. The Picts, Scots, and Attacotti, and ultimately other tribes from beyond the German Sea, breaking over Hadrian's wall, on which not a single legionary now kept guard, swept on into the heart of the fair land, hardly encountering any resistance, slaying, spoiling, and burning, in short, enacting within the narrow limits of our island, the same upturnings and cruelties which the Goths, the Huns, and so many other barbarous nations were perpetrating at that time on the wider theatre of Europe.

The truth is, that the government of the Romans, which worked so beneficially at the beginning for Britain, became destructive in the end. The tendency of despotism is to grow ever the more crushing. The Roman tyranny, after a continuance of five centuries, produced a Britain of spiritless men. Denied all local government, and held in serfdom, they had no heart either to cultivate or to fight for a country which was not theirs, but their masters'. When the Romans withdrew, they were virtually without a king. There remained neither order nor industry in the land. The consequence of their neglect to plough and sow was a mighty famine. Hunger drove them to resume the pursuits of agriculture. After its rest, the earth brought forth plenteously; but the overflowing harvest brought down upon them their old enemies the Picts, who emptied their barns as fast as they filled them. It was from the depth of this manifold misery that the Britons uttered their "groan" to Ætius. But the Roman governor could only give them the counsel which had already been tendered them: "Take courage, and fight your own battle." This is one of the few distinct historic incidents of that unrecorded time.

When these silent years, with all their untold sufferings, draw to an end, vast political and social changes are seen to have taken place in Scotland. Here, then, at this well-defined epoch of our country's history, we resume our narrative.

Britain, on again emerging into view, has a settled look, instead of landmarks perpetually shifting, and tribes always on the move, our island has become the dwelling-place of four nations—the Britons, the Picts, the Scots, and the Saxons—each in the main content to abide within definite limits. It will help us to realise the Britain of that age, and the relative position of the four nations that occupied it, if we shall figure to ourselves an oblong area, with a line drawn through its centre from north to south, a second line drawn from east to west, and cutting the former at right angles, and so dividing the area into four compartments. In each of these four distinct and separate compartments is a nation. In the north-eastern division are the Picts, and in the north-western the Scots; in the south-eastern are the Anglo-Saxons, and in the south-western the Britons. This is a rough outline of the Britain of the sixth century. Let us go over the ground a second time, tracing out a little more precisely the boundaries of these four nations.

We stand beside the cradle of a great power: a future, which the boldest imagination would not then have dared to picture, is here just beginning. If the birth-place of great rivers strike the mind with a certain awe, how much more the fountain-heads of nations destined to arrive at imperial sway. The command had now gone forth with regard to Rome, "Remove the diadem!" How astonished would she have been had she been told at this hour, "Here is your successor." Yet so it was eventually to be. The lesson has often been taught the world, but, perhaps, never more strikingly so than in this instance, that "what is destined to be great must begin by being small."

Of the four nations which had partitioned Britain amongst them with their swords, we begin with the Anglo-Saxons. This was a people from the other side of the German Sea. They occupied the low country lying along the coast of North Germany, beginning at the Rhine. Their original seats were Holstein, Schleswig, Jutland, and the islands at the mouth of the Elbe, and their transference across the sea to the English shore, which was effected in successive bands or expeditions, took place in the middle of the fifth century, and continued during great part of the following one. Gildas and Nennius, the earliest British writers, have recorded their arrival in our country, with substantial truth doubtless, but it may be also with some admixture of fable. They say that they were invited over by the Britons, who beheld with alarm and terror, their Roman defenders being now gone, the Pictish swarms gathering on their northern frontier. The Saxons crossed the sea at the first as allies, but in the end, and mainly, as invaders. They had heard tell that the Romans had quitted Britain, or were preparing to do so, and they hoped to serve themselves heirs, with their swords, to the fruitful land the legions were leaving. Their own country was penurious and infertile. In order to subsist, they were compelled to betake themselves to the ocean and prey upon its commerce. In these circumstances it was not unnatural that they should wish to possess a country which lay so near to them, and the wealth of which would so well reward the trouble of conquest. The invading host was made up of three tribes, the Angles, the Jutes, and the Frisians, to which is given the general name of Saxons, but all three belonged to a common race, laboured under common disadvantages, and addicted themselves to common pursuits; in short, they were sea-pirates, and, it is unnecessary to add, hardy and adventurous. They are said, by the writers to whom we have referred, to have followed the standard of two famous leaders, Hengista and Horsa. They advanced, driving the Britons before them, who would seem to have been much enervated by their long subjection to the Roman power, and unable to make any successful resistance. The vanquished Britons retired into the west and north-west of England, where we shall find them forming a distinct kingdom by themselves. The boundaries of the Saxons in Britain extended from the Wash south to Portsmouth. Future conquests, as we shall see, enlarged their dominion on the north at one time as far as to the shores of the Firth of Forth, infusing the Anglian element into the shires of Lothian and Berwick, which is still found in that population.

The new kingdom of the BRITONS lay along the west coast of the island, extending from Cornwall, and running northward by Wales, the counties of Westmoreland and Cumberland, and onwards to the Clyde. The capital of this kingdom was the strongly fortified position on the rock Alcluith, the Dumbarton of to-day. On the east the forest of Ettrick divided between them and the Angles who dwelt from the Tyne to the Forth. The ancient boundary between these two peoples can still be traced on the face of the country in the remains of the huge earthen dyke, known as the Catrail, which, beginning near Galashiels, holds on its course over the mountainous land till it ends at Peel hill in the south of Liddesdale. The Britons were of Celtic origin; no history records their arrival in the country: the Romans found them in it when they invaded it. But early as their coming must have been, they were preceded by a still earlier race. So do the sepulchral monuments of England testify.

The PICTS, or Caledonians, are the third in order. Speaking generally, they occupied the whole eastern half of Scotland from the Forth to the Pentland Firth. They dwelt within well-defined boundaries, their limits being the German Sea on the east, and on the west the towering ridge of the Argyllshire and Perthshire mountains, a chain of hills to which was given the name of Drumalban. Tacitus describes them as "large limbed and red-haired." They were at first ranged in fourteen independent tribes; latterly they came to be grouped into two great bodies, the Southern and the Northern Picts, so called according as they dwelt on this or on the hither side of that great mountain chain which, running from Lochabar to Stonehaven, parted their territories. In the latter half of the sixth century they embraced Christianity, and became united into one nation under a powerful king.

Ample and goodly were the territories of the Picts. Theirs were the corn-lands of Fife; theirs was the rich carse of the Tay; theirs was Strathmore, the queen of Scottish plains, which spreads out its ample and fertile bosom between the Sidlaws on the south, and the towering bulwark of the Grampians on the north; theirs were the wooded and picturesque valleys which the Dee and the Don water; theirs was the plain of Moray, blessed with the climate of Devonshire; theirs the rich grassy straths of Ross-shire; theirs the gigantic platform of moorland and mountain, with its not infertile border, which constitutes the counties of Caithness and Sutherland. Rounding Cape Wrath, theirs were the giant headlands, with the islands dispersed at their feet, which nature would seem to have placed here as a bulwark against the great surges of the Atlantic, as they come rolling up before the tempest from the far-off shore of a then undiscovered world. In a word, theirs was nearly all that was worth possessing in Scotland, the Lothians excepted.

We turn last of all to the SCOTS. They were as yet strangers in the land to which they were afterwards to give an imperishable name. Of all the four nations, the possessions of the Scots were the most diminutive and the least fertile. The corner of Scotland which they had appropriated, appeared a mere assemblage of rocky mountains, parted by arms of the sea, liable to be deluged by torrents of rain, and obscured by frequent mists. An inhospitable land it must have seemed, compared with the rich and level country of Ulster, from which they had come. Either they were straitened in their former home, or abridged in their dearly-prized independence, or they were inspired by the love of adventure, and cherished the confident hope of becoming in the end of the day the lords of this new land, when, forsaking the green shores of Loch Neah and the fertile plains of Antrim, they chose for their dwelling this region of gloomy hills.

The limits of the Scots were strongly marked. On the south their boundary was the Firth of Clyde. On the east it was the long and lofty mountain chain termed Drumalban, the "dorsal ridge of Britain," as Adamnan, the biographer of St Columba, terms it. These hills are, in fact, the watershed of the district, parting the rivers that flow to the west from those that flow to the east, as at this day they part the counties of Argyll and Perth. At a point in the Drumalban chain—the precise point it is impossible to say, but as far to the northward as to include the Crinan Moss—the boundary line struck westwards through Morvern, and climbing the shoulder of Ben More in Mull, it came out at the Atlantic. So petty was the Scotland of that day. It comprehended Kintyre, Cowall, Lorn, and the islands of Islay, Jura, Colonsay, and Iona—names which remain the ineffaceable imprints of the chiefs who led thither the first Scottish occupants of this soil.

We have traced the narrow boundaries—identical almost with those of the modern county of Argyll—which then enclosed the kingdom and nation of the Scots; this brings us to a more important question, Whence came the people whom we now see planting themselves amid the fiords and rocky promontories of south Argyll? All agree in saying, They came from Ireland. The early chronicler, whose guide is tradition, and the modern historian, who walks by the light of ascertained facts, tested by ethnological and physiological proofs, are at one here. They show us a little band of colonists crossing the narrow strait that divides the north of Ireland from the Mull of Kintyre, in their leathern coracles, under the leadership of Fergus Mor, son of Erc. This was in A.D. 502. From what more remote country they came originally, we have already shown. We now join their company where history brings us acquainted with them as a settled people, and that is in that part of Ireland which now forms the county of Antrim. At some remote period, not now ascertainable, a body of wanderers had arrived in the north of Ireland. About the time that Rome was laying the first stone of her capital in the marshes of the Tiber, this people, it may be, were establishing themselves on the shores of Loch Neah, or clustering around the basaltic cliffs of the Giant's

Causeway. In course of time one of their number had the influence or the art to make himself be elected king. The name of this chief was RIADHA; his sons succeeded him in the government; and those over whom they reigned were called Dalriads, from the name of the founder of the dynasty, and the territory which they occupied came to be known as Dalriada. This is the territory which figures as *Scotia* in the pages of the chroniclers; for it is always to be remembered that when the early historians speak of Scotland, it is the Irish Dalriada, in other words, the present county of Antrim, which they have in their eye. The name *Scotia* began to be of more general application, and to be given to the whole of Ireland. It was not till the tenth century that the name of Scotland was applied to the country on this side the channel, that is, to the Scotland of to-day.

It was a descendant of this early king of Ulster who, according to the testimony of the oldest Irish chronicler, Abbot Tighernac, led a body of these Dalriads or Scots from Antrim, across the channel, to find for them new homes amid the friths and mountains to the south of Loch Linnhe. The name of this chieftain, we have said, was Fergus Mor. Thus was founded a new Dalriada, and we now behold a Scotia on both sides of the Irish Channel.[1] The capital of the new Dalriada, or hither Scotland, was situated at the head of Loch Crinan. In the middle of what is now the great Moss of Crinan rises an isolated hill. On its top are the vestiges of former fortifications of great strength, while the wastes around are strewn with a miscellaneous debris of stones and cairns. These remains are supposed to mark the site of the earliest capital of the early Scotland. It stood on the banks of the Add, a streamlet that still winds through the morass; hence its name, Dunadd.

[1] Tigh., 502-574. *Chron. Picts and Scots*, p. 130. Adam., *Vit. Colum.* (Reeves), App. 2, p. 435. Bed., *Eccl. Hist.*, lib. iii., c. 3.

This infant colony carried in its bosom a seed of great power. These Dalriads, whom we see crossing the sea in their modest wherries, were Christians. Their Christianity, we grant, may have been very elementary. It had not been built up into system by the learning of the exegete and the labours of the commentator; it was the simple faith of the early ages, and would not be expected to furnish those bright examples of evangelical virtue which may be looked for where a fuller knowledge is enjoyed, and where, consequently, the influence of the truth is greater. To whom little is given, from him little will be demanded. But between a people under the influence of Christianity, though only partially so, and a people sunk in the practices of heathenism, as were the Pictish populations around these new settlers, there will ever be found a mighty intellectual and moral difference. This difference was seen to exist in the present instance. Naturally hardy and brave, with a noble independence of spirit, these settlers brought with them yet higher qualities, even such as are engendered by that living faith which they had embraced. There was henceforth a divine force acting in Scotland. The seed of the new life, it is true, had been deposited in only a corner of the country. It had been entrusted to the guardianship of but a little community, but it took root in the soil; it germinated, it sprang up, and every year it spread wider through the land. It had a fair spring-time in the ministry of the Culdees. Under the missionaries of Iona, this young vine began to shoot forth its branches so widely, as to touch the Alps on the one side, and the shores of Iceland on the other. But that goodly tree was destined to be visited by furious tempests before attaining its full stature. A winter intervened: its boughs were rifled; its trunk was stripped bare;

but, despite these ravages, its root still remained in the ground. When the sixteenth century came, a plenteous dew from above descended upon it, and awoke into mightier energy than ever the life that lingered in the old trunk. The sapling of the Culdean era became the giant of the Knoxian period.

Fergus Mor, when he crossed from Antrim to what is now the Scottish shore, was accompanied by his two brothers, Angus and Loarne. They were the fathers of three tribes, termed " the three powerfuls of Dalriada," among whom the new Dalriada was partitioned. Cowall and Kintyre fell to the lot of the descendants of the great-grandson of Fergus, Comgall by name, and that name, slightly altered, we can still recognise in the " Cowall " of to-day. The islands of Jura and Islay formed the possessions of the descendants of Angus. They had the sea for their border; and their territories were neither infertile nor wanting in picturesqueness of landscape, the fine outlines, and the rich purple colourings of the mountains of the former island in particular often tempting the tourist of to-day across the troubled strait that separates it from the mainland. To the descendants of Loarne was assigned the district that still bears the name, scarcely altered, of their ancestors. In a central position, between the territories of Cowall and Lorn, was placed, as we have already said, the capital of the little state, Dunadd.[1]

Each tribe was subject to the immediate authority of its chief. While owning the limited claims of chieftainship, the tribes recognised at the same time the superior and larger authority of the king, who exercised sway over the whole confederacy. The sovereignty among the early Scots was not confined to a single family, in which it descended as a hereditary possession. Each tribe, in its turn, supplied an

[1] Skene, *Celtic Scotland*, vol. i. p. 229.

occupant for the throne when it became vacant. At first the prerogative of furnishing a king was divided betwixt the tribe of Comgall and the tribe of Fergus, afterwards it came to be shared between the two tribes of Comgall and Loarne. It was in accordance with the Irish law of Tanistry that the sovereign power passed thus alternately from the one tribe to the other. This division into tribes became, in after days, a source of frequent calamity. When these tribes came to be split up into others, and the nation was parted into numerous subdivisions or clans, feuds often sprang up touching the boundaries of their respective territories, and furious battles were fought over the question of who should possess this tract of barren moor, or who should call himself the owner of that mountain, whose rocky soil and steep sides bade defiance to the operations of the plough.

The fortunes of the Scots of Dalriada had their ebb and flow; but though chequered, their affairs were in the main progressive. They lived at peace with their powerful neighbours the Picts, and they reaped the benefit of this wise policy in a century of almost unbroken prosperity and progress. During this, the happiest period of their early annals, they built up their country into a compact and, viewing it in relation to the tribes bordering upon them, powerful state. Set free from the exacting and impoverishing demands of war, they were at liberty to concentrate their energies on bringing their territory under tillage, so far as its mountainous character permitted. The area which their boundaries enclosed was a narrow one, but they strove to augment its fertility with the plough rather than to extend its limits by the sword. Better, they judged, a rich though small, than a great but barren domain.

Their petty kingdom was shut in at almost all points by

the far ampler possessions of the Picts. The territory of that warlike people ran up along the entire eastern boundary of the Scots, and then sweeping round on the north, it descended along the shore, and partially enclosed them on the west, leaving open only the short line of the Clyde, and the seaboard looking towards Ireland. Scottish Dalriada lay in the embraces, as it were, of Pictland. The Picts, as the more numerous and the more powerful people, might, if they had had a mind, driven the colonists into the sea or across the channel. They did, indeed, soon after their settlement, make some attempts to dislodge them, but whether they thought these new neighbours too few and too insignificant to be at pains to expel them, or whether they deemed their mountains not worth the trouble of subjugating, or whether they encountered a stouter resistance than they had reckoned upon, it is now hard to say; but one thing is certain, the Scots kept their ground, and refused to withdraw or rectify their frontier in presence of the Picts. There would have ensued, in all probability, a series of raids and fights between the two nations, which would have occasioned great effusion of blood, and left no record save the cairns that would have dotted the moors and the hill-sides, but for the occurrence of an event which powerfully influenced the relations of the two peoples, and formed so beneficent a bond between them, that for a hundred years thereafter never was Pict seen fighting against Scot, nor Scot against Pict, nor did either covet a foot-breadth of the territory of the other, nor was there battle or bloodshed between the two nations.[1] Let us turn to that event.

[1] Skene, vol. i. 276.

CHAPTER XXIII.

KINDLING OF THE LAMP OF IONA.

ONE day, about half a century after Fergus Mor and his two brothers had crossed the channel to find for themselves and their companions new homes amid the blue lakes and the heath-clad hills of Argyllshire, a solitary coracle might be seen approaching the Scottish shore. As the tiny craft rose and sank on the swell of the Atlantic, nor token nor badge of any sort was discernible from which one might infer the rank of those on board, or guess the errand on which they were bound. No pennon floats at the mast-head of the little ship, no blazoned shield is hung out at its bows: humbler wherry never crossed the sea. It draws near: it is rowed into a little shingly bay that opens amid the rocks of Iona, and now its occupants drop the oar and make ready to disembark. As they step on shore, one after one, we can count them. They are thirteen in all; a little company, verily! and then their garb, how plain! their air, how void of assumption; and yet there is a loving look and a conscious dignity in their faces which bespeak them more than they seem, and make it manifest that they have crossed the sea on an errand of peace and blessing. There is, moreover, about one of the number that which reveals the master, and in the deportment of the others is that which befits the character of scholars and disciples; but disciples that follow not from authority, but from reverence and affection.

The ripple of the calm sea on the pebbly beach, so musical and soft, as the feet of these venerable men touch the shore of the little island, sounds in the Sabbath-stillness like a hymn of greeting. We see the newly-arrived strangers cross the narrow strip of meadow that lines the bay, and we hear their voices in sweet converse as they proceed to explore the island. One of their number, leaving the group, climbs with slow steps the little hills and seeks the highest point. Having gained the summit, he halts and looks around him. Islet, and narrow firth, and long line of rocky coast, with the mountain-tops of Mull, and the western ocean stretching away to unknown regions, lie spread out beneath the warm beams of a Whitsuntide sun. The tranquil, loving gaze which the venerable man bestows on the scene falls like a benediction on land and sea. His survey finished, he comes back to his companions. The strangers have had their first sight of their future home. Here, they well know, there await them long years of privation and toil, for they have come to work for the emancipation of Pictland. But here, they also know, there await them glorious triumphs. And the thought of these triumphs kindles the light of a deep joy in their eyes : not the fierce light that burns in the eye of conqueror, for not with the sword are their victories to be won : the faces of these men glow with the serene light that shines in a higher sphere. "Break out into singing, ye dark mountains," we hear them say, "for fairer morning than ever yet gilded your summits is about to break upon you. And ye woods, clap your hands; for no longer shall Druid make your recesses horrible with his sacrifices, or crimson your oaks with the blood of his victims. We come to cleanse your glades from deep pollution and make your solitudes vocal with songs. Hearken ye islands of the western sea: listen ye shores, ye heath-clad plains, ye blue hills of the ancient Caledonia: Fallen is Druid: Broken is his yoke: Your redemption is come."

The passage of this osier-built craft, with its venerable freight, across the Irish Channel, is one of the great voyages of history. From the moment its keel touched our strand we date the commencement of a new era to Scotland, and also to lands far away, beyond the limits of that little country on which we see these voyagers planting their first footsteps.

The arrival of Columba and his fellow-labourers — the second founders of the Scottish nation—is deserving of more space than we have here given it. Our aim at this stage is hastily to note that event as one in a chain of causes which powerfully contributed to place the relations of the Scots and Picts on a right footing: *first*, by inspiring both nations with a common sentiment; *second*, by imparting to both the latent capacity of fighting the battles of freedom and religion: and *thirdly*, by leading on the country to its first great landing place, namely, the union of the two peoples under one crown, and the consolidation of a land partitioned among independent clans, weakened by rivalries, and torn by tribal feuds, into one powerful state. At its proper place, which will soon occur, we shall dwell more at length, and with fuller enumeration of incident, on the arrival of Columba on the Island of Iona, and the vast consequences that grew out of that event. Meanwhile we wish to pass rapidly on to the era of the union of the two crowns, without lingering over the intervening transactions, or wasting our time with the phantom kings that occupied the Scottish and Pictish thrones—if we may dignify these paltry seats by such lofty terms—or the battles in which they so freely shed the blood of their subjects: occurrences of a class which, though each, doubtless, contributed its modicum of influence to make

Scotland what it is, and what it has since done, or may yet do, nevertheless merit only the most general narration, and were we to attempt a minute and lengthy recital regarding kings of uncouth name, and battles where the slaughter was as great as it was useless, and which, moreover, are encompassed by such a mythical haze, the reader, if he did not turn away, would forget the story as soon as he had finished its perusal. "The annals of the Dalriads," says Mr Robertson, "are totally devoid of interest before the reign of Conal, fourth in succession from Fergus Mor, who, by the shelter he afforded to the exiled Abbot of Durrow, furthered the conversion of the northern Picts to Christianity."[1]

Two years did Columba expend in erecting buildings and framing rules for the regulation of the brotherhood over which he presided, and now he was ready to begin the great evangelistic campaign for which he had crossed the Channel. He made a commencement in his own neighbourhood. The Pictland of that day, from the Grampians northwards, was sunk in the gross and cruel superstition of Druidism. Thither, therefore, did the great missionary of Iona direct his steps (A.D. 565). He obtained an interview with the Pictish king, Bruidi, son of Malcolm, at his Dun or castle, on the banks of the Ness, near where the river issues from its parent loch. The barbarian monarch took the missionary into his cabinet, and shut the door behind him. The conversation that passed—the objections that Bruidi may have urged, and the reasonings and explanations with which Columba was able to remove his difficulties, we do not know. The issue only is known to us. When the door of the royal closet opened, and the king and the missionary walked forth, Bruidi declared himself a convert to

---

[1] *Scotland under her early Kings*, vol. i. p. 6, Edin. 1862.

Christianity. The Pictish king had become a Christian sovereign.[1]

In those days the conversion of a king was the conversion of his people, for no subject ever dreamed that he had a right to be of a faith different from that of his prince. King Bruidi, in his closet, had renounced Druidism and embraced Christianity. With him the whole nation of the northern Picts had passed from the altars of Baal to the Christian rite. They were no longer a pagan people. So did the age account it. But Columba did not bow to the maxims of his age. He knew that no rescript from cabinet of monarch could rend the veil of darkness on the intellects and hearts of a people. Light from the book of Heaven only could do this; and the chief value of Bruidi's conversion, doubtless, in Columba's eyes, lay in that it opened the gates of his kingdom to the entrance of the light-bearers. Columba made haste to send thither the missionaries of Iona. Opening the Book of Life, they taught the Picts therefrom the story of the Cross. The sacrifice of the Druid was forsaken: his stone circle fell into ruin, and in its room rose the Christian sanctuary. Schools were planted, and the youth educated. The darkness of an ancient barbarism gave way before the twin civilising powers of Christianity and letters.

Before this time, as we shall afterwards see, the southern Picts had embraced the Gospel. The northern portion of the nation, however, had still continued pagan; the chain of the Grampians being the boundary between that part of the kingdom on which the light had arisen, and that where the darkness still brooded. But now the whole country to the shores of the Pentland Firth, as the results of Columba's

[1] Tighernac, 563; Bed., *Hist. Eccl.*, lib. iii. c. 4, 5, 26; Adam., *Vit. Colum.*, lib. i. c. 37.

efforts, had become professedly Christian. Another watch of the long night was past.

With the conversion of the Picts came important political and social changes—consolidation at home and peace beyond the frontier. Pagan Pictland had been blotted out. It was as if the chain of the Grampians had been levelled. In the suppression of a pestiferous superstition a source of irritation and division had been extinguished, and the whole nation now met around one altar. But this was not all. The most friendly relations were established between the Picts and the Scots. From the day that the missionaries of Iona had been seen crossing Drumalban no warlike host had mustered on the banks of the Spey, or on the moors of Ross-shire; and no cry to arms had sounded along the shores of Loch Awe, or awoke the echoes of the mountains of Dalriada. The hates and passions which set nations at variance had been trodden out, and the sword rested in its sheath for many a long year thereafter. "During the entire period of a century and a half which elapsed since the northern Picts were converted to Christianity by the preaching of Saint Columba," says Mr Skene, "there is hardly to be found the record of a single battle between them and the Scots of Dalriada."[1]

We must avert our eyes for a moment from Scotland and fix them on a country which has not yet come to be known by the name of England, but is soon to be so. Here we are met by a very different spectacle from that which we have just been contemplating. In North Britain a lamp of singular brightness is seen to shine out in the darkness, and hostile tribes are beheld walking in its light and dwelling together in peace. While this is taking place in the north, in the south an ancient people are suddenly plunged into all the

[1] *Celtic Scotland*, vol. i. p. 266, Edin. 1876.

horrors of barbarian war. There seems, at first sight, but small relation between the peaceful labours of the Columban brotherhood at the one end of our island, and the furious tempests which are seen to devastate it at its other extremity. But no event in history stands alone, and sometimes events most dissimilar in their outward form are closely connected in their inward relations. The kindling of the lamp of Iona, as regards both the hour when, and the spot where, it was lit, has a close reference to the terrible revolution which at this same epoch was being accomplished in southern Britain. We must bestow a momentary glance on that revolution.

The light of Christianity, as we have seen, broke on England not later than the middle of the second century. We trace its continued existence through the third and fourth centuries by the presence of British pastors in the Councils of the age. But the Christianity which the disciples of the apostles had planted in South Britain, and which had withstood the terrible tempest of the Dioclesian persecution, was fated to disappear before the yet fiercer storms that were about to burst upon it from the north. Or should it survive, in any feeble measure, it would be only in those remote corners of the land, such as Wales and the kingdom of Strathclyde, where a feeble remnant of the ancient Britons, saved from the sword, were to find hiding from the face of their cruel invaders. We shall not repeat the often told story of the Anglo-Saxon conquest. The Jutes, the Saxons and the Angles were invited over by the Britons, now abandoned by the Romans, to repel the Picts and Scots, whose inroads had become incessant. They came and did their work; but the Britons had soon more reason to be afraid of their new allies than of their old enemies. Their deliverers had cleared the land not for the Britons but for themselves. Entering by the Isle of Thanet, they held open the door, and troop after troop of fierce warriors from the same prolific sea-board rushed across to swell the Anglo-Saxon bands already in the country. Starting with the conquest of East Kent (A.D. 449), they advanced westward and northward into the very heart of the land, fighting battle after battle, following up sanguinary battle with still more sanguinary massacre, and those whom it was their pleasure not to kill they reduced into slavery. It was a war not of conquest but of extermination. Of all the provinces of the world-wide empire of Rome, now overrun by Goth and Vandal and Hun, and enduring the miseries of fire and sword, not one was so terribly scourged, or so entirely revolutionised, as the province of Britain. Here the ancient inhabitants were exterminated, and the new races took sole possession of the country. The two remote districts we have already named excepted, England was now occupied by the Anglo-Saxon race from the German Sea to the mountains of Wales on the west, and from the shores of the English Channel to the Forth on the north. So fell the Roman province of Britain; and with it would have fallen the ancient Caledonia, and Scotland, whether name or people, would have found no place among the nations, but for the stubborn resistance of its inhabitants to Agricola and Severus.

But along with the expulsion of the Britons from a country which they had occupied for five, and it may be ten centuries, before our era, there came an entire change of religion. Their conquerors were pagans. The gods whom the Anglo-Saxons worshipped were Wooden and Thor. Their hatred of the Christian faith was greater even than that of the Germanic tribes that overturned the empire, for the latter permitted themselves to be conquered by those whom they had vanquished with their swords when they consented to be led to the baptismal font and conducted within the pale of the Christian church. But not so the Anglo-Saxons. Contemning the gods of the Britons, they mercilessly slaughtered the clergy, razed the churches, and on their site erected temples to Thor. England was again a pagan land.

It is the bearing of this unexpected and mysterious occurrence on Scotland that it chiefly concerns us to note. What is it we behold? It is the early Christian day of England overtaken by sudden eclipse, and a wall of heathenism drawn between Scotland and continental Europe. For a brief space, Scotland is a second time isolated from the rest of the world. For what purpose? Evidently that the pure evangelism of Iona may be shielded from the now corrupt Christianity of the Western Church. Ere this time the tide of declension in that church had begun to flow. But now it was vastly accelerated by the admission of the northern nations within the Christian pale. These nations were received without undergoing any instruction in the faith, and without evidencing any renewal of nature or any reformation of manners. The church, within whose open gates we behold them passing with all their superstitions, incorporated their rites into her worship, and even erected a Christian Valhalla for the reception of their deities.[1] Instead of lifting them up, she stepped down to them. How changed the church of the seventh century from the church of the second! Her pastors had grown into princes; a brotherhood had been converted into a hierarchy, the mem-

[1] This is confessed by the Benedictine monks in the *Histoire Littéraire de la France*, tom. iii., Introduc., pp. 8, 11, 13. Gregory the Great, in the orders given to the Anglo-Saxons, permits them to offer the same sacrifice to the saints on their respective holidays they had been accustomed to offer to their gods. *Epist.*, lib. xi., lxxvi., p. 1176, tom ii. App. edit. Benedict. See also Wilkins' *Concilia Magnæ Britanniæ*, tom. i. p. 18. Chateaubriand (*Etud. Hist.*) and M. Beugnot admit the same thing.

bers of which stood in graduated ranks round a centre which was liker the throne of a monarch than the chair of a minister of the Gospel. The spirit of the first Rome had entered into the second. "Conquest" was her cry, even as it had been that of her predecessor. She sought to reduce all nations to her obedience. And in that age it was not difficult to make such conquests as she coveted; and had the road been open into Caledonia, had no such partition wall as this new-sprung paganism in south Britain barred her way, she might have advanced her standards farther into the north than the first Rome had been able to do. The feeble Christianity of south Britain would have been an easy conquest to her art, her missionaries, her pompous rites. Instead of obstructing, it would have facilitated her advance on Iona, where she would have replaced the Bible with Tradition, and the doctrine of Columba with the teaching of her Pontiff. But the Anglo-Saxon conquest of England, and the darkness that ensued, delayed her advance into the ancient land of the Scots and the Picts for two centuries.

But Iona stands related—a relation of contrast and antagonism—to an event of even greater consequence than the sudden irruption of Anglo-Saxon paganism into Britain. About the same time that Conal, king of the Scottish Dalriada, was giving Iona to Columba (A.D. 563), that he might there kindle a lamp of evangelical light, the emperor Phocas was giving Rome (A.D. 606) to Bishop Boniface, that in the old city of the Cæsars he might consolidate the papal power, and set up his throne as the Vicar of Christ. The contemporaneousness of these two events, though far separated in point of space — for the whole of Europe well nigh lies between—attests the ordination of Him who is the creator both of the light and of the darkness. At the same epoch we behold the day breaking at the one extremity of Europe, and at the opposite we see the night beginning to descend. From Rome the shadow continues to creep northward. It threatens the world with universal night. But in the opposite quarter of the sky the day all the while is steadily waxing, and we know that the light will conquer. The nations are rushing to and fro; the seats of ancient and powerful kings are being overturned, but here, at the extremity of the earth, shut in from the great winds that are shaking the world, there is found a little territory where the evangelical lamp may burn in the calm, and where for nearly two centuries it continued to diffuse its brightness.

The men of Iona were not dreamy enthusiasts, but energetic workers; and the work they did was such as the times needed. Iona was more than an evangelical church, it was an active propaganda. It was a training school of missionaries; for Iona, like Rome, aimed at making conquests, though conquests of a different sort, and it was here that soldiers were provided for carrying on the war. The plans of this mission-church were wide. Her own country had of course the first claim upon her; and no long time elapsed till churches were planted in numerous districts of Scotland, supplied with pastors from the theological school of Iona, where the text-book of study was the volume of Holy Writ. Before Columba died, he had the satisfaction of thinking that the ancient Caledonia, for even in his time it had not come to be known by the name of Scotland, might be regarded, both north and south of the Grampians, as a Christian country. The Druidic darkness had not indeed been entirely dispelled, but there were now few districts in which the light had not been kindled.

But the labours of these evangelists were not restricted to Caledonia. The mission-field of Iona was Christendom.

Surveying Europe from their rock in the western sea, they saw the cloud of paganism coming up from the south and projecting its dark shadow over lands once enlightened with the truth. Rome, instead of combating was, they saw, courting the rising superstition, and unless Iona should throw itself into the breach there would be none to fight this battle of a beleaguered Christianity. Columba was now in his grave: but his spirit lived. The fame of his institution was extending year by year, and hundreds of youth, athirst for knowledge, divine and human, were crowding from the Continent to sit at the feet of its doctors. When their studies were finished, and "the hands of the elders of Iona had been laid upon their head," they returned to their native land to communicate to their countrymen what they had learned in this famous school of the west. The youth of Caledonia and of Ireland, too, enrolled themselves among its pupils, and when duly qualified they swelled the mission bands which from this renowned isle travelled far and wide, spreading the evangelical doctrine. They attacked the darkness of England, carrying the olive branch to those who had offered only the sword to the Britons. Crossing the Channel they might be seen, staff in hand, and wearing long woollen garments, traversing France, the Vosges, the Alps, and the northern plains of Italy. They pursued their labours, surrounded by the manifold distractions and miseries of the time—plague, battle, fanatic mobs, barbarous tribes, and the wolves of the deserts and the woods. Turning to the north, they traversed Germany. They were not content that the dry land should be the limit of their missionary tours. Embarking in their leathern coracles, they launched out on the unknown seas of the north, and sought out the islands that lie beneath the star of the pole, that they might proclaim to their inhabitants the message of the Great

Father. No age has witnessed greater zeal and intrepidity. The countries they visited were more inaccessible to them than India and China are to us, and the labour and peril attendant on their missionary tours were unspeakably greater than those which the missionary of our day, unless in very exceptional cases, has to encounter. The details of this great movement will come before us at a future stage. We note it briefly here as a step in our country's progress. For undoubtedly the Christianity that emanated from Iona was one of the main forces that acted on the "rude and undigested" masses of the then Scotland. It cemented Scot and Pict, and of the two peoples made in due time one nation. This was the first great landing-place of our country.

CHAPTER XXIV.

BATTLES, POLITICAL AND ECCLESIASTICAL.

COLUMBA is not the first light-bearer who appeared amid the darkness of Caledonia. He had pioneers as early as the second century. But history has found no place on her page for the humble names of the men who first carried the message of Heaven to our shores. In the fourth and fifth centuries there were evangelists among the southern Picts, who may be regarded also as predecessors of the great missionary. An hundred and fifty years before the light of Iona was kindled, a Christian sanctuary rose on the promontory of Whithern; and the gleam of its white walls greeted the eyes of the mariner as he steered his vessel amid the tides of the Irish Channel towards the Scottish shore. This was the scene of the ministry of Ninian, who strove to diffuse the evangelical light along the shores of the Solway, and over the wilds of Galloway. When Ninian rested from his labours, there appeared, in the same region, Kentigern, or, as he is sometimes called, St Mungo. His memory still survives in the West of Scotland, where, humble and courteous, he evangelised, and where he is popularly revered as the father of a long line of pastors, which have been the glory of a city whose cathedral church bears his name. To this age, too, belongs Palladius. Of him we know little beyond the name. He has left no distinct foot-prints, and his story belongs to legend quite as much as to history.

Servanus was another of these early pioneers. He established his hermitage on the north shore of the Forth, at the point where the waters of the firth, issuing through the strait at Queensferry, expand into an inland lake, encircled by banks of picturesque beauty. He is said in latter life to have travelled as far as to Orkney, preaching the " crucified " at the very threshold of the high sanctuary of Druidism, whose rugged grandeur lent dignity, as its ruins now impart an air of melancholy to those northern wilds. There is another name we must include in this roll of early Scotch evangelists. That name is Patrick. True, the scene of his labours was not the land of his birth. Nevertheless it was Scotland that in the end reaped the largest benefit from the achievements of her illustrious son. In our judgment, Patrick was the greatest of all the reformers which arose in the church of Britain before Wickliffe, not even excepting Columba, for the mission of the latter to Iona was a reflex wave of the great movement which Patrick set on foot on the other side of the Channel. In boldness, in popular power, in elasticity of mind, in freedom of action, and in the grasp with which he laid hold of Divine truth, he resembles rather the reformers of the sixteenth century, than the men of his early day, whose light was dim, and who seldom permitted themselves a wider range in their evangelistic efforts than the maxims and canons of their age prescribed. But the subject of Patrick is a large one, and place will be found for it afterwards.

The men of whom we have spoken, the evangelists of the fifth century, Patrick excepted, were, no doubt, men of genuine piety, of ardent zeal, and of holy life ; but they were men of small build, and moved in a narrow groove. They were lights in their several localities, and the age owed them much, but they stood apart and lacked the appliances which organisation would have furnished them with for making their influence wider than the sphere of their personal effort, and more lasting than the term of their natural life. To them the Gospel was not a kingdom—the figure under which its Divine Founder had set it forth, it was a life, a holy life; but their piety had a strong tendency to run into asceticism, and asceticism is often but another form of self-righteousness. There is abundant evidence that these men had their own share in the weaknesses and superstitions of their age, and there could not be a greater mistake than to speak of them as the giants of an early time, who were sprung of a virgin soil, the virtues of which, having since waxed old and feeble, can no longer produce as aforetime, and therefore it is vain to look for men of the same lofty stature now as were seen upon the earth in those days. The truth is, that these men were not above but below their successors. Nevertheless they towered above their contemporaries, and their names deserve, and will receive, the reverence of Scotchmen in every coming age, as the lights of a dark time, and the pioneers of a better day, inasmuch as they were among the first to tame the rudeness and instruct the ignorance of their country.

The first attempt on a large scale to Christianise Scotland was that of Columba. He was no solitary worker, but the centre of a propaganda. Around him were twelve companions, who had drunk into his spirit, and had voluntarily placed themselves under his rule, the better to carry out the great enterprise to which he and they had become bound by a common consecration. This organisation was consonant with the methods of the age, and was the only form of church-life which the circumstances of Columba made possible. He stood in the midst of his fellow-labourers, not as a master among his servants, but as a father amongst his family. The preliminaries settled, the work was begun in earnest. It consisted of two parts: first, the training of missionaries; for the little staff on Iona was not sufficient to do the service at head-quarters, and at the same time occupy the mission fields of the mainland. The second was the actual evangelisation of the country by personal visits. As yet no Christian missionary, so far as is known, had crossed the Grampians. We trace a feeble dawn in the south, but not a ray had penetrated the thick darkness that still shrouded northern Scotland. Columba, as we have seen, was the first in person to venture into that region over which, till his coming, the Druid had reigned supreme. The door which Columba had opened he succeeded in keeping open. Band after band of missionaries, from the feet of the elders of Iona, poured in and took possession of the land. Following the course of the rivers on the banks of which the thin population of that day was mostly located, the evangelists kindled the light in numerous districts, both highland and lowland. That light was a new life in the hearts which received it. There was a sweetness in the hut of the Caledonian, and a brightness in the faces of his children, till then unknown. He flung down sword and lance, and seized hold of mattock and plough, and soon a blooming cultivation clothed valley and strath. After the church came the school. Letters and arts grew up beneath the shelter of Christianity. Columba had enriched the world by calling a new civilisation out of barbarism. One fruitful century — from the middle of the sixth to the middle of the seventh — had sufficed to enrol a new nation under the banners of knowledge and liberty. As if the limits of Caledonia were too narrow, these light-bearers carried their torch into England in the south, and Ireland on the west, and for a century and a half Iona continued to be looked up to as the mother church by institutions which followed her rule and owned her sway in all the three kingdoms.

We have already said that a century of comparative quiet followed the first kindling of the light on the Rock of Iona. With its rays a spirit of peace seemed to breathe over the land. Animosities died out, feuds were forgotten, and battle ceased between Pict and Scot. This calm was the more remarkable, inasmuch as outside the borders of Caledonia the fiercest storms of barbarian war had been let loose on the world. England was in the throes of the Anglo-Saxon invasion; the sky of Europe, from side to side, was dark with northern tempests; around the lamp of Iona alone the storm slept. The solution is not far to seek. It was Iona that had chained the winds in this northern land, where before they were seldom at rest. Columba was the friend of both the Pictish and the Scottish monarchs—both were now converts to Christianity, and their joint consent had been given to the planting of his institution at a point that was intermediate as regards the territories of both. His purity and nobility of character made him be looked up to by both kings; his counsel was often sought, and his advice, doubtless, was always thrown into the scale of peace. His sagacity would anticipate, and his meekness would compose, quarrels before they came to the arbitrament of the sword. Besides, every branch institution that was planted in either the Pictish or the Scottish kingdom was a new bond of amity between the two peoples; an additional pledge of peace. But it is not in a day that the passion of war is to be rooted out of the heart of a nation; and though at this period there is no recorded outbreak betwixt the Scots and Picts, the sword did not entirely rest. Both peoples indulged themselves with an occasional raid into the neighbouring territories of the Britons of Strathclyde and the Angles of the Lothians, and had to suffer the unavoidable penalties of retaliation.

It is now that the kings of Scotland—the little Dalriada—come out of the dubious light in which they are hidden before the days of Columba, and that the work of tracing the transactions of their reign becomes a not altogether ungrateful task. Conal, king of the Scots, gifted, as we have said, the little island to the great missionary; Bruidi, king of the northern Picts, most probably concurring. Dying three years after (A.D. 566), he was succeeded by his brother Kinnatell, who, old and sickly, reigned only a few months. After him came Aidan. Before his accession, Aidan had entered the Monastery of Iona, and put himself under the tuition of Columba; and when he mounted the throne the abbot-missionary anointed him as king, charging both monarch and people, says Buchanan, "to remain stedfast in the pure worship of God, as they valued His blessing and dreaded His chastisement." A clearer historic light falls on the reign of Aidan than on that of any Scottish monarch before the union of the Picts and Scots. We have it on the concurrent testimony of Tighernac and the "Saxon Chronicle," as well as of Adamnan, that he was endowed with princely qualities, that his policy was wise, and that his reign on the whole was prosperous. His first labours were undertaken for the internal pacification of his kingdom. He made an expedition against the robbers of Galloway, punished and suppressed them. He held conventions of his Estates. He renewed an old league formerly existing with the Britons. He strengthened himself on all sides; but the England of the day was too full of broils, confusions, and battles, to make it easy for even the most peace-loving ruler to escape entanglements, and keep war from his borders.

The throne of Northumbria, at that time the most powerful kingdom of the Heptarchy, was filled by Ethelfrith. His territories extended from the Humber to the Forth, and from the rock of Bamborough, across the chalk downs of York, westward to the border of Wales, in which the Saxon sword had cooped up the Britons. The restless ambition of the pagan Ethelfrith made him the terror of his neighbours. Seized with the lust of extending his dominions, he led his army against the Britons, whose kingdom extended from the Clyde to the Dee. Cadwallo, their king, demanded of Aidan, who had renewed with him the league mentioned above, that he should send him help. He obeyed the summons and sent him a contingent. Meanwhile the terrible Ethelfrith held on his way to Chester. The inhabitants trembled as he approached. Twelve hundred and fifty monks belonging to the Monastery of Bangor, after preparing themselves by a three days' fast, came forth and posted themselves betwixt the city and the Northumbrian army. Kneeling on the ground and extending their arms to heaven, they besought help of God. The heathen Ethelfrith, observing them in that unusual attitude, asked who they were, and what they did. Being told that they were praying, he answered, "Bear they arms or not, they fight against us when they pray to their God." In the rout that followed, twelve hundred of these British clerics were slain. The Scotch contingent, carrying arms, suffered less than the poor monks, who were butchered without striking a blow.[1]

A more fatal field for Aidan and the Scots was that of Dægsastan, fought a few years later. It was a terrible blow to the Britons of Cumbria and Strathclyde as well. The engagement was a bloody one; the allied host of Briton and

---

[1] Extinctos in ea pugna ferunt de his qui ad orandum venerunt viros circiter mille ducentos.—Beda, lib. ii. cap. 2.

Scot was completely overthrown, and the power of Ethelfrith more firmly established than ever, and his name made a word of terror, both on the Forth and on the Clyde. About the same time that Aidan sustained this defeat he received intelligence that Columba was no more. The death of his faithful counsellor affected the king even more than the loss of the battle. Unable to bear up under these accumulated misfortunes, he retired, Fordun informs us, to Kintyre, and died about the age of eighty.

When Aidan went to the tomb, the line of the Scottish kings becomes again only dimly traceable. But if the royal house falls into the background, the Institution of Iona, though Columba was now in the grave, comes to the front, and for a full century after the death of its founder, stands full in view, shining with a light undimmed, and working on the country with power undiminished.

Iona was the heart of Caledonia. It was the nurse of the nation. It met the successive generations of Scotchmen, as they stepped upon the stage, and taking them by the hand, lifted them up to a higher platform; and when the sons succeeded their fathers, it started them on the higher level to which it had raised their progenitors. Thus, storey on storey, as it were, it built up, steadily and solidly, the social pyramid. As an illustration of the duality that is often observable in the world's affairs, at that very time an event of precisely the opposite significance was taking place at the other extremity of the island. Augustine and his monks from Rome were entering England (A.D. 597) by the very door by which Hengista and his warriors had entered it a century before—the Isle of Thanet. The pomp that marked the advent of Augustine and his forty-one attendants is in striking contrast to the quiet and unostentatious arrival of Columba and his twelve companions on the shores of Iona.

Preceded by a tall silver cross, on which was suspended an image of Christ, and chanting their Latin hymns, the missionaries of Gregory marched in triumphal procession to the oak beneath which Ethelbert, King of Kent, had appointed to receive them. The interview with the pagan king, held in the open air, for fear of magic, resulted in the grant of the ruinous chapel of Durovern for their worship. On the site of this old fabric, once a church of the Britons, there stands at this day the stately pile of Canterbury. Despite that these two occurrences are parted by the whole length of Britain, there is a close relation betwixt them. Augustine and his monks stand over against Columba and his elders. It may seem to be one and the same faith that is being planted at this epoch at the two extremities of our island; and we do not deny that in this mission host there may have been some sincere lovers of the Gospel honestly bent on the conversion of the pagan Saxons. But this band comes from one who has begun to scatter tares in the field, and the intentions and wishes of the sower, be they ever so earnest and good, cannot prevent the seed flung from his hand bearing fruit after its kind. The moment when that seed is deposited in the earth is not the time to prognosticate what will certainly come out of it. We must wait till the tree has grown and its fruits have ripened, and then we shall be able to judge betwixt seed and seed. When we unroll the sixth and the thirteenth centuries, and hang up the two side by side, we find that it is a contrasted picture which they exhibit. In the sixth century the legate of Pope Gregory is seen bowing low before King Ethelbert, and accepting thankfully the gift of an old ruinous building for his worship. In the thirteenth century it is King John who is seen kneeling in the dust before the legate of Pope Innocent, and laying crown and kingdom at his feet. The seed planted in the sixth century has become a tree in the thirteenth, and this is its fruit.

When we return to Iona, it is to experience a surprise. Among the scholars, from many lands, seated at the feet of the elders, and drinking in the doctrine of the sacred volume, is a pupil, of all others the last we should have looked to find here. He is of royal lineage, but not more distinguished by birth than he is for his loving disposition, his diligence, his reverence for his teachers, and his readiness to share with his fellows the labours of the field as well as the studies of the school. Who is this youth? He is the son of the cruel, ambitious and blood-thirsty King of Northumbria, the pagan Ethelfrith. Ethelfrith has been slain in battle in 617. Edwin has seized his throne and kingdom; his children, chased from their native land, have found asylum among the Scots, and the youth before us is Oswald, the eldest son of the fallen monarch. We shall again meet him. Meanwhile Edwin, whom we now behold on the throne of Ethelfrith, gave a new glory to the English race. His success in war raised Northumbria to the first rank in the Heptarchy, and made its sovereign over-lord of its seven kingdoms. He displayed not less genius in governing than bravery in fighting. He made security and quiet prevail from end to end of his realm, which reached from Kent to the shores of the Forth, where he has left a monument of his reign in a city that bears his name, and is now the capital of Scotland.

Ethelbert, King of Kent, gave Edwin his daughter to wife. With his bride came Paulinus, one of the missionaries of Augustine, "whose tall, stooping form, slender aquiline nose, and black hair, falling round a thin, worn face, were long remembered in the North."[1] There followed frequent discussions at court betwixt the two faiths—that of

---

[1] Green, *History of the English People*, p. 19, Lond. 1875.

Woden, and that of Rome. These discussions resulted in the baptism of Edwin. The conversion of the King of Northumbria woke up the slumbering zeal of the worshippers of Thor. A strong reaction set in on the side of the old paganism. The converts of Augustine, though somewhat numerous, had not strength to stem the tide. Augustine was now dead, and of the bishops whom he had appointed to carry on his mission in England, all fled save one, leaving their flocks to face the gathering storm as best they could. Penda, the pagan King of Mercia, stood forth as the champion of the Thunderer, his zeal for his ancestral gods being quickened, doubtless, by the prospect of throwing off the lordship of Edwin and recovering the independence of his kingdom. The quarrel soon came to the battle-field. The two armies met at Hatfield, A.D. 633. Edwin was slain in the fight, and victory remained with Penda.

Tidings soon reached Oswald, the son of Ethelfrith, in the quiet retreat of Iona, of what had happened on the battle-field of Hatfield. The young scholar had given his heart to his Saviour by a real conversion. All the more was he prepared for the task to which the fall of Edwin summoned him. He panted to kindle in Northumbria the fire that burned at Iona, but in order to this he must first seat himself on the throne of his ancestors. Inheriting the courage though not the paganism of his father Ethelfrith, he set out for his native land, and gathering round him a small but resolute band of Northumbrians, he began the struggle for the throne. The distractions into which Northumbria had been thrown by the fall of Edwin favoured his enterprise. Planting with his own hands the Cross as his standard on the field on which the decisive battle was about to be fought, and kneeling with his soldiers in prayer before beginning the fight, he joined battle with the enemy, and when it was ended he found himself master of the field and of the throne of Northumbria (A.D. 634). Oswald's reign of nine years was a glorious one. To the bravery of his father Ethelfrith, and the wisdom and magnanimity of Edwin, he added a grace which neither possessed, but which alone gives the consummating touch to character—genuine piety. Northumbria speedily rose to the pre-eminence it held under Edwin in the new England.

We have seen that it was good for Oswald that, instead of being on the throne of Northumbria, he was sitting all these years at the feet of the elders of Iona. We are now to see that it was good also for his subjects. A little space sufficed to allay the tumults amid which he had ascended the throne, and then Oswald turned to what he meant should be the great labour of his life, and the crowning glory of his reign. He longed to communicate to his people the knowledge which had illuminated his own mind. The bulk of the Northumbrians were still worshippers of Thor. The Christianity which Gregory had sent them through Augustine, had not power in it to cast out their pagan beliefs, and dethrone their ancestral deities. Oswald turned to the north for a Christianity drawn from an apostolic source and instinct with divine fire. He sent to the elders of Iona, begging them to send a missionary to preach the Gospel to his subjects. They sent him a brother of the name of Corman. The choice was not a happy one. Corman was an austere man, who would reap before he had well sowed. He soon returned, saying that so barbarous and stubborn a people were not to be converted. "Was it milk or strong meat you gave them?" enquired a young brother sitting near, and conveying by the question as much reproof as a sweet and gracious voice could express. All eyes were turned on the questioner. "Brother, you must go to the pagans of Northumbria," said they all at the same moment. Aidan, for so was his name, joyfully accepted the mission. He was straightway appointed to the charge, Bede tells us, adding, that "Segenius, abbot and *presbyter*, presided at his ordination."[1]

Bishop Aidan, as Bede calls him, whom we now see ordained by Presbyter Segenius, and sent to King Oswald, had a wide diocese. He had all Northumbria, and as much beyond as he could overtake. But a fellow-labourer came to his side in the cultivation of this large field : and that fellow-labourer was no less than the King of Northumbria. Oswald and Aidan made their missionary tours in company, the missionary preaching and the king acting as interpreter.[2] Never was there a more beautiful exemplification of the fine saying of Lord Bacon, "Kings are the shepherds of their people." Ultimately there arose a second Iona on the coast of Northumberland, in the Monastery of Lindisfarne, or Holy Island. The missionaries that issued from it, the lands they visited, chasing before them the pagan darkness, and kindling the light of the Christian revelation, belong to the Celtic evangelisation of the seventh and eighth centuries, which will find a place farther on.

There was peace betwixt Northumbria and Scotland all the days of Oswald. That noble and gracious monarch was too sensible of what he owed to the elders of Iona, in sheltering his youth and opening to him the springs of Divine knowledge, ever to think of invading their country. But when Oswald was succeeded on the throne by his brother Oswy, the relations betwixt the two nations began to be strained. The preponderating power of Northumbria

---

[1] Aydanus accepto gradu episcopatus quo tempore eodem monasterio Segenius abbas et presbyter præfuit.—Beda, lib. iii. cap. v.

[2] Beda, lib. iii. cap. 3.

pressed heavily upon all its neighbours, the Scots and Picts included. The latter wished to recover from the Northumbrian monarch the Pictish provinces on the south of the Forth, though they refrained from pressing their demands to open rupture. But religious affronts came to embitter the feeling growing out of political wrongs. Wilfrid, a young Northumbrian, educated at Rome, and a zealous devotee of the Latin rite, appeared at the court of Oswy, and began to proselytise in the interests of the Pontiff. Crafty and ambitious, expert alike at planning an intrigue or conducting a controversy, he succeeded, after several conferences and disputations, the famous Synod of Whitby among the rest (664), in inducing the king and his court to renounce their allegiance to the church of Iona and transfer it to the Bishop of Rome.[1] As the first fruits of Oswy's perversion, the Scotch missionaries were driven out of his dominions. By this time Aidan was dead; but Colman and Finan had been sent in his room from the Presbyters of the Western Seas. The enforced return of the missionaries to their own country was felt as an affront by the Picts and Scots, and intensified the feelings rankling in their hearts, and engendered by other causes. Nevertheless, during the lifetime of Oswy, the peace remained unbroken. At this period a plague desolated all Europe, "such as has never been recorded by the most ancient historians; the Scots and Picts alone are said to have escaped."[2]

Oswy dying in 670, he was succeeded on the throne by Egfrid, and now the storm which had lowered so long burst. With "the doves of Iona" peace would seem to have taken flight from the realm of Northumbria. The reign of the new king was little else than a continual succession of wars, in

---

[1] Wilkins, *Concilia*, p. 37; Beda, lib. iii. cap. 25.
[2] Buchan., *Hist.*, lib. v. cap. 55.

the midst of which Rome worked unceasingly to consolidate in England her ecclesiastical supremacy, ever the foundation of her political dominancy. First, the Scots and Picts broke in to regain their independence, but the attempt was premature. Next, Egfrid turned westward, invaded Galloway, and drove the Britons out of Cumbria, annexing the district, of which Carlisle was the chief city, to the dominions of Northumbria, and enriching the Monastery of Lindisfarne, from which the Columban missionaries had already been expelled, with part of the spoils. His success in arms having brought him to the shores of the western sea, Egfrid crossed the Channel and invaded Ireland. The Irish of that day were cultivating, not arms, but letters, especially divine letters. They were reaping the harvest which Patrick had sowed, and their schools were the glory of their country, and the light of Europe. But their church was not of Roman planting, and their nation found no favour in the eyes of the Northumbrian king. He ravaged their sea-board, and would have carried his ruthless devastations into the interior had not the peaceful Irish, stung into sudden passion, taken arms and driven him out of their country. He next turned northward on an expedition from which he was never to return. At the head of a mighty army he crossed the Forth. The Picts pursued the same strategy to entrap Egfrid by which their ancestors had baffled Agricola. They drew him, by a feigned retreat, on through Fife, and across the Tay, and into Angus, luring him nearer and nearer the mountains. Pursuing a flying foe, as he believed, he marched on to the spot where the Pictish army waited for him in ambush. The place was Lin Garan, or Nectan's Mere, a small lake in the parish of Dunnichen, Forfarshire. The battle that ensued was decisive (685). Egfrid lay dead on the field, and around him, in ghastly array, lay the corpses

of his nobles and fighting men.[1] A few fugitives, escaping
from the field, carried to Northumbria tidings which too
sadly realised the presentiment of evil which weighed upon
the hearts of his subjects when they saw their king setting
out. The woes denounced by the Irish pastors, as he sailed
away from their ravaged coast, had in very deed fallen
upon the unhappy monarch. The consequences of the
battle were important. The fetters of the Scots and Picts
were effectually broken. Never again, Nennius tells us, was
Northumbrian tax-gatherer seen in their territory. From
the height of its fame as a military power, Northumbria fell,
never more to regain its supremacy. The Northumbro-
Roman bishopric, which had been established at Abercorn
on the southern bank of the Forth, was swept away by
the same victory which wrested the Lothians from the
sceptre of the Northumbrian kings, and its bishop, Trum-
wine, fled, panic stricken, on receipt of the news from
Nectan's Mere, nor halted till he was within the walls of
Whitby. This bishopric was an advanced post in the army
of aggression which was marching slowly upon Iona with
intent of garrisoning that evangelical citadel with Roman
monks, or razing it to the ground. The lesser Institution of
Lindisfarne had been captured, and was now being worked
in the interests of Rome; but the victory was not complete so long as the parent institution retained its independence. Had Egfrid triumphed at Nectan's Mere, the extinction of Iona as an evangelical school would have speedily
followed: its teachers would have been driven out as those
of Lindisfarne had already been. But the defeat of the
king gave it a respite, and for half a century longer it
remained a fountain of Divine knowledge to the Picts and

[1] Buchan., *Hist. of Scot.*, lib. v. cap. 56; Robertson, *Early Kings of Scot.* vol. i. p. 12.

Scots, and to lands beyond the sea. The blood spilt on this Pictish moor was not in vain.

Nectan's Mere killed others besides those whom the Picts slew on the field with the sword, and history sometimes imparts its finishing touch to a national disaster by singling out an individual woe. At the time of the battle the good Cuthbert was bishop at Lindisfarne, or Holy Island, and waited tremblingly for news from the battle-field. When tidings came that king and army lay cold on that fatal moor, the aged Cuthbert sickened and died. The circumstances of his last days have a deep pathos. Cuthbert was born at the southern foot of the Lammermoors. Meditative from childhood, when he grew up he entered the Monastery of Melrose, a branch of that of Iona. Daily he wandered by the banks of the Tweed and the Teviot, instructing all he met, whether young or old, in the truths of Holy Writ. He climbed the hills and talked with the shepherds, as they tended their flocks amid the Cheviots; he crossed the wide moors, where the silence seemed holy, and entered the lonely huts with the message of life. The fame of his sanctity spread through all the region. Happy would it have been for Cuthbert if his last years had been passed amid these peaceful scenes, and in the pursuit of these pious labours. But it was fated to be otherwise. King Oswy, as we have seen, at the Council of Whitby, declared in favour of Latin Christianity. The Columban monks were expelled from Holy Island. "Ichabod" was written upon the walls of the monastery. And now the question came to be, where could one be found of so great repute for piety, that his appointment as Bishop of Lindisfarne would bring back the glory that had departed. Cuthbert was sought out and installed in the office. Disgusted with the atmosphere of intrigue and selfishness which he here breathed, he fled from the monastery and built himself a hermitage on the mainland. He was dragged from his retreat, and brought back to his post in the island. He had not long returned till the crushing news of the death of the king at Nectan's Mere, and the consequent distractions of Northumbria, came upon him and broke his heart. He retired to his hermitage on the mainland to die. They who watched at his dying bed agreed to notify by signal to the monks on the island the moment of his departure. They would place a candle in the window of the hut in which he lay. One of the brotherhood, stationed on the tower of the monastery, remained on the outlook. At last the eventful moment came. Peacefully Cuthbert drew his last breath. The faithful attendant by his bedside rushed to the window with a light. The pale gleam, carrying the fatal tidings, shot across the narrow belt of sea that parted the island from the mainland. It was caught by the watchful eye of the monk on the tower. Hurrying down to the chapel, where his brethren were assembled, he announced to them that their bishop was no more, just as it happened to them to be chanting, with dirge-like voices, the mournful words of the sixtieth Psalm, "O God, thou hast cast us off, thou hast scattered us, thou hast been displeased. Thou hast shewed thy people hard things, thou hast made us to drink the wine of astonishment."

CHAPTER XXV.

IONA AND ROME ; OR, THE SECOND ROMAN INVASION.

AFTER these commotions the three nations—the Northumbrians, the Picts, and the Scots—settled down into what might be termed, in that era of world-wide revolution, tranquillity. Nectan's Mere—the Flodden of the seventh century—had adjusted and sweetened the relations betwixt all three. The humiliating defeat on the Pictish moor had purged Northumbria of its ambition, and made it content to abide within narrower limits. The Picts had recovered their corn lands on the south of the Forth. The Scots of Dalriada were no longer struck at through the side of Galloway with the Northumbrian spear; and the Cymric Britons were allowed to possess in peace the vale of Strathclyde, all that was now left them, Wales excepted, of a country once wholly their own. The Lamp of the North, the Latin corps having been arrested in its covert advance to inflict eclipse or extinction upon it, continued to burn and to diffuse, among the two nations of the Picts and Scots, its vivifying and healing influences. Of all the instrumentalities which combined to lift up the country, this was the first and greatest, and pre-eminently so. Without it the rest would have been powerless to subdue the barbarism of the people. The touch of Iona had in it a plastic power that was omnipotent. It planted a conscience in the breast of the savage ; and conscience is the first thing to sweeten the bitterness of humanity, by curbing its selfishness and passion. Every decade that Lamp continued to burn was an inestimable gain, not only to the country in which it shone, but to every land to which its rays extended.

At that juncture, moreover, two princes, exceptionally enlightened and wise, exercised sway over the two nations of Northumbria and the Scottish Dalriada. This helped to deepen the peace that happily prevailed, and prolong the period of its duration. Egfrid, who had fallen in the great battle with the Picts, was succeeded by his brother Alfred. The Alfred whom we now see mounting the throne of Northumbria is not to be confounded with the Alfred of the ninth century, whose name has come down to us across the ten intervening ages in the pure glory of leader in the Divine work of Bible translation. Nevertheless this earlier Alfred was a learned and magnanimous prince. Eschewing the war path, in which his brother had found only destruction, he sought in the pursuit of peace and letters the glory of his reign and the welfare of his subjects. It was now that English literature had its spring-time, and ventured to put forth its earliest buds, though the air was not as yet genial enough to expand them into blossom. It was under this king that Bede—the venerable Bede, as we now style him—the father of English ecclesiastical history, flourished. He lived in the convent of Jarrow, and spent his whole life in the tranquil grandeur of study. His fame for learning drew round him six hundred scholars, to whom he ministered daily instructions. His school rose into great repute, rivalling those earlier seminaries in Ireland, which had been the glory of a former age. Now that their light was waning, the school of Bede was beginning to take their place in the eyes of the nations of the West. His life was one of unbroken labour; he was monk, schoolmaster, and historian all in one;

upwards of forty volumes from his pen, on all the sciences, as his age knew them, are the monument of his prodigious industry. His favourite study was Holy Scripture; and his last labour, as is well known, was the translation of John's Gospel; the last line was dictated with his last breath, and written down by a young scribe with the last ray of eve— Bede and the day setting together, but the one as sure to reappear as the other, and to have dark night turned into glorious morning.

But truth compels us to add that the great scholar and devout Christian did not wholly escape the blight which the Latin Church, ten years before he was born, at the Conference of Whitby, had begun to inflict on England. The shadow of Rome was upon him. But for this how much clearer would have been his vision, and how much wider his sympathies! He speaks lovingly, it is true, of the Columban missionaries who came to enlighten the pagans of Northumbria: he awards them the praise of humility and piety, and lauds the exemplary diligence with which they travelled from village to village instructing the ignorant; but one thing was lacking to their perfection, the Roman tonsure even. It was hard for those who had not received the mark of the bishop of Rome to enter into the kingdom of heaven. So Bede thought. Nor has he a word of condemnation for the cruel slaughter by the pagan Ethelfrith, instigated by the Romanising party of the twelve hundred clergy of Bangor who had stood up for the independence of the British church by refusing to have their heads shorn by the agent of Pope Gregory's missionary. The same cause abridged the good flowing from his labours after he was gone. When the great Alfred arose in the middle of the next century, he found that the goodly promise of the school of Jarrow had come to nothing. It had been mown by the sword of the Dane, who descended on the coast of England after Bede's death; but its premature extinction had been mainly caused by the breath from the cemeteries of ancient paganism on the banks of the Tiber, now creeping over England. Christian products cannot flourish in the air of the grave. The pious king, without very clearly perceiving what had wrought the ruin he lamented, sought how he might remedy it. He began working on the lines of Bede, but his own labours, in their turn, crumbled into dust in the same poisonous air which had blighted those of the monk of Jarrow, and which, so far from being purified and healed, became, century after century, only the more deadly and killing.

It so happened at that epoch (about 690) that there was, as we have already said, a scholar on the throne of Scotland also. He figures in the list of our early kings as Eugene the sixth. Congeniality of taste and study cemented the bonds of friendship between him and Alfred of Northumbria. Accordingly, during their reigns, there was peace betwixt their kingdoms. "Both kings," says Buchanan, "were profound scholars, according to the literature of the times, especially in theology."[1] Fordun, speaking of the Scottish king, says, "He was, for those times, a learned prince, being educated under Adamnan, abbot of Icolm-Kill." Fordun affirms of Alfred of Northumbria also, that he was trained in the Monastery of Iona; a not improbable occurrence, seeing his youth was passed in adversity, and at a distance from the Northumbrian court. The western world of that day may be divided into three great zones in respect of knowledge. There was a broad and dark belt in the middle space, and on either side a zone of light. The Gothic nations had brought night with them into Europe, extinguishing the lamps of ancient learning, and obscuring

[1] Buchanan, lib. v. cap. 57.

those of the Christian faith before they were well kindled. On the south, science, art, and philosophy flourished among the Saracenic nations—a distinction which they owed to their possession of the writings of the Greeks and of the eastern nations, which strengthened their minds and stimulated their inventive faculties. On the north of the central zone was, too, an illuminated region, in which sacred letters especially were studied. It owed its light to its possession of a Book of all others the most powerful in quickening and enriching the mind and expanding the soul. In the southern region the light was scientific and artistic solely. In the northern it partook largely of the humanistic and moral element, and the civilisation based on it was therefore deeper and more varied. We can give full credit, therefore, to Fordun and Buchanan when they tell us that in the North, scholars were to be found, not only in the church and school, but even on the throne itself.

The reign of Eugene VI. of Scotland lasted ten years. The peace betwixt him and the king of Northumbria was profound. His relations with his neighbours the Picts, whose kingdom had become of late very powerful by the accession of the Lothians, so as greatly to overshadow the little Dalriada, were less satisfactory and at times critical; but the occasional quarrels that threatened the peace betwixt them were adjusted without the intervention of a pitched battle. Ever as either king put his hand on his sword's hilt, a voice was heard from Icolmkill in the interests of peace, before the weapon could be unsheathed or blood spilt.

The eighth century of our country rises in a hazy light, and that haze overhangs it to its close. Its kings, Scottish and Pictish, pass before us without individuality, and therefore without interest. Doubtless some of them, perhaps many, were worthy princes, and did worthy deeds, but they have failed to find a historian who was able to do more than cite their names and say of a particular king, that he fought so many battles, reigned so many years, and died. It does not follow that these kings lived in vain. Not one of them but helped to make Scotland what it is; each brought his stone to the building; although now it is impossible to assign his stone to the individual king, or award the measure of praise due to him for placing it there, and contributing thereby to the solidity and grandeur of the edifice.

It is with events, rather than men, that our history has to do, and from the shadowy potentates of Dalriada—for the Scotland of the eighth century was still enclosed within the narrow boundary of the Clyde and the Drumalban chain—we turn to a transaction which we see taking place on the larger stage of the Scotland of the future, known as yet as Pictland. The occurrence we are about to narrate did not receive great attention or awaken much alarm at the time—the loss of a battle would have occasioned more—but its consequences did not die out for nine centuries. We have already animadverted on the extraordinary eagerness of the first Rome to occupy Britain. The second Rome was not less eager and persistent in her attempts to seize our country. The imperial legions had hardly left our soil till the feet of an army of monks were planted upon it. The burden of the mission of these foreign propagandists was the supremacy of the Roman See, and the authority of the ecclesiastical constitutions. The badge of submission to these two powers, on the part of the convert, was the Roman tonsure on his crown, the same which distinguished or dignified the priests of Isis and Osiris. The Columban missionaries labouring in Northumbria did not object to have their heads shorn after any pattern that seemed good in the eyes of the monks of Augustine. It was a matter of indifference to them what form the tonsure took, whether a circle, or a square, or a triangle. What they objected to was the yoke thereby imposed upon their conscience. The tonsure in the form proposed—the coronal, to wit—was the badge of subjection to a strange bishop, and of the reception of constitutions which they had not examined, and which, for aught they knew, might contain things contrary to Holy Scripture. Would not this new obedience be a manifest renunciation of their prior vow to their own church, and especially to the Word of God as the supreme and infallible standard of faith and duty? They would virtually perjure themselves. It was the sheerest tyranny to exact such a thing; and compliance would have been cowardice and treachery. The Columban missionaries resolutely stood their ground. Mindful of the honour of Iona, on which their submission would have entailed disgrace, and mindful, too, of the honour of their brethren, on whose integrity their fall would have brought suspicion, they chose to quit their adopted country and the work they were so zealously and successfully prosecuting in it, rather than submit their heads to the scissors of Rome in token of passing under the crook of the shepherd of the Tiber. Finan, Colman, and their brethren disappeared from the halls of Lindisfarne and the mission-walks of Northumbria, and their place was taken by men whose heads bore the orthodox tonsure, but whose words were strange. By this victory the Latin pale was extended to Edinburgh and the Forth, the farthest limit of the old empire.

But the chief of that church was not content that this should be the final boundary of his spiritual dominions. Beyond that limit there burned in the northern sky a star of apostolic brightness, and till its light should be extinguished he deemed that his own kingdom was not secure. The order was now issued to march on Iona. Accordingly, in the second decade of the eighth century (about 717), we find the Italian monks at the court of Nectan Macderiloi, king of the Picts, and there setting on foot the same manœuvres which had resulted in the Roman victory at Whitby half a century before. Nectan, on a certain day, assembled the nobles of his court at Restenet, Forfarshire, and gave audience to the papal envoy and his attendants. Nectan and his people, according to the envoy, whose name is said to have been Boniface, were sunk in three deplorable heresies. They celebrated Easter on the wrong day; their clergy lacked the true tonsure; and their churches were not so constructed as to permit of an efficacious administration of the Christian rites. The Picts were in peril of losing their salvation by indulging in these gross and wicked courses. They might be ever so well instructed in the doctrines of the faith, but to what avail when they sinned so grievously in the all-important matter of form? What benefit could they hope to receive through Christ's death, unless they commemorated His passion on the anniversary of the day on which it was endured? And what power to convert could possibly be possessed by a clergy whose crowns were not shorn, or not shorn in the orthodox fashion? Was it not immense presumption in Nectan and his Picts to set themselves, in these vital matters, in opposition to the whole of Western Christendom? Was he not cutting off himself and his people thereby from the body of the church and from the channels of grace, for what grace could the Eucharist contain if celebrated on the wrong day, or by a heretically-tonsured clergy? These were pertinent interrogatories, and Nectan felt that there was great weight in the arguments which they implied. The Christian system, he saw, had been wonderfully simplified! All its doctrines were here gathered into the one great doctrine of the Eucharist, and all the duties of the Christian life were comprehended and summed up in the one cardinal virtue of keeping Easter on the right day of the moon. It was not the Bible but the Calendar that must be Nectan's guide. It was not the one anointed priest in the heavens to whom he was to lift his eyes, it was a tonsured priesthood on earth which was to be to him and his people the fountain of grace. So did Boniface teach him.

In an evil hour for himself and his kingdom the Pictish monarch permitted himself to be persuaded by Boniface. Nectan exchanged the Gospel which Columba had preached to his predecessor, Bruidi, for the sweeter doctrine and the easier yoke, as he believed it, of Rome. He issued an edict from the "Hill of Faith," at Scone, appointing Easter to be observed henceforward on the day fixed in the calendar of the Roman Church, and commanding all the clergy of his dominions to receive the coronal tonsure. To complete the reformation of his kingdom, Nectan sent to Ceolfred, abbot of Wearmouth, for architects skilled to build churches so constructed as that all that was said, and especially all that was done in them, might be efficacious. The ecclesiastical revolution was now complete. The three instrumentalities by which Nectan had effected his new reformation were the calendar, the scissors, and the architects![1]

The first fruit of the new faith was persecution. The Columban clergy were required to have their heads shorn in the orthodox way, and from this time forward to take their instructions, not from Iona, but from Rome. On their non-

[1] Bede, *Eccl. Hist.*, bk. v. c. 21; Skene, bk. i. c. 6; Robertson, *Early Kings*, vol. i. p. 9, 10,

compliance they were straightway separated from their flocks and driven across Drumalban into the Scottish kingdom of Dalriada, where the lamp of Iona still continued to burn, though with decaying brightness. The livings left vacant by their expulsion were filled by priests from the kingdom of Northumbria and the south of Ireland. In both countries the novel doctrines and rites of which Boniface was the propagator, had already taken root and were flourishing.

The second consequence of these ecclesiastical changes was the interruption of the peace which had so long existed between the two nations. For a full century, as we have already seen, after the arrival of Columba, hardly was there a battle betwixt Scot and Pict; but now the period of amity comes to an end, and it is Rome that is seen stirring the embers of strife. Those whom the evangelist of Iona had united in one Christian confederacy the emissaries of the Vatican again part into two rival and hostile kingdoms. The flag of battle is again unfurled, and an element of intenser bitterness is infused into the strife than had ever been known even in the days of Druidism.

What success these new teachers who filled the vacant charges and walked so straightly by canon and rubric had in convincing the ancient Caledonians that they could not be saved unless they observed the great Christian festival on the right day, and were soundly instructed by a tonsured clergy, we know not. One thing is certain, however, that Nectan did not much prolong his reign after these events. On the seventh year after he had driven out the Columban pastors, he vacated his throne and entered a monastery. Whether, in assuming the cowl, he sought escape from the cares of government, or whether he was drawn to the cell in the hope of doing expiation as a monk for the sins he had committed as a king, or whether he simply yielded to the importunities of his monkish advisers and masters, who may have wished to place a more pliant ruler in his seat, we know not, but the fact is that Nectan adopted the fashion, even then becoming prevalent, and since his time followed by mightier monarchs, of forsaking, in their last days, crown and courtiers, for the sombre, if not sanctified, companions of the cloister, and engaging in the mortifying but not purifying observances of asceticism.[1]

From this date there opens an era of trouble and convulsion in the Pictish kingdoms. The conversion of Nectan to the Roman rite had disrupted the bond which joined the two peoples in one. The flight of the pastors of the old faith across Drumalban into Dalriada, carrying thither the tidings of the spoliation to which they had been subjected in the Pictish realm, had also inflamed the wrath of the Scots. That mountain barrier, virtually annihilated so long as the faiths of the two peoples were one, was upreared again; and instead of the feet of those "who bring good tidings, and publish peace," there were now seen upon these mountains heralds bearing the flag of defiance, and blowing the trumpet of war. Armies crossed and recrossed Drumalban, carrying into the territories of Pict and Scot battle and bloodshed. It were unspeakably wearisome to recount the story of these savage and sanguinary conflicts, even were it possible. Who could dwell with interest over such a recital, or who could be the wiser or the better for it? We look down into a mist, as it were: we see combatants rushing to and fro, we see host encountering host, we hear the din of battle perpetually rising; anon there comes a cloud that hides all, and when it again lifts and the light is let in, new champions are seen struggling on the stage, and new battles are going for-

[1] Tighernac, Skene, vol. i. p. 284.

ward, but the cause in which they originate, and the interests they advance, we find it hard, often impossible, to ascertain. The ages seem running to waste. Now it is the Picts and Scots that are seen contending with one another. Now it is the Scottish clans that have fallen out among themselves, and are laying waste their country by intestine broils. Now the Dalriadans are seen rushing across the Clyde to assail the Britons of Strathclyde. And now the Picts and Scots make peace between themselves, that they may join their arms against the Angles of the kingdom of Northumbria. But what fruit comes of all these bloody encounters does not appear; nor of many of them does there remain record or memorial, save the cairn which has come down to our day through the tempests of a thousand winters, and the sepulchral urn which the plough or the mattock lays open, to tell that here warrior fought and died, though his name and deeds have long since passed into oblivion.

CHAPTER XXVI.

UNION OF THE SCOTS AND PICTS—THE SCOTTISH NATION.

In A.D. 787 new troubles came from without to complicate the affairs of the four kingdoms into which Scotland and England were then divided, and to add to the miseries with which they were already full. Ships of ominous look, from beyond the sea, appeared suddenly like a flock of vultures off the coasts of Britain. They made their appearance simultaneously on both the eastern and western shores of the island. Their prows moulded like beak of eagle, and their sterns tapered and curling like tail of dragon, gave dismal presage of the errand on which they were bent. Their long narrow build, and the rows of oars by which they were impelled, made their passage through the waves like that of bird hasting to the prey. They were the terror alike of the Scot and the Pict, of the Angle of the eastern kingdom, and the Briton of the western, all of whom suspended their mutual feuds to wage united battle against this common and formidable foe. From Norway and Denmark had come this horde of ravagers. The old chronicler, Simeon of Durham, who alone relates the occurrences of these unhappy times, tells us that fearful prodigies heralded the arrival of these sea pirates. Dragons of fire and warriors in flame filled the night skies, and shook with terror the men of Northumbria and Mercia. And when at last these frightful prognostications received but too terrible fulfilment in the arrival of the Vikings, Simeon goes on to give us a harrowing description of the slaughter which they inflicted. It is singular that the first burst of this northern tempest should have fallen upon the two great religious institutions of the age. The riches known to be hoarded in these establishments was what, doubtless, drew thither these spoilers. "In the same year," (793) "the pagans from the northern region came with a naval armament to Britain like stinging hornets, and overran the country in all directions like fierce wolves, plundering, tearing, and killing not only sheep and oxen, but priests and levites, and choirs of monks and nuns. They came, as we before said, to the church of Lindisfarne, and laid all waste with dreadful havoc, trod with unhallowed feet the holy places, dug up the altars, and carried off all the treasures of the holy church. Some of the brethren they killed, some they carried off in chains, many they cast out naked and loaded with insults, some they drowned in the sea."[1]

A few years thereafter a like calamity befell the older institution of Iona. The northern storm-cloud was seen to divide in two when it approached the shores of Britain. One tempest made its descent southward along the English coast, its track marked by the ruins the old chronicler so graphically describes. The other tempest crossed the Orkneys, swept round Cape Wrath, and descended on the western shore of Scotland, expending its destructive rage on the Hebrides. The marauders bore off to their ships the spoil of the wretched inhabitants, destroying what they were unable to carry away, and after slaughtering the owners, and setting fire to their dwellings, they departed, leaving the western isles and the adjoining coast a scene of desolation. The sanctuary of Iona had no exemption from these awful

[1] Sim. Dun., *Hist. Regum.*, ad an 793 ; Skene, i. 303.

calamities. Neither its fame, nor the inoffensive lives of its inmates, could procure it reverence or consideration in the eyes of these barbarians. It was spared on occasion of their first visit (794), but in four years the Vikings returned to harry and slay; and in A.D. 802, as the Annals of Ulster record, Ikomkill was burned by these sea robbers, and in A.D. 806 its destruction was completed by the slaughter of its whole community, amounting to sixty-eight persons.[1] This beacon of evangelical light, which had burned for two centuries, redeeming the land from pagan darkness, drawing to the feet of its elders scholars from other and distant countries, and so wonderfully shielded amid the tempests of battle between Pict and Scot which had raged around it for a hundred years past, but the light of which had begun to wax faint and low, was now finally put out by the hand of violence.

But the fallen Institute rose up again, though not on its old rock, nor in its former glory. Iona, up to the period of its suppression, had continued to be the recognised head of the Columban church in both Ireland and Scotland. But the authority in the Columban church, which till now had been *single*, was henceforth *dual*. The question had come to be, Shall the seat of supremacy in the communities of Iona be placed in Scotland or in Ireland? That question was determined in a way not to give umbrage to either nation. It was resolved that henceforth there should be two parent or presiding institutions, one at Kells in Ireland, and another in Dunkeld in Scotland. In the little cup-like valley where the Tay struggles through the southern range of the Grampians, Constantine, king of the Picts, laid the foundations of a second Iona, a very few years after the destruction of the first. The relics of Columba were afterwards dug up

[1] *Ul. Ann.*, Skene, i. 304.

and brought from the island of Iîi, to sanctify the soil on which the new temple stood; for men had begun to believe in a holiness that springs out of the earth, rather than in that which comes down from heaven. It was easier consecrating the soil with the bones of Columba, than animating the new institution with his spirit; easier rearing a new temple than rekindling, in its first brightness, the old lamp.

The conversion of the Pictish monarch in 717 to the rite—we say the *rite* rather than the faith of Rome; and the enforced exodus of the Columban pastors from his dominions, were, there is reason to think, the originating causes of those political changes and social convulsions that were immediately consequent on the change of religion, although few of our historians appear to suspect the connection between these two events. In order to see how these two things stood related, let us glance a moment at what Scotland had now become.

We do not hesitate to avow it as our belief that Scotland at the end of the seventh and the opening of the eighth century was the most Christian country in Europe. Perhaps we might venture to add the most civilized, for Christianity and civilisation are never far apart. The Christianity of Scotland, unlike that of Italy and of most Continental countries at that same period, was drawn from the Bible, and was of that kind which goes to the roots of individual and national life, and instead of expending itself in rites and ceremonies of hierarchical magnificence, develops in the quiet and enriching virtues of purity, truth, industry, and sobriety—the true civilisation. Iona had now for a century and a half been shedding its evangelical light over the country. Five generations of Scotsmen had been reared under it. The land was fairly planted with churches, its thin population considered. The pastors who ministered in them were thoroughly trained in Divine learning, and were a race of pious, humble, laborious, and, in many instances, studious and scholarly men. The education of youth was cared for. The population, happily relieved from the distractions of war, cultivated the arts of the time, both ornamental and useful. The same men who interpreted Scripture to them taught them how to use the pen and the chisel, how to construct their dwellings and cultivate their fields. The sons of princes and nobles were proud to enrol themselves as pupils in the school of Iona. Scholars from abroad came to visit a land that had become so famous, that thereby they might increase their stores of knowledge; and kings when dying commanded that their bones should be transported across the North Sea, ferried over to the island of Icolmkill, and laid beneath the shadow of its saintly towers. Where, in the Europe of that age, is there seen another country with a halo like this round it, unless it is Ireland in the fifth century?

But soon after the opening of the eighth century we find this fair picture deformed by sudden tempests. Whence and of what nature were these storms? The Dane had not yet set foot on our soil, and even when his piratical hordes appeared off our coasts, the nation rose and drove him away, or limited his ravages to the islands and parts of the sea-board. The convulsions of this era had their origin within the country. Who or what was it that set Pict against Pict, and Scot at times against both? Historians have been unable to discover any cause for this sudden outbreak, and have spoken vaguely of it as referable to the wildness and barbarism of the age. But the age in Scotland was not barbarous: on the contrary, it was pious and peaceful; this being the fifth generation which had given the plough the preference over the sword, and cultivated peace rather than war with their neighbours. It begins now to be seen that these disturbances had a religious origin, and that they grew out of the visit of the papal envoy to the court of King Nectan of the Southern Picts, and his attempt to impose, at the sword's point, on the pastors of the Columban church, the badge of submission to the new faith and the foreign authority which he sought to instal in the country. It is here, too, that the solution lies, as is strongly suspected, of what is so startling and inexplicable, even that when the troubles we now see beginning come to an end, the numerous and powerful nation of the Picts have entirely disappeared, if not from the soil of the country, yet from the page of history, and the comparatively small handful of Scots in Dalriada have come to the front and grasped the supremacy, and henceforward give their name to the nation and to the country. The point is a curious one in our history, and deserves a little examination.

It is to be noted, first, that the commencement of these troubles is coincident with the arrival of Boniface at Nectan's court, and the expulsion of the pastors from the Pictish territory on their refusal to have their heads shorn in the Roman fashion. This raises a presumption against the strangers as mischief-makers. But, farther, at this same time, we find a great political revolution or convulsion within the Pictish kingdom apart from the troubles to which the expulsion of the clergy across Drumalban into Dalriada may have given rise with the Scots. We see the two great divisions of the Picts, north and south of the Grampians, bursting into sudden flame, arraying themselves in arms against each other, and this is followed by a century of strifes and bloody battles. We know of no political occurrence which could have so suddenly and violently disrupted the bonds betwixt the two. But in the change of religion in southern Pictland we have a sufficient solution. It rallied the Pictish people under two creeds, and parted them into two churches. The Picts of the northern kingdom continued loyal to Iona. Their pastors, unaffected by the decree of the southern king, continued to feed their flocks as aforetime, preaching the evangelical faith of Columba, whereas those on the south of the Grampians had forsaken the faith of their fathers for novel rites and doctrines, and wore the coronal tonsure in token of their submission to a foreign master. War is just what we should expect in the circumstances. The animosities and hatreds which this great secession from the Columban church engendered could not fail to provoke it. The crisis would be rendered more acute by the consideration that it imperilled the political independence of the country, as well as undermined its ancient faith. It opened the door to invasion from Northumbria, with whom the southern Picts had become one in religious rite; and ambitious chiefs on both sides, under pretext of religious or patriotic aims, would find the occasion favourable for enlarging their territories or acquiring greater personal authority.[1]

The fact that the Scots appear as the allies of the northern Picts throughout this tumultuous and bloody century, corroborates the idea that religion mainly had to do with its troubles. The Scots, it is to be remembered, never fell away from Iona, and they would naturally sympathise with their co-religionists, the northern Picts, and be ready to help them in their conflicts with their Romanised countrymen on the south of the Grampians. The sudden and unexpected reappearance of Nectan from the monastery to which he had retired, the moment he saw a chance of

[1] Tighernac, Skene, i. 287, 288.

recovering his throne, is also suggestive of the religious element in these complications, and shows that the foreign monks were pulling the wires that plunged the Pictish tribes into murderous internecine war.

It helps to throw light on the condition of our country, and the opinions that agitated it at that era, to reflect that when the establishment of Iona was plundered and burned by the Norsemen, the foundations of a new church were immediately thereafter laid in the realm of the Picts by the hands of a Pictish monarch. Plainly the old faith had still many adherents among the southern Picts, for Constantine, who founded the new Columban sanctuary at Dunkeld, would not have adventured on showing so decided a mark of favour for the apostle of Iona unless he had known that among his subjects were many to whom the memory and doctrine of the abbot of Icolmkill were still dear. The act was a virtual revocation of the ban pronounced against the Columban clergy by his predecessor Nectan, and a virtual permission to the extruded shepherds to return and feed their former flocks. Some—perhaps many—did, doubtless, return, and found admission into the heritages and livings which their predecessors, a century before, had been forced to vacate. In what way their influence would be employed it is no ways difficult to guess. It would be put forth for the re-establisment of the Columban faith, and by consequence the ascendancy of the race by whom mainly that faith was held—the Scots, to wit. "The Pictish chronicle," says Mr Skene, "clearly indicates this as one of the great causes of the fall of the Pictish monarchy."[1] So long as both branches of the Columban church, the Irish and the Scottish, was governed from one centre, and that centre Iona, the Scots must have felt that they were one with the

[1] Skene, *Celtic Scotland*, i. 315.

Irish, being linked to them by the most sacred of all bonds, but when that bond was broken by the erection of two parent institutions, the Scots doubtless felt that they were parted as a church, and parted as a nation, and that henceforth their thoughts must be turned more exclusively to the acquisition of influence and territory in the country where they had fixed their abode.

The Roman rite, we have said, does not appear to have made its way beyond the Grampians. The spirit of Columba still predominated in the North, and the pastors, sent forth from Iona, continued to feed their flocks, though, we fear, not in the same simplicity of faith, nor with the same fulness of knowlege and zeal, which had characterised them in an earlier and better age. But even among the southern Picts there would appear to have been two powerful religious parties all along during the dark century that intervened between the conversion of Nectan and the founding of the church at Dunkeld. We cannot otherwise account for the transference to the Pictish territory of the northern Institute. Rome would not have suffered such a monument of the old faith and the old liberty to exist, had she been quite mistress among the southern Picts. The policy of King Constantine, in founding Dunkeld, was plainly one of conciliation. He aimed at securing the good will of those of his subjects who had not yet been brought to believe that Easter was more honoured by being kept on this day rather than on that, and that the chief glory of a pastor lay not in the depth of his piety, but in the form of his tonsure.

The conciliatory policy of Constantine, king of the Picts, was followed up by Kenneth Mac Alpin, the first Scot who reigned over the two peoples, when he brought the relics of Columba to consecrate the new church at Dunkeld—a proceeding which, he must have judged, would gratify his new subjects, and tend to consolidate his government over them. Nor was this all. Kenneth Mac Alpin took a still more decided step in the same direction. He set the Abbot of Dunkeld over the church of the Picts.[1] This was to undo the work of Boniface, and to restore the supremacy of the Columban Church over the whole of Scotland. The peace and quiet in which this revolution was accomplished may be accepted as a proof that the faith of Rome had not gone very deep among the southern Picts after all, and that a goodly portion of them had continued to cling to the old doctrines of the north, and refused to yield their faith to the novelties which the Roman missionary had brought with him from the sensuous and ritualistic south.

It is now the opening of the ninth century, and Scotland is in sight of its first great landing place. Constantine, able and patriotic beyond the measure of the sovereigns of his age and country, is on the throne of the southern Picts. He reigned thirty years, dying in A.D. 820.[2] He was succeeded in the government by several kings whose reigns were so short, and whose actions were so obscure, that their names hardly deserve, and seldom receive mention.[3] The Pictish kingdom had now for some time been on the decline. When the southern and northern Picts were united, and one king ruled the land from the Firth of Forth to the Pentland, the Picts were a powerful people. Their numbers, and the surpassing bulk of their territory, quite over-shadowed the Scots in their little domain of Dalriada. But from the day that Columba arrived on the western shore and kindled his lamp on Iona, the disproportion between the little Dalriada and the greater Pictland gradually grew less. The moral

[1] *Chron. Picts and Scots*, p. 361; Skene, i. 316.
[2] *Ann. Ulster*, Skene, i. 305.
[3] Robertson, *Scotland under her Early Kings*, i. 20.

influence which radiated from Icolmkill, and the scholars it sent forth, gave power at home and influence abroad to the Scots, despite their foot-breadth of a kingdom. The names of greatest literary glory in France in that age were those of Scotsmen. When the emperor Charlemagne founded the University of Paris, it was to Scotland he turned for men to fill its chairs of philosophy, of mathematics, and languages. Among Scotsmen in France eminent for their attainments in literature and piety, was Joannes Scotus, or Albinus its equivalent. He left behind him not a few monuments of his genius, one of which Buchanan says he had seen, a work on Rhetoric with his name inscribed.[1] Clement, another distinguished Scotsman, proved a thorn in the side of the popedom. He stood up in the centre of Europe in opposition to Boniface, whom Gregory II. had sent to the Germans, and maintained in public disputation the sole authority of the Scriptures against the traditionalism of Boniface.[2] The tide was turning against the Papal missionary, when the eloquent and undaunted Clement was seized, sent off under a safe guard to Rome, and never heard of more. We may venture to affirm that Scotland had the honour of furnishing the first martyr who suffered under the papacy. This by no means exhausts the list of Scotsmen who, by their learning and piety, placed their little country on a pedestal whence it was seen over all Europe.

But ever since the day the foreign monks appeared among the southern Picts, a process had been going on amongst them exactly the reverse of that which Columba originated among the Scots. The new comers introduced religious dissensions, and these eventually broke up the union betwixt

[1] Buchanan, *Hist.*, lib. v. cap. 53.
[2] Alter qui dicitur Clemens, genere Scotus est, Bonifacii epistola ad Papam, Labbei concilia ad ann., 745.

the northern and southern kingdoms. The dissolution of the union was followed by war. The strength of the Picts departed, and though a gleam of prosperity visited them in the days of Constantine, their power never fully returned, and what they had gained under Constantine they more than lost during the reigns of his feeble successors. Moreover, there was a party among the Picts themselves who from community of faith favoured the Scotch succession. As the result of these concurring causes there had come to be a crisis in the Pictish supremacy. Is it Pict or Scot who is to be the future ruler of the land? And by what name shall North Britain be known henceforward? By that of Pictland, or by that of Scotland? Such was the question now waiting solution in the ancient Caledonia.

At this juncture the male line of Angus, king of the Picts, became extinct, and the throne was claimed by Alpin. Alpin was a son of that Achaius, king of Dalriada, with whom Charlemagne of France is said to have formed an alliance. Achaius had for wife a sister of Angus, the Pictish sovereign. Thus Alpin, the claimant of the Pictish throne, was a Scot by the father's side and a Pict by the mother's. He advanced his claim in A.D. 832. Modern historians incline to the belief that the transference of the sovereignty of the Picts to the line of Dalriada was effected by peaceable means. Not so, say the older historians: the Pictish sceptre, they tell us, was not grasped by the Scottish line till after several bloody battles. We prefer to follow the historians who stood nearest the event, and who moreover have tradition and probability on their side. The greater people were not likely to yield up the rule to the smaller without bringing the matter to a trial of strength on the battlefield. The first encounter between the two armies took place at Restennet, near Forfar. When night closed the battle, the uncertain victory was claimed by Alpin; but even this doubtful success had cost him dear, for a third of his army lay on the field. The Pictish king was among the slain, but the Picts notified that they did not hold the death of their monarch as deciding the issue of the war, for they straightway proceeded to elect another in his room.

The second battle was fought in the neighbourhood of Dundee. It was the Picts who triumphed in this fight, and they won the battle by a stratagem similar to that which Bruce employed four hundred and eighty years after at Bannockburn. The camp attendants were instructed to mount the baggage horses and make their appearance on the heights around the field when the combatants should be in the thick of the fight. This make-believe of a second army advancing to the aid of the Picts threw the Scots into panic. They broke and fled: the king and his principal nobles were taken captive on the field. The nobles were slain on the spot; but Alpin was reserved for more ignominious execution. All ransom being refused for him, he was bound, led away, and beheaded, and his head, fixed on a pole, was carried in triumph round the army. This barbarous exhibition over the gory trophy was stuck up on the walls of the Pictish capital, supposed to have been Abernethy.

There followed a few years' cessation in the war.[1] Elated by their victory, the Picts broke out in fiercer dissensions among themselves than ever. It happened, too, about this time, that they were assailed by the Danes, and one of their most powerful tribes all but exterminated.[2] Thus the Scots had respite, and were able to recruit their strength, much impaired by their disastrous defeat. Kenneth, the son of

[1] Chron., *Picts and Scots*, p. 209; Skene i. 206; Buchan., *Hist.*, lib. v. c. 58.
[2] Skene, i. 387, 308.

the fallen Alpin, a brave and worthy prince, was placed on the throne. The young monarch was naturally desirous to prosecute the quarrel against the Picts, and his ambition to enlarge his realm by adding the Pictish territories to it was quickened by the cruel indignities to which his father had been subjected, and of which he was touchingly reminded by some adventurous youth, who took down the head of the murdered Alpin from the walls of Abernethy and carried it to the young Kenneth. He convoked an assembly of his nobles and strongly urged upon them a renewal of hostilities against the Picts; but the older and more experienced of the nobles, were averse, believing that the time for another trial of strength was not yet come. Kenneth allowed the matter to sleep three years longer.

But in the fourth year Kenneth revived the project, and succeeded in overcoming the reluctance of his nobles by the following extraordinary stratagem, as Fordun relates, and in which Boethius, Buchanan, and others follow him. He invited the nobles to a banquet in the palace, and prolonged the festivities to so late an hour that the guests, instead of departing to their homes, sunk down on the floor of the banqueting room overcome by wine and sleep. The king had previously selected a youth, a relation of his own, whom he instructed in the part he was to play, providing him at the same time with a luminous robe, made out of the phosphorescent skins of fish, and a long tube which was to serve the purpose of a speaking trumpet. It was now past midnight: all was dark in the chamber where the feast had been held, and the silence was unbroken, save an occasional interruption from the heavy slumber of the prostrate mass that covered the floor. Suddenly a terrible voice rang through the banqueting room and awoke the sleepers. On opening their eyes, they beheld with amazement a figure in the middle of the hall, in a blaze of silvery glory, speaking in a voice of more than mortal power, commanding them to gird on the sword and avenge the murder of King Alpin, and thundering in their ears dreadful maledictions should they not obey. No sooner had the spectre delivered its message than it disappeared as noiselessly as it had entered, leaving those whom it had dazzled, or terrified by its unearthly brightness, bewildered by its mysterious exit. When morning broke the nocturnal apparition was the one topic of conversation, and all were agreed that a celestial messenger had visited them in the night, and that it was the will of the Deity that they should renew the war with the Picts. They were confirmed in this conclusion by the king, who assured them that the same celestial visitor had appeared to himself, bringing with him a message which left him no alternative but a resumption of the war. The character of the times made the success of such a stratagem possible, and so makes the story credible.[1]

But whatever we may think of the story, we now find the Scottish nobles, who had hitherto held back, rushing into the field, and plunging, noble and soldier alike, into furious battle with the Picts. Crossing Drumalban, and advancing into the low grounds of Stirlingshire, the Scots, shouting their war-cry, "Remember Alpin," flung themselves upon the ranks of the Picts. The Pictish army was broken and routed. But one battle was not enough to decide the issue of the war. The Picts rallied; battle followed battle, and when we think how much was at stake, and how enflamed were the combatants on both sides, we can well believe that these encounters were as sanguinary as the chroniclers say. At last the matter came to a final trial of strength near

[1] Fordun, lib. iv. cap. 4; Buchanan, lib. v. cap. 60.

Scone. When this last battle had been fought the Pictish king lay dead on the field; and around him, in gory heaps, lay the bulk of his nobility and army. The Tay, which rolled past the scene in crimsoned flood, making flight impracticable, increased the carnage of the battle.[1]

That severities and atrocities were consequent on victory, to awe the conquered country, and prevent insurrection and revolt among the Picts, is highly probable. Submission was a new experience to this impatient and war-like people. But the legend that assigns to the Pictish race, as the result of its conquest by the Scots, the fate of utter extermination, is wholly incredible. Such an effusion of blood, even had it been possible, would have been as profitless as it would have been revolting. It was blood far too precious to be spilled like water. If that ancient and valorous race had been swept off, the Norsemen from across the sea, and the Anglo-Saxons from the other side of the border, would have rushed in and taken possession of the empty land. How sorely should the Scots have missed the Picts in the day of battle! They were of the old Caledonian stock, descendants of the men who fought the Romans at the roots of the Grampians, and their blood instead of being poured on the earth was to be mixed with that of the Scots, to the invigoration of both. Mixed blood is ever the richest, and gives to the race in whose veins it courses a notable robustness and variety of faculty. It was not extermination but absorption or incorporation that befell the Picts at this epoch. It is true that their name henceforward disappears from history; but so, too, had the earlier name of Caledonian at a former epoch. It as suddenly and completely disappeared as that of Pict does now: but no one supposes that the people who bore it suffered exter-

[1] Buchan., lib. v. cap. 62.

mination. In both cases it was the name only, not the race, that became extinct.

In A.D. 843 Kenneth Mac Alpin ascended the throne as ruler of the whole land. Under him the two crowns and the two peoples were united. The conquerors and the conquered gradually merged into one nation, and from the opening of the tenth century the only terms employed to designate the country and its inhabitants were SCOTLAND and the SCOTS.

END OF VOL. I.

THE SECOND VOLUME OF THIS HISTORY

Will be issued in <u>OCTOBER</u>, *and will embrace*

The Times and Labours of Ninian, Palladius, the Abernethy Brotherhood, Patrick in Ireland, Columba in Iona, and the Celtic Evangelisation, &c.

Fourth Thousand, Demy 8vo, Cloth, Price 8s. 6d.

THE PAPACY;
ITS HISTORY, DOGMAS, GENIUS, AND PROSPECTS.
BEING THE EVANGELICAL ALLIANCE FIRST PRIZE ESSAY ON POPERY.

By REV. J. A. WYLIE, LL.D.

"Dr Wylie's volume is learned, philosophical, and eloquent."—*British Quarterly Review.*

"This able and finished production combines at once the rare qualities of clear statement, vigorous logic, and eloquent style. Its tone and spirit are worthy of an Evangelical Alliance; and it is to the praise of the author that he could write upon a subject on which the public mind has been so excited, and, we may say, so exasperated, with such an absence of all passion and prejudice."—*Baptist Magazine.*

"It would be difficult to determine which to admire most,—the breadth and comprehensiveness of the plan, the method of the argument, the clearness and copiousness of the details, the vividness and tact of the grouping, the fine, healthy air of its high Christian philosophy, or the vigorous eloquence, rich imagery, and moral earnestness of its style."—*Glasgow Constitutional.*

"The volume is the substance of a whole Protestant library, in a form which rewards, instead of taxing, the patience of the reader."—*Witness.*

"One of the most massive and masterly productions in our literature on the subject."—*Report on Popery, General Assembly of the Free Church of Scotland.*

"The book of the age on the question."—*Rev. Mr Brocklehurst, in Corn Exchange, Manchester.*

"The most important work on Popery since the beginning of the century."—*United Presbyterian Magazine.*

"With all we have read on Popery, we have yet met with nothing in the English language which we regard to be so complete in itself, and so overwhelmingly destructive to Romanism, as the work before us."—*Evangelical Magazine.*

LONDON: HAMILTON, ADAMS, & CO.
EDINBURGH: A. ELLIOT, 17 PRINCES STREET.

By the same Author.

Second Edition, Price 6s. 6d.

THE GREAT EXODUS;

OR,

"THE TIME OF THE END."

"Dr Wylie does not follow the ordinary beaten path so commonly trodden by the feet of 'students of prophecy.' He is neither literalist, spiritualist, nor futurist. He thinks out his own method, and follows his own course, and is rather, if we might coin a word, a typologist. His scheme of interpretation is worked out with great skill, precision, and clearness."—*London Record.*

"This work is not only one of great ability, but it is in many respects a remarkable production: it is so with regard to the amount of research which is everywhere visible in its pages: it is, too, a remarkable work viewed in relation to the hypothesis, if we may use the word, which the volume developes, and which is so ably supported. In many respects Dr Wylie differs on important points connected with prophecy, and with the past history of the Church, from most, if not all, of our popular writers on prophetic questions. . . . The style of the work is, indeed, from the beginning to the end, characterised by great affluence. It is one of the most interesting and valuable which has appeared for a long time past on the subject of prophecy, and is destined to occupy a permanent place in the category of our Protestant theology."—*London Morning Advertiser.*

Crown 8vo, Cloth, Price 2s. 6d.

EGYPT AND ITS FUTURE;

A VISIT TO THE LAND OF THE PHARAOHS.

"There is just enough of what is personal about it to form a sketch, which is then filled in by bright, warm colouring; history, ancient and modern, physical geography, poetry, and even such dry things as statistics are interwoven with the facts that come under the writer's own observation in such an easy, and yet perhaps, therefore, artistic manner, that few readers will fail to be interested, and fewer still to be instructed. The journey out, the run through Italy, the passage from Brindisi to Alexandria, and the arrival in that ancient town just a little before the war broke out, all furnish materials which the writer turns to excellent account. Then Egypt itself, the land of the Pharaohs, is presented in such clear and graphic terms as if it stood out in a picture to the actual vision of the reader. Its soil, its people, its laws, even its dogs, and above all, its monuments of hoary antiquity, which connect the present with a far-distant past—all are made to pass successively under review. God hath set 'His signs and wonders in the land of Egypt, even unto this day.' An interesting account is given of the mummies lately discovered at Thebes. 'That the Pharaohs of early Bible times,' says Dr Wylie, 'the contemporaries of Joseph and Moses, should come out of their tombs, and that we of the nineteenth century should see the very faces of the kings who figure in the sad story of the Bondage and the terrible drama of the Exodus, is what no one looked for, and what, perhaps, no one deemed possible. Yet this most improbable and most unexpected event is what has taken place. . . . We saw these Pharaohs lying in their coffins, with their mortuary appendages and inscriptions around them. Sight amazing and well-nigh incredible! We gazed with an indescribable feeling, not being perfectly sure how this strange meeting had come about—whether they had come up to us, or we had gone down to them. This part of the volume is full of sacred and solemnising interest, and all through it will be read with great profit and satisfaction."—*London Record.*

LONDON: HAMILTON, ADAMS, & CO.
EDINBURGH: A. ELLIOT, 17 PRINCES STREET.

www.ingramcontent.com/pod-product-compliance
Lightning Source LLC
Chambersburg PA
CBHW020259240426
43673CB00039B/643